TYPOLOGIES OF HUMOR IN AFRICAN LITERATURES

AFRICAN PERSPECTIVES
Kelly Askew, Laura Fair, and Pamila Gupta
Series Editors

Typologies of Humor in African Literatures
Adwoa A. Opoku-Agyemang

*Between HIV Prevention and LGBTI Rights:
The Political Economy of Queer Activism in Ghana*
Ellie Gore

*Protest Arts, Gender, and Social Change: Fiction, Popular Songs,
and the Media in Hausa Society across Borders*
Ousseina D. Alidou

The Imaginative Vision of Abdilatif Abdalla's Voice of Agony
Abdilatif Abdalla, edited by Annmarie Drury

Congo Style: From Belgian Art Nouveau to African Independence
Ruth Sacks

Lagos Never Spoils: Nollywood and Nigerian City Life
Connor Ryan

Continuous Pasts: Frictions of Memory in Postcolonial Africa
Sakiru Adebayo

*Writing on the Soil: Land and Landscape in Literature
from Eastern and Southern Africa*
Ng'ang'a Wahu-Mũchiri

In Search of Tunga: *Prosperity, Almighty God,
and Lives in Motion in a Malian Provincial Town*
André Chappatte

*Power / Knowledge / Land: Contested Ontologies of Land
and Its Governance in Africa*
Laura A. German

A complete list of titles in the series can be found at www.press.umich.edu

Typologies of Humor in African Literatures

Adwoa A. Opoku-Agyemang

University of Michigan Press
Ann Arbor

Copyright © 2024 by Adwoa A. Opoku-Agyemang
All rights reserved

For questions or permissions, please contact um.press.perms@umich.edu

Published in the United States of America by the
University of Michigan Press
Manufactured in the United States of America
Printed on acid-free paper
First published October 2024

A CIP catalog record for this book is available from the British Library.

Library of Congress Cataloging-in-Publication Data

Names: Opoku-Agyemang, Adwoa A., author. | Michigan Publishing
    (University of Michigan), publisher.
Title: Typologies of humor in African literatures / Adwoa A. Opoku-Agyemang.
Other titles: African perspectives (University of Michigan. Press)
Description: Ann Arbor [Michigan] : University of Michigan Press, 2024. | Series: African
    perspectives | Includes bibliographical references and index.
Identifiers: LCCN 2024023134 (print) | LCCN 2024023135 (ebook) | ISBN 9780472077038
    (hardcover) | ISBN 9780472057030 (paperback) | ISBN 9780472221868 (ebook)
Subjects: LCSH: African literature—Humor—History and criticism—20th century. | African
    wit and humor—History and criticism—20th century. | African literature—History and
    criticism—20th century.
Classification: LCC PL8010 .O66 2024 (print) | LCC PL8010 (ebook) | DDC 809/./917096—
    dc23/eng/20240627
LC record available at https://lccn.loc.gov/2024023134
LC ebook record available at https://lccn.loc.gov/2024023135

This book will be made open access within three years of publication thanks to Path to
Open, a program developed in partnership between JSTOR, the American Council of
Learned Societies (ACLS), University of Michigan Press, and The University of North Carolina
Press to bring about equitable access and impact for the entire scholarly community, including
authors, researchers, libraries, and university presses around the world. Learn more at
https://about.jstor.org/path-to-open/

For Neil
and
Naana

CONTENTS

Acknowledgments	ix
INTRODUCTION	1
CHAPTER 1 Trickster	24
CHAPTER 2 Mimic	61
CHAPTER 3 Interpreter	98
CHAPTER 4 Deviant Norm	132
CONCLUSION	161
References	167
Index	177

Digital materials related to this title can be found on the Fulcrum platform via the following citable URL: https://doi.org/10.3998/mpub.12876792

ACKNOWLEDGMENTS

This book began as a random chat with Ato Quayson, who went on to give invaluable feedback throughout its different versions. Meda ase.

For being careful and insightful readers, I owe a massive thank you to Jeanne-Marie Jackson, as well as to Shoka Adenekan, Dan Newman, Susan Gall, and Uzoma Esonwanne.

I am grateful to the University of Toronto's Centre for Comparative Literature, especially Ann Komarami, Jill Ross, Aphrodite Gardner, Mary Nyquist, and Pushpa Acharya.

A significant part of the research that went into this book was supported by the Social Sciences and Humanities Research Council of Canada.

Thank you to the team at the University of Michigan Press: Katie LaPlant, Mary Hashman, Jill Hughes, and Danielle Coty-Fattal. My thanks also go to the University of Michigan's Department of African and Afroamerican Studies, particularly to Kelly Askew, Scott Ellsworth, and Omolade Adunbi.

For their support, and especially for their excellent and very different senses of humor: Akwasi Owusu, Ben Andagalu, Ch. Kwabena Opoku-Agyemang, Edward Annan, KTM, Nana Tandoh Nyankolmes, Papa Nyame Sam, Pearl Asomaning, Theresah Ennin, Trixie Akpedonu, and everyone else who regularly shows me something new to laugh about. You people do all.

Introduction

"WHO NOSE?"

A Ghanaian church is organizing a crowded, open-air crusade (or miracle) service. It is a nighttime gathering, but the setting is well lit and the congregation vibrant. The usual church groups are in attendance—the singing band, the choir, the women's and youth associations, the prayer warriors—with ushers stationed between the rows of plastic chairs. Completing the assembly is a visiting pastor, earnestly delivering his sermon from a dais. Though the pastor is Ghanaian, he does not appear to speak the community's Mfantse (one of the Akan languages); most seem not to connect with the English in which he expresses himself. As is expected in such situations, he resorts to consecutive interpreting, employing someone who understands both languages and can thus bridge him with his audience. In a country where any community can be home to several languages, it is not uncommon for interpreters to accompany pastors.

In consecutive interpreting, a speaker breaks up his speech in order to allow the interpreter to deliver the message to the audience, segment by segment and as faithfully as possible. This interpreter is undoubtedly respecting this framework by speaking to the congregation whenever the pastor pauses. But something unusual is happening here: from the moment he hears the pastor's greetings from the Church of Christ and announces that the pastor says he is here for those who "do not know Christ," it becomes obvious that he is decoding the English words according to his own very peculiar system inspired by phonetics, his oratory talent, knowledge of ready-made litanies, and a very healthy imagination. In any case, semantics has little to do with it.

During a chorus, he is seen consulting another person, an open *Oxford English Dictionary* in hand. This does not help. Mfantse words that bear the faintest rhyme with English ones are continually yanked into the conversation. When the pastor says, "Let us be glad and believe in him," the church is told, "Sister Gladys, if you have a hanky, take it out." In the video, a church member gladly waves her handkerchief in the air; "him" has a homophone in Mfantse that means "to wave." The pastor, as pastors are wont, also quotes the Bible: "Psalm 33 verse 12: blessed is the nation of which God is the Lord." The figures strike the interpreter as too familiar to be coincidental, and he infuses the text with a commercial bent: "Pastor says he is selling twelve [Nokia] 3310s. Come buy some and be amazed at how long the batteries last." Most notably, he nods along solemnly to the pastor's theological question-and-answer: "Who knows? Nobody knows. Only God knows." The interpreter then renders it thus: "Whose nose is it? It's nobody's nose! It's only God's nose."

This is the setup of "The Crusade," hiplife musician Kofi Kinaata's 2015 song and music video. Kinaata plays the interpreter, while the role of the pastor is played by the featured artist, Donzy. The most arresting feature of this brilliantly written song is its humor, the mechanism of which takes advantage of the flexibility of signifiers. Studies suggest that when bilinguals are speaking one language, the other one is active, so that they sometimes process one language in terms of another. Thus, to arrive at his meaning, Kinaata's interpreter looks for phonetic equivalencies between English words or between Ghanaian English and Mfantse. Languages and linguistics, as the song suggests, can be funny.[1] More important, that we can process a language in terms of another to create a novel, comic effect suggests that a similar procedure can take place with the cultures that produce those languages. There is humor in the tensions that occur when one way of seeing the world is imposed on another, when they rub elbows, or when said elbows bash into each other. These tensions and humorous potentials are worth studying from a literary perspective, particularly in such highly multilingual contexts.

It is also worth noting that the premise of the song and its video updates an older literary trope that may be traced at least to Ghana's tradition of concert party theatre. The concert party dates to 1920s itinerant theatre troupes and continues to be present in Ghana's literary landscape. As the audiences of television shows like the 1990s "Key Soap Concert Party" will attest, wordplay is integral to the humor. Concert party theatre was itself cobbled together from various sources, including traditional theatre, music hall performances,

---

1. Also attested to by the fact that some French speakers approach artificial intelligence (AI) with a sense of hilarity because "ChatGPT" sounds remarkably like "Cat, I farted" in French.

and the folktale. The folktale's most-cited setting—community gatherings in the evening—is that of Kinaata's video. In fact, the broader theme of inaccurate but funny interpretation may be traced even further back to traditional folktales—for example, "Tortoise and the Birds," retold in Chinua Achebe's *Things Fall Apart*. Also, concert party theatre regularly lampoons various social groups. Kwabena Bame recounts a scene where a Ghanaian pastor, fresh from training abroad, tries to impress his congregation by pretending to have forgotten how to speak the local language (incidentally, Mfantse). Unfortunately, the interpreter chosen for the task is not quite up to it and consistently mistranslates his homily. The pastor's frustration has been growing steadily, but it is when the interpreter pulls out the infamous "it's only God's nose," that the pastor bursts out (in his mother tongue) that "that" was not what he said, to the mirth of the audience (39).

What is it about the setup where two groups divided by language are brought "together" by an incompetent third, and where the dissimilarities between languages are given preeminence, that consumers of literature are still finding entertaining in the twenty-first century? Especially when some allegedly funny things seem like they should be left firmly in the past, and when some of the material that *we* are convinced is the height of hilarity will likely fail to convince future generations? If Kinaata has unearthed and personalized this framework, it is because some aspects of it still resonate with people and make them laugh. This raises questions about the nature of humor in African texts. Do these texts require familiarity with African cultures? Does their humor depend on knowing an African language? The primary impulse of texts like "The Crusade" is clearly humor. What do creators believe is funny, and what is the relationship between their texts and their audiences?

Humor is common to all cultures. That, at least, is something scholars in the field of humor studies can agree on. It should not seem strange that people everywhere laugh, though what sounds like a banal observation sometimes needs to be explicitly pointed out. On the relationship between humor and postcolonial societies, Susanne Reichl and Mark Stein note that "laughter is a central element [and] humor a key feature" of their literatures (1). Humor certainly enjoys a prominent profile in African literatures; it regularly sets the tone for traditional folktales,[2] theatre performances,[3] songs, and poetry.

---

2. As Naana Opoku-Agyemang observes in her study of Akan folktales, the creation of humor is one of "shared aesthetic criteria for a good narration" (117).

3. The title of Kwabena Bame's book on Ghanaian concert party theatre is, appropriately, *Come to Laugh*.

It was used to reflect on and subvert power imbalances in the colonial period.[4] It is equally present in more contemporary genres; it infuses radio and television programs, newspapers, and internet memes.[5] Yet, though we all know—instinctively, even—how to identify humor, and despite its acknowledged aesthetic value, rhetorical functions, and restorative and therapeutic qualities, it is difficult to isolate, analyze, and generalize the operations that add up to humor in a conclusive way.

While humor can be negative, we tend first to associate it with feelings like happiness and lightheartedness (or awkwardness when it misses the mark). Those positive elements would undoubtedly benefit from more attention from African literary criticism. David Adu-Amankwah, for example, observes that "very little research work" has been done on humor in African literature (2), while Ebenezer Obadare questions the "distinctive rarity" of such studies ("Uses" 244).[6] The impressive *Routledge Handbook of Language and Humor* acknowledges that it pays "very little attention" to non-Western scholarship (1). For its part, modern African literary history is mapped out according to core themes, such as decolonization, early postcolonialism, post-independence, and postcolonial disenchantment, which are fitted into a nation/narration model. Or it may be viewed through the lens of the diaspora (Afropolitanism, the Anthropocene, etc.). Though humor on its own is too amorphous to be a historical movement, it intersects with or runs through those models with a constancy that proves its value to African literatures. Still, despite the strong presence of humor in this corpus, studies have largely sidestepped it. On the analysis of literature produced in former colonies, Reichl and Stein note that humor and laughter may be treated as anything from "an uneasy bedfellow" to an "abomination" (2). That is because humor is assumed to treat serious topics lightheartedly and, sometimes, disrespectfully. On the other hand, literature from former colonies seems to lend

---

4. Elizabeth M. Perego notes that Algerian comedy makers created scenes of resistance against colonial forces (73). Similarly, Hermann Wittenberg posits that humorous Khoi folktales were used subversively against the colonial intruder (598, 607).

5. For instance, misquotes attributed to Robert Mugabe have been very popular over the past several years. Among many examples, see Shearlaw, Maeve. "Mugabe Falls: Comedy Memes of Zimbabwe's President Go Viral." *The Guardian*, 8 Mar. 2018, www.theguardian.com/world/2015/feb/05/mugabe-falls-comedy-memes-of-zimbabwes-president-viral. See also U, Fadamana. "56 Most Hilarious Relationship and Political Quotes by Robert Mugabe." AnswersAfrica.com, 18 July 2023, answersafrica.com/50-hilarious-robert-mugabe-quotes.html.

6. John Ball similarly says that satire is "prevalent but largely untheorized" even though "many Commonwealth writers have written novels that are largely or partly satiric" (ix–1).

Introduction • 5

itself to an inherently serious reading.[7] In an important study on postcolonial satire, John Ball's primary focus is not humor proper. He builds on the connection between the two terms by showing that postcolonial literature is distinguished by oppositionality and referentiality, while satire is similarly characterized by aggression and historicality (2). Modern African literature, after all, was born out of a context of opposition to colonialism and postcolonial realities (Gikandi 379). Even when humor is remarked upon, it risks being reduced to what Reichl and Stein label an "interventionist stance" (2).[8]

Undeniably, many classic African texts assume the self-proclaimed task of "writing back" to the colonial metropolis or are an indictment of postcolonial injustices. Twentieth-century African writers are typically regarded as "advocates of radical social change" (Lindfors 22).[9] In many cases, the criticism of African literature takes its cue from writers like Chinua Achebe, who famously declares that his aim is to teach his readers lessons about the worth of their history. It is likely because of the emphasis on timeliness and being useful to an audience deemed in need of education that the parallel notion of African literature as historical is so prevalent. What this means for humor is that, in terms of inspiration, criticism tends to be preoccupied with Africa's recent and largely unamusing sociopolitical history. In short, by virtue of the emphasis placed on didacticism and realism, it might initially appear that the writing and appreciation of African literature was a very serious business indeed.

---

7. Gérard Genette mentions Roberto Benigni's *La vita è bella* to discuss a similar phenomenon. For Genette, the only way the part of the film set in Auschwitz can maintain "laughter through tears" is to sanitize reality. This technique, he admits, offends historical truth. However, we must consider that the reality of an extermination camp is, by definition, strictly impossible to reconstitute (414).

8. We can note, for example, that Mongo Beti, although masterful with humor, is primarily described in terms of resistance and conflict (book titles like *Langue d'écriture, langue de résistance; Mongo Beti: Le Combattant fatigué*, while not at all inaccurate, are expressive of this tendency).

9. Some writers, such as Alain Mabanckou, balk at the blanket descriptions applied to African writers, and at the expectations often placed on them (Mabanckou 148). Bernth Lindfors shows that writers have served as "chroniclers of contemporary political history" (240), in this way associating their texts with factual accounts. Accordingly, when Bienvenu Nola declares that, for Ferdinand Oyono, colonialism was "*la source principale de sa création romanesque*" [the principal inspiration for his fiction] (69), he could be speaking of virtually any African writer of the period. More measured, Kolawole Ogungbesan likewise states that the African writer being "much influenced by politics," "African literature has tended to reflect the political phases on the continent" (43).

6 • TYPOLOGIES OF HUMOR IN AFRICAN LITERATURES

While it would be purposefully myopic to undermine these perspectives, they should not be read as an invitation to distill the continent's literary output to its sorrows. Africa is multilayered, and that unique diversity means her comedic output is disposed to excel in ways it will not elsewhere. Not only does implicitly excluding other modes and perspectives (including humor) impede a thorough reading of African literatures, but in the end, it also perpetuates the marginalization of those very literatures and perspectives. Yet, even the texts that consider the gravest themes can have a persistently comic flair. Ferdinand Oyono's classic *Le Vieux nègre et la médaille*, published during Cameroon's time under colonial rule, addresses racism and the violence of colonialism; the title alone indicts these things. Yet the entire novel comes to life through a tongue-in-cheek narration that is striking for its sharp humor. For example, the plot routinely builds up to crucial scenes between French colonial officers and members of the African populace. It then pans to dutiful but chronically blasé African interpreters trotted out by the French for communication. Consider one such professional on the job at a very highly anticipated award ceremony. Having been announced to much joyful hysteria, the ceremony and reception are replete with pomp, frenzy, medals, and a selection of colonial representatives including a "great Chief" who has specially come from France to address the people. After all the buildup, this is how the interpreter renders the Frenchman's—undoubtedly impressive—speech:

> —*Le grand Chef* . . . *a parlé de la guerre que vous avez faite ensemble contre les autres Blancs de chez lui* . . . *et il a terminé en disant que nous sommes plus que ses amis, nous sommes comme des frères, quelque chose comme cela* . . .
> *Tout le monde se mit à applaudir, l'interprète rejoignit sa place.* (*Le Vieux nègre* 118)

> ["The great Chief . . . spoke of the war which you made together against some other white men in his country. He finished by saying that we are more than friends, that we are like brothers. Something like that . . ."
> Everybody began to clap and the interpreter went back to his seat. (*Old Man* 105)]

The thrust of the humor, "*quelque chose comme cela,*" suggests an unimpressed, shrugging professional who was not paying much attention to begin with and is not particularly bothered if others remark on his apathy. With his clear preference for brevity and approximations; casual dismissal of the war as the

Introduction • 7

business of random, faraway white men; and polite disbelief in dubious declarations of brotherhood—in short, with the air of delightful indifference that he wafts over the occasion—the interpreter meets the much-harped-upon event and unceremoniously deflates it. The obliging applause only makes it more amusing. This and similar scenes, the focus of my intervention in this book, illustrate the prevalence and importance of such humorous modes in African literatures across the twentieth century. I do not intend so much to discuss audience reception of texts but to analyze what the texts themselves reveal.

LAUGHING IN THE GRAY AREAS

Humor is no longer considered a uniquely human phenomenon—apes apparently have the capacity for it. The humorous laughter among us humans implies a common culture, even if diluted—some shared perspective to throw the material into relief and implicitly explain how to judge it. That is why translating humor is notoriously complicated or why there can be studies on something as culturally specific as Jewish humor. This book reads texts from across the twentieth century from a variety of authors from different countries and cultures and with different styles. So, then, what is "African" about the humor of the primary material?

It is not, as I may seem to be suggesting with my examples so far, that such humor must involve bilingual interpreters doing questionable things with language. When American president Barack Obama made a speech in South Africa in 2013, the sign language interpreter for the occasion offended much more than he amused when he "translated" Obama's speech into gibberish. The protocol at the event was intense—high-profile personalities had gathered to eulogize Nelson Mandela—and the arm-waving fellow was roundly criticized; when he was called a "clown," it was *not* in jest.[10] Still, interpreting does offer insight into the workings of modern African literary texts. If we

---

10. Bruno Peter Druchen, head of the Deaf Federation of South Africa, tweeted "Please get RID of this CLOWN interpreter, please!" during the memorial: Mufson, Steven. "Interpreter for Deaf at Mandela Memorial Service Was a Fake, Advocates for Deaf Say." *Washington Post*, 11 Dec. 2013, www.washingtonpost.com/world/africa/interpreter-for-deaf-at-mandela-memorial-service-was-a-fake-advocates-for-deaf-say/2013/12/11/fc35cc12-628e-11e3-aa81-e1d-ab1360323_story.html. See also Memmott, Mark. "'Fake' Sign Language Interpreter Marred Mandela Memorial." *NPR*, 11 Dec. 2013, www.npr.org/sections/thetwo-way/2013/12/11/250179179/fake-sign-language-interpreter-marred-mandela-memorial.

wanted to find humor in the South African interpreter's delivery, we might consider it a failed attempt at spoofing a formal event. There are similar frictions between high promise and dubious results in the examples I have given so far.

More important, however, interpreting is useful because it highlights a peculiar uncertainty and elusiveness; as a practice, it inserts itself into the often-ambivalent status of the things and people in these narratives. Protocols, for instance, are not always clear-cut, and words do not always mean what they seem to mean; the religious leader of the concert party should not take it for granted that his congregation is looking to him for spiritual guidance any more than the colonial leader can safely assume that applause means approval. It is not a given, either, that the interpreters or their audience are privy to or aim to expose some higher truth about their society.[11] If humor has lagged behind other areas of African literary criticism, it is partly due to the trickiness of Africa's social granularity and the intricate social details reflected in its comic literatures. Humor certainly engages with opposition, resistance, and derision, but it also goes beyond these to lie in the new realities created when different worldviews or frames of reference collide, as they frequently do in these texts. At the risk of overworking my earlier metaphor, elbows, when they bang into each other, tickle the funny bone.

In other words, the literatures exploit the wealth of comic potential in the imbrication of different classes, political factions, belief systems, (un)officialdoms, and, of course, languages. I read writers—Ferdinand Oyono, Chuma Nwokolo, Wole Soyinka, Kobina Sekyi, Amadou Hampaté Bâ, Athol Fugard, Ola Rotimi, Okot p'Bitek—whose texts play with ambivalence in different ways and to comic effect. Their humor can be simultaneously subversive *and* conservative or critical of difference or newness. It resides in the tug-of-war between preserving the status quo and challenging it. These writers thus paint images with fascinating layers of ambiguity: a career fraudster bitterly chastising his victim for dishonesty; an Mfantse colonial subject earnestly proclaiming her Britishness in broken English; an interpreter hearing a text and blithely proclaiming the opposite message; or a clown bearing the trappings of a capable leader. Their amusing ethos comes through in narration and action.

---

11. In *Humor, Silence, and Civil Society in Nigeria*, Ebenezer Obadare studies the role of humor as an "irregular" weapon of resistance and subversion as well as a coping mechanism for the marginalized. He still notes, rightly, that among "ordinary people," humor is not meant exclusively to subvert (63).

Introduction • 9

In terms of narration, it must be noted that Africa's multilingualism is due to her own internal variegations as well as the infamous repartitions imposed by colonialism. Transnational and regional boundaries do not necessarily respect national borders. Also, countries may share borders and local languages but not the languages that international exchanges are now written in. Some nations leapfrog their closest neighbors to form trade agreements or treaties with others due to the conditions created by a shared French, English, and (for a smaller number) Portuguese colonial past.[12] On the continent, therefore, a country's or region's concerns are sometimes expressed as well—or better—by a distant neighbor as an adjacent one. To an extent, then, by adopting a comparative frame, this study reflects the reality of the crisscrossed connections among African countries and cultures. As I read a primary corpus composed of anglophone and francophone texts, I refer occasionally to secondary literary texts from different authors, spaces, and times for thematic emphasis or contrast.

While English and French are used officially in many countries on the continent, African languages existed before their arrival. They continue to evolve alongside and mutually influence each other. The anxiety of the concert party preacher to impress his listeners has historical roots: English, both a product of colonialism and a mark of modernity, is "displacing native languages, by installing itself as a 'standard' against other variants which are constituted as 'impurities'" (Ashcroft et al. 283). Linguistic hierarchization generates tensions that may reshape, deflate, or invert established orders. Though they are the medium employed by most African writers, English and French must regularly intermingle with the local languages, which have their own standards and leave their own imprint on stories. We have glimpsed, for instance, the possibilities that lie in the confusion of meanings. Interactions among languages have led to the growth of new variants—such as pidgins and Ghanaian or Nigerian English—and code switching. These provide more fodder for the humor of malapropisms, solecisms, and misreferences. Terms like "anglophone" and "francophone" are thus employed here with an awareness that African literary texts are not always written in "official" or "standard" English or French. Then, among the speakers of local African languages or dialects, there is playful mockery for reasons including pronunciation, vocab-

---

12. To give one example, eight francophone countries using a common currency came together to form the UEMOA (the West African monetary and Economic Union): Benin, Burkina Faso, Côte D'Ivoire, Mali, Niger, Senegal, and Togo.

TYPOLOGIES OF HUMOR IN AFRICAN LITERATURES

ulary, and the play-fighting that comes from pecking orders. Bame observes, for instance, that the version of Twi spoken by the Yoruba and the Mossi is "exceedingly amusing" to Twi viewers of concert parties (38). In Achebe's *Things Fall Apart* as well, the foray of English missionaries into the village of Mbanta involves an interpreter who speaks a different Igbo dialect; the people of Mbanta laugh at his unfortunate pronunciation and choice of words ("myself" in his dialect means "my buttocks" in theirs).

Furthermore, modern African fiction is typically understood to "happen" in one of those African languages; we know that Oyono's interpreter is not speaking French to his African audience. But the text is rendered in French (many also read an English translation). Yet, everything, seemingly, reaches us with no remainder. The French reader is meant to understand the joke against the French speaker, while the English reader is also to assume that there is smooth transmission and full cooperation between the "standard" and the "impure" languages. The fact that readers must take things at face value, rather like Oyono's clapping audience, creates another gray area where writers have leeway to amuse themselves with readers' expectations.

After how these stories are told, we can turn to the what, or the humorous phenomena encountered or created by comic characters. These include (1) the plot devices common to many modern African narratives—boastful "big men," younger second wives, the politics of the belly; (2) the conflicts peculiar to postcolonial contexts—cultural in-betweenness, subversion, and resistance; all consolidated by (3) the social value of humor—survival, a reprieve, establishing solidarity, or subversiveness. Though this list may not seem especially hilarious at first glance, it, too, underlines the tensions and ambiguities generative of humor.

• • •

THE KNOTTINESS OF HUMOR: "THE DRAMATIC IS FIRST"

To be fair to scholarship, especially as summed up so far, critical uninterest in the funny side of African literatures reflects an older, more pervasive trend in literary criticism generally. Comedy, since antiquity, has often been juxtaposed with tragedy and, in light of the latter's gravitas, treated with carelessness, if not condescension.[13] Humor is often held as too slippery or

---

13. (Hokenson 13). Antony J. Chapman and Hugh C. Foot confirm that "humour has often

Introduction • 11

unserious to study earnestly. There is also the notion that comic material lacks enough depth to be studied or, worse, that to scrutinize humor is to kill it. Then there is the issue of subjectivity. Such comments are not new—Aristotle observes in the *Nicomachean Ethics* that "tastes differ as to what is offensive and what amusing," forewarning that to tackle humor is often to wade into discordant waters.

We like to experience humor but do not bring the same enthusiasm to its study[14] ("I cannot criticize, I can only laugh," said one critic with refreshing frankness, if somewhat unhelpfully, upon reading P. G. Wodehouse[15]). It does bear recalling how the comical atmosphere of the interpreters from the previous sections effortlessly makes nonsense of words that take themselves too seriously. Or we may take a cue from Nwokolo's main character, who would likely object to being thrust into an overly theoretical undertaking: "What I don't like," Calamatus declares, "is for people to be laughing on my time." If humor has been called a "permanently unsolved" problem of literary study (Schilling 12), that may be partly because of the assumption that the enjoyment obtained from comic material is inversely proportional to any scholarly attention paid to it. Some discussions on humor thus seem to go out of their way to be as dry and humorless as possible, opening their writers up to some ironic commentary.[16] Others stand by the lack of funniness in studies on humor: Victor Raskin, editor of *Humor*, points out that in the same way

---

been characterized as base and degenerate, fit only for the ignorant and foolish" (1). John Morreall, whose work has made a significant impact on the field, adds that, traditionally, humor has been "the proverbial elephant in the room of human experience, ignored by the social sciences, whose attention was focused on the twin 800-pound gorillas of aggression and depression" (x).

14. Humor is frequently viewed as "a peripheral, leisure activity which lacks the more obvious significance of literature" (Ross 2). McGowan notes that, especially compared to other "extreme" experiences like loss and love, comic material invites us to enjoy the experience itself and not to scrutinize it; it is considered, by its very definition, *antithetical* to reflection (3).

15. Max Eastman might term that critic's approach to Wodehouse's humor as the "agnostic attitude" (130).

16. Baudelaire counters the inevitable objections from those he calls "*professeurs jurés de sérieux, charlatans de la gravité, cadavres pédantesques sortis des froids hypogées de l'Institut*" [staunchly serious professors, charlatans of gravity, pedantic cadavers taken from the chilly hypogea of the academe]. For his part, Voltaire remarks that "*ceux qui cherchent des causes métaphysiques au rire ne sont pas gais*" [those who investigate the metaphysical causes of laughter are not gay] (1832). Similarly, Georges Minois has described debates held by "*certains spécialistes dénués d'humour à propos de l'usage du mot 'humor'*" ["certain specialists devoid of a sense of humor, about the use of the word 'humor'"] (qtd. in Noonan 93). As Ross warns, books about humor are "unlikely" to be funny themselves (1).

12 • TYPOLOGIES OF HUMOR IN AFRICAN LITERATURES

that a journal on schizophrenia would not be expected to print abuse, humor scholars should not be expected to be *funny* (Weems).

Truthfully, it is difficult to speak about the comic without evoking "seriousness" or "drama" as the other side of the narrative coin. When Étienne Souriau presents over two hundred thousand possibilities for dramatic plots in *Les Deux cent mille situations dramatiques*, he wonders if there are situations that are intrinsically dramatic and that can be treated only by tragedy or drama and others that are completely comic. He decides that none is comic or tragic in itself; the comic aspect of a situation is arrived at through an active reduction of its dramatic dimension. He can then conclude that his book provides as many comic situations as dramatic ones. Still, he says, the dramatic comes first.[17] Gérard Genette also recognizes that humor is not typically our default mode.[18] However, he also contends that every situation is "dramatic" in the neutral sense of having an action as its departure point. A situation is thus open to an affective reception that is more or less serious or amused (428): when we think of a church service, we picture a thoughtful gathering before imagining rogue interpreters.

If we follow Souriau and Genette, which can be a productive choice, then a comic reading is almost always generative.[19] That means that even if African literature strove to be a reflection or "spectacle" of intense sociopolitical incidents (Ndebele 42), a comic bias would yield interesting results. Nevertheless, this book is not setting out to reexamine random texts from contrived comic angles. Nor will I mine obviously tragic texts for some humor in order to prove a point. Instead, I will read texts that explicitly seek to make their readers laugh and in which humor occupies a primary position. As Genette admits, some objects and styles are better suited to forming comic connections than others (429).

---

17. "*le dramatique est le premier . . . elles sont dramatiques d'abord, originellement, essentiellement*" [the dramatic is first . . . originally and essentially, plots are dramatic before anything else" (Souriau 50–53).

18. "*C'est le sérieux, en somme, qui serait premier, et il serait plus fréquent (plus naturel?) de passer, comme dit Boileau, 'du grave au doux,' que 'du plaisant au sévère'*" [It is the serious, in short, that appears to come first. It seems more frequent (more natural?) to go, as Boileau puts it, "from the grave to the sweet," than "from the pleasant to the harsh"] (436–437).

Though they aim to emphasize humor's "desirability" and "popularity," Chapman and Foot, by saying that it fulfills emotional needs in "our everyday humdrum lives," implicitly confirm that humor is not the first medium one turns to when faced with a text or situation.

19. Best resumed by Genette's response to the "classic" question "*Peut-on rire de tout?*" [Can we laugh at everything?]: "*De quoi d'autre voulez-vous qu'on rie?*" [What else would you like us to laugh at?] (424).

THEORIES OF HUMOR AND THEIR LIMITATIONS

So far, I have used the words "humor" and "comic" and "laughter" without defining them. This is partly because it is possible to discuss such everyday phenomena without explicitly stating what they are beforehand. "Everyone thinks he knows" what humor is, remark Anthony Chapman and Hugh Foot in *Humour and Laughter: Theory, Research and Applications* (3); at the same time, it seems that nobody quite "nose." We must apply caution, since even the most well-intentioned attempts at definitions can lead to what Will Noonan calls the "age-old trap" of circular definitions (94).[20] Even English and French, with shared origins, do not have neat translations between them.

Though a lot more can be (and has been) said about this state of affairs, I am employing "humor" in a relatively restrictive sense. Here, it is not the subcategory of a larger classification. Nor will this study emphasize laughter's aggressively negative connotations. The primary texts, if they do not stimulate physical, "good-tempered laughter" (Chapman and Foot 3), are at least intended to invoke a milder reaction—perhaps, good-tempered *smiles*. While humor can be both impetus and response, I place less emphasis on a visible response, since that can depend on random external factors (company, mood, physical well-being, etc.). Moreover, reading is generally a solitary exercise, and studies have shown that we are thirty times more likely to laugh at an experience when it is shared.[21] Even if I will not place too high a premium on a visible or audible response, I will consider the texts' engagement with their audience and the creation of a mutually enjoyable dialogue. And though we can laugh at something whose humorous dimension was not deliberately created, I consider that the reader of the texts I have chosen is under the impression that his laughter is a welcome reaction and even the texts' ambition.

Some studies use "comedy" interchangeably with "humor," but the same will not be done here.[22] However, I do employ "comic" as a synonym of

---

20. Deep dives into definitions risk aporia and entanglements that can be amusing in themselves. Terminology is "at once mind-bogglingly extensive and still insufficient: One woman's humor is another's laughter; one man's wit is another's joke" (Reichl and Stein 4). Jean Sareil also recognizes "*Cette difficulté d'isoler et de définir la satire, l'ironie, l'humour explique, à mon avis, pourquoi . . . dans les études consacrées à ces figures, on trouve tant de catégories, tant d'essais de définition*" [This difficulty in isolating and defining satire, irony, humor . . . explains, in my opinion, why . . . in studies dedicated to them, we find so many categories, and so many essays with definitions] ("La Démolition" 2).

21. Notably, Robert Provine's "Laughter" in *American Scientist* 84, no.1 (1996): 38–45.

22. "Comedy" suggests a history as a theatrical genre with rules and traditions that date to Ancient Greece. "Humor" is obviously not being used to refer to olden concepts about human

"humor" (even though "comic" sometimes refers to stand-up comedians). The meaning here is taken from the *Merriam Webster Dictionary*: "causing laughter or amusement; funny."[23] The object of humor/the comic in this book is what Noël Carroll terms "comic amusement," a kind of pleasure that, among other things, activates the brain's reward system (4). Laughter is often an external sign of this condition. Here, too, people sometimes laugh at things they do not find funny at all; at other times, though they are extremely tickled, they do not even crack a smile. I am therefore limiting laughter to its role as the physiological response to humor and adhering closer to Jean Sareil's opening claim in *L'Écriture comique*—"*Le rire est à la gaieté ce que les larmes sont à la tristesse et le bâillement à l'ennui*" (5) [Laughter is to gaiety what tears are to sadness and yawning to boredom].[24]

Given that the terms used are not always fixed, it should not be surprising that the theories conceived of to explain laughter are themselves varied. Much ink has been spilled over the millennia to explain why people laugh, resulting in a plethora of texts that range from passing comments to entire volumes. These days, many studies on laughter and humor are multidisciplinary, shaped by fields from philosophy through neuroscience and psychology to literature. Each of these areas is constantly making new discoveries. Currently in humor studies, a consensus has it that in terms of a uniting theory that captures the "essence" of humor and laughter, there is little by way of consensus.[25] Sareil sums up the situation succinctly: "*J'appelle comique ce qui me fait rire*" [I label as comic whatever makes me laugh] ("La Démolition" 1).[26] Nevertheless, the field categorizes the existing theories in the field of humor studies under three main umbrellas: Superiority, Relief, and Incon-

---

character (choleric, sanguine, etc.).

23. In psychoanalysis, however, "humor" and "comic" are not to be used interchangeably (Chapman and Foot 2).

24. Voltaire is less subtle: "*Que le rire soit le signe de la joie comme les pleurs sont le symptôme de la douleur, quiconque a ri n'en doute pas*" [Nobody who has laughed doubts that laughter signals joy, just as tears are the symptom of pain] (1832).

25. "Humor studies" refers to an interdisciplinary field with studies from specialties as varied as neuroscience and psychology. A significant portion of the most influential theories come from literature and philosophy. There are now journals, conferences, and associations dedicated to the academic study of humor.

26. Genette echoes him, perhaps inadvertently, and puts emphasis on the subject and direct object as though to highlight the subjectivity of the exercise: "*j'appelle comique ce qui* me *fait rire*" (429).

gruity.[27] Even though it is common to approach the three theses as a tripartition, many of their theorists did not write full treatises on the subject and were not aware of consciously participating in a movement.

Though studies on humor are not obliged to be entertaining, many do emphasize its positivity and cheer.[28] That optimism is not shared by proponents of the Superiority theory, which carries an air of disapproval about it. This thesis implies that where there is laughter, there is a victim, and that humor must be approached warily because laughing involves unrefined behavior, excessiveness, and ascendancy. Plato, commonly cited under this theory, specifies that laughter can be a pleasure but condemns it for being tied to a lack of self-control. In an ideal state, as he sets forth in *The Republic*, men "shouldn't be lovers of laughter" (Plato and Bloom 66). Thomas Hobbes, the most-censorious philosopher under the Superiority theory, is even more categorical. In *Leviathan*, he declares that laughter is a sign of selfishness and cowardice.[29] The Superiority theory thus holds that laughter is largely suspect, a somewhat puritan interpretation that finds echoes in some interpretations of Christianity, particularly in the Middle Ages and during the Protestant Reformation. It may also seem extreme.[30] John Lippitt, however, shows that there is "no shortage of evidence that people are amused by 'the infirmities of others.' As late as the eighteenth century, it was common for the wealthy to visit lunatic asylums to laugh at and taunt the inmates for fun" (54). One can

---

27. Morreall offers comprehensive overviews of the different theories over the centuries and categorizes them first under these three schools. It is worth noting that there are other (less prominent) theories.

28. As Chapman and Foot state, "To laugh freely and frequently at humorous and pleasurable events is regarded as thoroughly healthy and desirable by virtually all those who have concerned themselves with the subject of humor. The average man is also firmly committed to the belief that having a reputation for a keen sense of humor is something to be treasured" (1). Carroll even calls up the fact that we frequently pay for humor to be created for us (6).

29. He also remarks that laughter springs from scorn and pride: "Men laugh at mischances and indecencies . . . Men laugh often, especially such as are greedy of applause from every thing they do well . . . The passion of laughter proceedeth from a sudden conception of some ability in himself that laugheth. Also men laugh at the infirmities of others, by comparison wherewith their own abilities are set off and illustrated. Also men laugh at jests, the wit whereof always consisteth in the elegant discovering and conveying to our minds some absurdity of another: and in this case also the passion of laughter proceedeth from the sudden imagination of our own odds and eminency" (qtd. in *Cyclopedia of English Literature* 268).

30. Morreall cites one of the rules of the Monastery of Columban: "He who smiles in the service . . . six strokes; if he breaks out in the noise of laughter, a special fast unless it has happened pardonably" (5).

also point to cruel playground teasing and Henri Bergson's claim that laughter serves as a social corrective. If we were to look at "The Crusade" through this lens, the viewer's laughter would be at the expense of the pastor or the congregation.

Nonetheless, the Superiority tradition does not always hold. After all, what of laughing at oneself, which many of us are perfectly capable of doing? Also, as Francis Hutcheson points out, a rich person is more likely to weep than to laugh at the sight of beggars in the street (qtd. in Morreall, 9). Sareil confirms, "*Les agressions de ce type sont innombrables, mais il existe autant de cas où le comique est dépourvu de toute marque d'hostilité . . . L'analyse n'est pas fausse, elle est incomplète*" [Attacks of this type are countless, but there are just as many cases where the comic is devoid of any sign of hostility . . . The analysis is not false, it is incomplete] (*L'Écriture comique* 8–9).

Moreover, superiority does not explain "the very odd movements" that are laughter itself (Spencer 395). The Relief theory addresses the physicality of laughing and is traced by some thinkers to Aristotle. Given his ideas about catharsis, they postulate that in the lost half of the *Poetics*, Aristotle proposes humor as a way of releasing pent-up emotions (Carroll 38).[31] Similarly, the Earl of Shaftesbury's "The Freedom of Wit and Humor" (1711) posits that resourceful men, when controlled or imprisoned, will rebel against their constrainers to avenge themselves.[32] Scientists of the eighteenth century viewed the nervous system as a connection of tubes that transported so-called animal spirits. The venting would thus occur after a buildup of these in the body. John Morreall likens this to excess steam building up in a steam boiler. The analogy is likewise appropriate for Herbert Spencer, who assimilates emotions to nervous energy. Past a certain intensity, this energy begets muscular motion and bodily actions. Fear will lead to flight, while anger will lead to clenching of one's fists and then attack. Laughter, on the other hand, serves as the release of *excess* energy.[33] Outside of this function, Spencer declares, laughter has no purpose. Freud's definition of humor is similar: psychic energy is summoned for an incident that calls for feelings like sympathy or

---

31. This is speculative. Other scholars believe that Aristotle's take on humor rather fits "primarily" into the Incongruity theory (Perks 122).

32. This is the first published instance of "humor" being used with the sense that it has today (Morreall 16).

33. Energy is "readied," for example, for a situation we think calls for pity. But that prepared energy is found to be inappropriate or unnecessary for the situation. The excess energy is vented as laughter.

pity. When these feelings are found to be inappropriate, the energy is vented as laughter.[34]

The Relief theory is also criticized, mainly for its mechanical aspect and the idea that energy is summoned for a task and then dismissed as laughter. While Freud's propositions are certainly methodical, the implication that psychic energy is directly proportional to physical energy is one of their weaknesses. Morreall criticizes this "theory of mimetic representation," according to which "we expend a great amount of energy to understand something big and a small amount of energy to understand something small" (19). Moreover, it is possible, he points out, to be amused without feeling pent-up emotion that is then found to be inappropriate. Overall, the "hydraulic" or "pressure valve" theory of emotions and thinking is not always plausible (21).

Morreall calls Incongruity the dominant theory of humor (10). For Lisa Glebatis Perks, it "describes the most basic building block of humor" (121). Quite fittingly, the notions categorized under this theory do not always agree.[35] However, as varied as they are—linked to Aristotle, Cicero, Alexander Bain, Immanuel Kant, and others—they have a fundamental concept in common: perceiving (and possibly resolving) an incongruity. For Schopenhauer, it is about a mismatch between a concept and an empirical entity. *Congruere*, Morreall reminds us, means "to come together, to agree." At the heart of the *In*congruity theory, then, are things that "do not go together, match or fit in some way" (10). We perceive and are amused by "a thing whose parts or features violate [the] mental patterns" we form in relation to each of those parts (11). Going by this lens, for "The Crusade," humor comes from the mismatch between the interpreter's confidence and inaccuracy. There is also an obvious lack of "fit" between meaning and output.

It is for the sake of incongruity that Horace claims we could not "refrain from laughing" if we were presented with a painting depicting the head of a beautiful woman joined with the body of an ugly fish (qtd. in Morreall 10). Aristotle's take is that "the thought is startling, and . . . does not fit in with the ideas you already have." He adds, the "effect is produced even by jokes" and

---

34. In *Jokes and Their Relation to the Unconscious* (also translated as *Wit and Its Relation to the Unconscious*). For Freud, "the original material of all comedy is pure obscenity" (McGowan 56). He distinguishes "joking" from "humor" and "the comic." Jokes are of a sexual or hostile nature. In telling jokes, the psychic energy that society obliges us to use to repress libido and hostility is released. The comic also involves releasing energy that was amassed but found to be unnecessary.

35. The term is often misused (Morreall 10).

18 • TYPOLOGIES OF HUMOR IN AFRICAN LITERATURES

illustrates this with his own idea of a joke: "*Onward he came, and his feet were shod with his—chilblains*, where one imagined the word would be 'sandals'" (*Rhetoric* 160). After pausing for comic effect, Aristotle introduces something incompatible with the initial narrative.[36] Scholars continue to accord importance to that notion of the unexpected and so apply this theory to stand-up comics, given their tendency to round off a joke with a punch line. Incongruity would thus suit the following anecdote by South African comedian Trevor Noah, set during the "Fearbola" crisis:[37]

> It was honestly one of the worst flights I've ever taken in my life. It was so tense! I coughed once. The plane shook. There was one guy who couldn't even hold it—I couldn't hold it any longer and *he* couldn't hold it and I was like [*mild coughing*] and he was like: [*manic pointing and screaming*] "Ebola! Ebola!"
>
> I was like: "Calm down, calm down! It's just AIDS."[38]

Noah's audience bursts into laughter. They undoubtedly did not expect that his persona, after appealing for "calm," would try to defuse his interlocutor's panic by bringing up another transmissible and incurable disease.

TYPOLOGIES

Here is another intersection with "The Crusade": the risk of being like Kinaata's interpreter, who always applies something that does not quite fit. This pertains not only to the use of earlier theories but also to my own overarching conception of humor. Theories are not irrelevant. But they are not universally applicable.[39] Since all three umbrella theories can be given an African

---

36. Jerry Palmer notes that Aristotle is *not* offering a theory of humor (94). But Perks opines that the second part of the *Poetics* might have given a more detailed impact of Greek influence on the Incongruity theory. She cites scholars who have reconstituted Aristotle's text and who allude to incongruity as a central part of the philosopher's take on humor (122).

37. What Tara C. Smith calls "in the United States—the out-of-proportion panic at the possibility of Ebola cases": Smith, Tara C. "Ebola Panic Peaked in America a Year Ago. What Were We Thinking?" *Slate Magazine*, 6 Oct. 2015, slate.com/technology/2015/10/ebola-panic-anniversary-predictions-of-a-u-s-epidemic-didnt-come-true.html.

38. Transcribed from "Stand-up set by Trevor Noah." *YouTube*, uploaded by Comic Relief: Red Nose Day, 14 March 2015, https://www.youtube.com/watch?v=v76B8GUYflk.

39. There is also significant overlap. Kant's assertion that "laughter is an affect resulting from

Introduction • 19

inflection and are relevant to a colonial and postcolonial context, I will refer to them every so often over the course of the book. During colonialism, for example, the laughter generated by superiority and victimhood has a political charge; it makes a difference whether we laugh at the uneducated man for his mistake or the colonizer for his cultural ignorance. Regarding Relief, humor can be read as the release of the pent-up anger and frustration of those who are powerless to act or strike out in overt ways. Incongruity can be seen in clashes between cultures or in the relations between centers of power and their peripheries. That said, not everything is distilled to the colonial encounter, and we must not completely ignore indigenous attitudes to laughter. This book explores the ways in which humor in modern African literatures articulates a pursuit of balance between contrasting worldviews and frames of reference. I use that notion of equilibrium not as a sine qua non of humor but to trace out typologies for modern African literary humor.[40]

I refer throughout to remarks by Mikhail Bakhtin, Henri Bergson, Gérard Genette, Achille Mbembe, and Jean Sareil because their approaches to humor have largely literary applications. Given the proven insufficiency of single theses, the necessary complementarity of theories, and the slipperiness of humor itself, declarations about the workings of humor are more worthwhile when they serve the primary material than the other way around: Superiority, Relief, Incongruity, and so on, as well as my own ideas, are relevant insofar as they reveal something interesting about the corpus. Thus, many of the analyses in this book build on close readings. Furthermore, postcolonial scholars caution against applying notions "uncritically" to African literature so as not "to substitute one mode of neocolonialism for another" (Gates, "Writing 'Race'" 15). This book, however, is written with the confidence that to apply theory derived from elsewhere to African material can illuminate both the literature *and* the limits of the theory. It may help us understand African lit-

---

the sudden destruction of the tension arising from an expectation" has only to be held up to another light, as Genette does, to see that it could pertain just as well to tragedy or even death (Genette 417–418). For his part, Bergson offers a "genetic" description—a "recipe" for fabricating the comic (Genette 424): laughter is stimulated by imposing the mechanical on the living. In that sense, the Reverend Father Drumont in Beti's *Le Pauvre Christ de Bomba* is comic in that he spends decades imposing religious conversions on Africans like a distracted automaton, unaware of the reality best exemplified by the prostitution ring booming in the backyard of his own church. Bergson's recipes, of course, do not always hold; *Things Fall Apart*'s Okonkwo is obsessive but does not at once jump to mind as a comic character.

40. The typologies contain variations, and this book must leave out much material worth studying. Besides other writers who merit analysis, this book does not study oral literary texts.

erature better. At the same time, the use of African literature can assess the cultural and conceptual limitations of those theories.[41]

• • •

At the heart of the primary texts is some form of imbalance, ambivalence, or tension manifesting in ways that are generatively chaotic and funny. The product of these rowdy relations, I argue, are the characters populating the African comic universe, who take the weirdness and run with it. My typologies, thus, build on the four recurrent character archetypes I have already hinted at: the *trickster*, who "recurs with startling frequency" in postcolonial literature (*Signifying Monkey* 4) and who is unapologetically amoral and entertaining; the *mimic*, whose iterations are inherent to the colonial experience (Bhabha, *Location* 85) and whose ethos exudes ambiguity; the (by now infamous) *interpreter*, who mediates between two groups and does a terrible job of it; and the *deviant*, a burlesque figure cutting across strata in African societies (Mbembe 133), questioning and reinforcing norms.

Kinaata's persona reveals the flexibility of these typologies. As a trickster, the interpreter's role in "The Crusade" to indulge his appetite; when he feels that the sermon has dragged on enough, he prompts the pastor to take up the collection. When the song ends, the crowd is dispersed and the expectation is that the video will end as well, the camera pans to him sitting with the huge basin between his legs, exclaiming over the amount, and insulting the pastor. His body language and abusive remarks call to mind Kweku Ananse, the quintessential Akan trickster, whose ethos is marked indelibly by greed and the hoarding of communal wealth. As a mimic and interpreter, Kinaata's character stands between the pastor in ecclesiastical dress, bringing a message of salvation exclusively in English, and the mass of believers. The humor depends on incongruities in his botched reproduction of formal codes. The fact that interpreting is traditionally considered a secondary task is called

---

41. So far, most major studies have been illustrated by texts sourced from standard European languages. Many of Freud's examples are German. Sareil is adamant about limiting his study to French literature. Even then, his attention is on a restricted group of great authors, excluding "minor" writers and anything in a foreign language (*L'Écriture* 17).

Bergson's theories apply effectively to vaudeville and to French theatre; many of his illustrations come from Molière. When Bergson waxes eloquent on how hilarious the face of a black person can appear for its seeming unnaturalness (24), it becomes even clearer that not all theories should be applied wholesale.

into question (in the simple fact that *he* signals the pastor to speak by opening the song with "*Sɔfo, yɛnkɔ*" ["Pastor, let's go"]). Finally, his deviancy comes to life especially in his relationship with "the people." The congregation does not seem to want a more "sensible" outcome, nor are they bothered by funding a suspiciously un-Christian activity. In one brief scene, a disgruntled young man storms up to the duo on the dais, but is smoothly intercepted and led away by ushers. The other worshippers are thus free to sing and dance. They are happy to catch the Holy Spirit, nap, take selfies, flirt, and nod along to a sermon that tells them that having received the Bread of Life, it is now time to demand fruit juice. In the end, the message is mostly incidental, while performance is everything.

The trickster is omnipresent in the literary landscape and can often be counted on for laughs.[42] Chapter 1 will discuss the con man and the fake pastor as iterations of the trickster in Chuma Nwokolo's *Diaries of a Dead African* and Wole Soyinka's *Jero* plays. The chapter explores a connection between the trickster ethos and superiority to show how laughter is ultimately a tool in the trickster's repertoire. Furthermore, by infusing his narration with his problematic personality, the trickster invites us to consider our own reading.

The mimic represents linguistic and cultural mediation. This typology embraces failed communication and the awkwardness of different cultures interacting in an uneven setting. It highlights the vacillations between "official" and "formal" spaces—vestiges of colonial structures, including churches and courts of law—and "unofficial" cultural elements, such as the so-called informal educational skills and laws.[43] Chapter 2 will read Kobina Sekyi's *The Blinkards* through character development, nascent nationalism, and Sekyi's sociohistorical context, before turning to Ferdinand Oyono's *Le Vieux nègre*

---

42. In the Akan tradition, the art of storytelling is named after Ananse the trickster, which gives an indication of his importance to the framework of creating and appreciating literary texts.

43. In his discussion of the institution of law in postcolonial contexts, Neil ten Kortenaar underlines the fundamental differences between the law and elements from the "unofficial" realm: "That the law is a foreign institution is obvious wherever indigenous understandings have tried to engage it. The law imposed by the colonizer, like the institution of literature, is based on writing: on the signature, fine print, the archive, the contract, the act of parliament, and the constitution. It does not know what to do with, say, oral testimony: claims to territory or to authority based on inherited memories. The law assumes private property and shies away from collective property. It protects individuals but does not know respect collectives. It cannot conceive of overlapping sovereignties" ("Law and Literature" 1).

et la médaille as a comparison. The chapter will focus on the unfolding of an exaggerated form of didacticism and contrast it with another technique, which balances its lessons against a simultaneously vivid and subtle humor.

Interpreting supposes a significant amount of trust. After all, if neither side understands the other, then some serious and possibly naïve assumptions are being made regarding the interpreter's integrity. The comic interpreter calls into question the assumption that interpreting is a subordinate task. He approaches his job with little regard for scholarly ideals or standards, so that what becomes important is the plainly material. Chapter 3 will focus chiefly on Amadou Hampaté Bâ's *L'Etrange destin de Wangrin*, but it will also discuss the interpreter's role in Achebe's *Things Fall Apart*, Oyono's *Le Vieux nègre et la médaille*, and Athol Fugard's *Sizwe Bansi Is Dead*.

The interpreter is funny because he behaves unexpectedly; humor turns normal situations on their head. Chapter 4 will look at unfettered idiocy and the release and relief that accompany it. This typology will also query our expectations of normalcy as well as our readiness to laugh. The chapter will read Ola Rotimi's *Our Husband Has Gone Mad Again*, Okot p'Bitek's *Song of Lawino*, and Wole Soyinka's *The Lion and the Jewel*. It will examine various leaders as comic characters while investigating "norms": social and literary conventions, the assumptions that we bring to comic texts, and the interactions between men and women.

The four figures, each in his own way, hint at the condition that the African comic writer might find himself in. African writers writing in English or French inevitably act as interpreters, are conscious that they might be judged as mimics, and have something about them of tricksters or deviants. Also, humor works if we understand both ends of the conversation. As consumers of African literature written in English or French, our laughter is possible because we trust the author to offer us an overview of the situations and the dialogues, which are often understood to take place in local languages that we may not have access to. As readers, we therefore find ourselves as dependent on the transmitter of the text as the congregation or the pastor that we are invited to laugh at. As the following chapters will show, the conversation between the writer and reader manifests itself in different ways. Among other things, there is the potential for mockery *and* self-mockery on the part of the author.

Several of the comments so far—that humor is intrinsic to human culture, that it is subjective, and so on—seem obvious once articulated but must be stated regardless. It must also be noted that even the choice of material for

Introduction • 23

this book could prove problematic if the reader does not find it particularly amusing. It is true that certain basic conditions make it easier for people to perceive material as comical, including a willingness to be entertained. But it must also be admitted that these texts are quite simply "the best examples of a certain view of life" (Schilling 12). For, as Freud elaborates, it only makes sense for the writer to use the examples that have most struck and entertained him over the course of his life (12). The writer can only hope that others find them striking as well.

CHAPTER 1

Trickster

A condensed version of Chuma Nwokolo's *Diaries of a Dead African* first appeared in the *London Review of Books*. The novel tells the stories of Meme Jumai, a farmer, and his two sons, Abel and Calamatus. Recounted as entries in the same diary, the action reveals a Nigeria on the cusp of the new millennium wrestling with rural and urban life, new technologies, and evolving definitions of morality. Of the three main characters, the colorfully named Calamatus stands out as the quintessential trickster inspired by West African folklore. The trickster is many things: simultaneously "deceiver, thief . . . inventor, creator, benefactor, magician [and] perpetrator of obscene acts" (S.G.F. Brandon as quoted by Robert Pelton 5). Calamatus puts particular emphasis on "thief"; he is a 419-confidence man,[1] who exhibits these ageless trickster attributes in a modern context by incorporating newer technology into his schemes. He does all this while showcasing a feature that Pelton makes brief reference to but that is of fundamental importance to this chapter—the "essentially comic nature of the trickster" (11).

Having earned thousands of dollars through advance-fee fraud, Calamatus keeps his home village of Ikerre-Oti humming with news of his ostentatious spending. It is because of his flashy lifestyle—activities include but are not limited to "spraying" the hungry crowds with money and bathing with a bucket of wine—that, as the first of his many apprentices reports to Calamatus, his neighbors are convinced he must be a con man. A flea, as the hard-up but lucid villagers reason, cannot be fatter than the dog who houses him. This is Calamatus's response to those rumors, as paraphrased in his diary:

---

1. This is a term for advance-fee fraud. The name comes from the section of the Nigerian Criminal Code it falls under. Some Western embassies in West African countries now put up strong warnings against scammers looking to land foreign victims.

I explained to him that I was a con-artist, not just an ordinary conman, and that anybody who thought it was easy to tell lies and get rich was welcome to try it. After all, there's no Chartered Institute of Fraud signing only fifty certificates a year to keep their members rich. It wasn't like medicine where they take seven years worth of examinations for the right to wear stethoscopes. (Nwokolo loc. 798)

For all that humor has no specific domain, rhetorical devices are enlightening (Sareil, *L'Écriture* 10, 14). There is a strong sense of irony in Calamatus's righteously indignant tone as he dares anybody to try swindling. It is also in the ease with which he relegates otherwise respectable specialists to a backdrop whose function is to display his own ingenuity. Through understatement, or meiosis, business service providers have become hostages to their higher-ups. Those in charge have a stranglehold on their presiding body—and, it is implied, are clever by virtue of operating in ways reminiscent of scam artists. By artificially limiting certificates, they manufacture desire and control value. Not only would con men be conned by their own institute if they had one, but also, Calamatus is saying, the less adventurous professionals of the world are constantly conned by theirs. Doctors in training are reduced to examination-writing, stethoscope-wearing automatons. Clearly, the trickster lives by and profits from his conviction that the institutions of this world are intended to deceive, and he is at heart no worse than anyone else who is successful.

An important difference is that none of those occupations offers quick financial returns. Calamatus, a thief, can therefore dismiss what looks like a lot of foolish and disproportionate years of training, indefinite waits for certification, or seven years of examinations, for the anticlimactic opportunity to wear a stethoscope. Small wonder, then, that the con "artist" gains apprentices even without recruiting. A fundamental lesson for them is that they can gain far better returns on the investment of their time if they can lie. The scam artist's inventiveness is treated with overemphasis, since he stands head and shoulders above others; the words "just," "ordinary," and "only" certainly do not apply to him, and he is not on the same level as con men, thieves, followers and dupes. He is a creator who has elevated fraud into a lucrative calling that is the perquisite of only the most talented.

Taking what appears to be inordinate pride in scamming and yet making a case for creative and artistic genius, the trickster has eloquently and humorously imposed his own vision on the world and how it works. This chapter explores the intersections between the trickster and humor in Nwokolo's *Dia-*

ries of a Dead African and Soyinka's *Jero* plays. How does the trickster wield the laughter he incites? When do we laugh *with* the trickster at the foolishness of those who accept the world at face value, and when do we laugh *at* the trickster and his brazen self-regard? How does his singular vision manifest its humor, and, given his preoccupation with creating opportunities out of the ordinary, to what end is humor tied to his ethos? Where do we, as upstanding members of our communities who would be most opposed to being scammed, stand?

Trickster figures abound in various literatures, from Coyote in Native American cosmogony through Hermes in Greek mythology to Leuk-le-lièvre and Kweku Ananse. Ubiquitous in African folktales, the trickster is as complex as he is entertaining. The tales he features in serve different purposes, such as instructing their audience about social mores; in many cases, they also moralize. Paul Radin goes as far as to suggest that the civilizing process begins within the framework of the trickster myth.[2] Lewis Hyde likewise cites instances across cultures where the trickster is the one who gives mankind fire, teaches them agriculture, and provides other benefits. West Africa's famous Ananse stories serve various purposes, not least of which is allowing the listener to live vicariously through the kinds of exploits that are normally not permitted but that, through the medium of the story, are indulged and treated as a source of entertainment.

LAUGHTER AND THE TRICKSTER

Persuasive and cheekily unapologetic about the havoc he regularly wreaks on his community, the trickster is often cited as being equally at the margin of society and in its center.[3] Calamatus is determined to be a prominent (and rich) fixture of his community and yet thumbs his nose at whatever constraints do not suit him, all the while making a laughingstock of his neighbors. The trickster is all at once "fooler and fool" (Pelton 3); he is the "creative idiot, therefore, the wise fool, the gray-haired baby, the crossdresser, the speaker of sacred profanities . . . the mythic embodiment of ambiguity and ambivalence,

---

2. See "The Trickster and the Messiah" in Vine Deloria Jr.'s *Spirit & Reason: The Vine Deloria, Jr. Reader* , which offers a comprehensive explanation as to why this cannot be the case.

3. "These trickster characters display . . . gifts of creative expression that enable them to act more freely than others within and around restrictive societal codes" (Lynn 153). Hyde agrees with this (7).

doubleness and duplicity" (Hyde 7). There is an intriguing mishmash of traits in Calamatus's self-portrait—earnest dishonesty, ironic disdain, calculated disingenuousness. Given his multitude of often-contradictory characteristics, the trickster is said to defy social logic (Pelton 1). Maybe so. Or perhaps his take on notions like society and logic is more elastic. Soyinka's Jero and his congregation, like Calamatus's dismissal of professional institutions, make their case for a *kind* of social logic other than the version we would all likely stand behind if questioned by a magistrate of the peace.

Laughter, much like the logic of the trickster, "a rock upon which many . . . have foundered" (Pelton 5), notoriously defies logical attempts to classify it. Bergson opens *Le Rire* with deceptively simple questions: What does laughter *mean*? What is laughable? Freud's *Wit* indicts philosophers for being "far" from delineating the role of wit in human life (7). Others even more frankly admit their own shortcomings up front (Genette 425). Given that the very framework against which this chapter reads him can be so convoluted, the trickster fits into a study on laughter in interesting ways. Though a shared thorniness does not make a full case, there are enough instances of the trickster acting as instigator of humorous scenarios to deserve a closer look. While it might be complicated to pin a definition onto the trickster, he is often reliably funny, a trait springing from his "originality of vision" (Lynn 164). Indeed, broadly speaking, humor lies in the very dishonest techniques that, ordinarily, society should discourage. The activities eliciting laughter are "anomalous. When we're out for a laugh, we break social conventions right and left. We exaggerate wildly, express emotions we don't feel, and insult people we care about. In practical jokes, we lie to friends and cause them inconvenience, even pain" (Morreall 2). We may chuckle at the peacocking of a 419 con man, even though his actions have real consequences.[4] Oral folktales likewise showcase the trickster in his element as he taunts and hoodwinks innocent characters and random passersby.

Beyond folklore, several studies examine how writers successfully rewrite the trickster figure into newer texts. "Numerous traits possessed by West African mythic tricksters . . . are exhibited by modern West African literary characters," writes Thomas Lynn (153). For her part, Pascale de Souza classi-

---

4. While it is still difficult to calculate exact figures, it was proposed, even in 2005, that losses from 419 crimes "characteristically run into millions of dollars" (Oriola 241). To quote a slightly uncharitable but effective title from arstechnica.com, "~~Suckers~~ Victims lost $9.3 billion to 419 scammers in 2009." Jacqui Cheng, 29 Jan. 2010, https://arstechnica.com/information-technology/2010/01/victims-lost-93-billion-to-419-scammers-in-2009/

fies the hero of Alain Mabanckou's *Black Bazar* as a trickster due to the presence of recurring elements from trickster tales: "life in liminal spaces, shape-shifting abilities, and Signifyin(g) powers" (103). Henry Louis Gates famously traces the "startling" recurrence of the African trickster figure in Caribbean and African American culture in his *Signifying Monkey* (4). He posits that the black trickster has been able to "emerge intact from such traumatic crossings" (23) and continue to thrive. It is not surprising to note the persistence of the trickster, given his great ability to adapt. "If we accept that each society has its own tricksters and culture heroes," states Katrien Pype, "then we may expect that these characters alter over time" (119). In that light, Pelton asks what it means to study the trickster in a particular culture: "Do we already know what he is so that every study is merely a search for a new embodiment of him? Or is it just the other way around, so that we understand the word 'trickster' to be merely a *nomen*, purely a work of the mind that we apply to a vast array of more or less similar phenomena which remain nevertheless irreducibly particular?" (14). Though he acknowledges that he has raised "one of the knottiest of philosophical problems," Pelton does not aim to resolve it. He does, however, advise against trimming material to fit a ready-made form or analyzing the material like an encyclopedist. He is also right to point out that the trickster pattern seems "more suited to asking questions than to answering them" (17)! Still, I propose, for the rest of this chapter, an analysis of how the trickster, an intensely pragmatic being, translates his liminality into freedom from social mores and his superiority into laughter. He provokes amusement at the expense of others and sometimes becomes an object of it despite himself. As a starting point, I look to a remark by Hyde, who, in a bid to identify modern-day instances of tricksters, names the confidence trickster in literature as a very likely candidate (11).

CALAMATUS—THE TRICKSTER AS COMIC WRITER IN *DIARIES OF A DEAD AFRICAN*

Divided into three sections, Nwokolo's novel follows two generations, a father and his sons. Meme Jumai is a desperate, lonely farmer who falls further and further into malnourishment as he waits for the harvest. In these his last days, he is obliging enough to record his activities, thoughts, and impressions in the diary that becomes his sole companion. After a slow slide into what looks like death by starvation, he dies. Upon his death, his son, Calamatus Jumai, euphemistically labeled an "adventurer," returns to Ikerre-Oti and follows his father's practice of writing in the diary. After an equally violent death, his older brother, Abel Jumai the writer, does the same until his ambiguous disappearance.

Reduced to the bare bones of its plot, *Diaries* does not come across as a particularly heart-warming story, nor does it seem funny. Yet Calamatus, the advance-fee fraudster, invites the reader to consider how the *telling* of a trickster story can be a source of humor, recalling but also building on the spontaneity and creativity of oral storytelling. Additionally, the written word is of particular importance to the *Diaries of a Dead African*, where the hero of each tale is also its narrator, using the medium of a diary. This has interesting implications in Calamatus's case, when the storyteller is essentially an untrustworthy character advancing the cause of scammers.

Autobiographical narrative is a strong vehicle for humor, and it is worth pausing over Meme, the father, because he sets the stage for Calamatus to enter. Meme uses an eye-catching mix of Englishes and imagery to make the reader laugh even through themes that are not immediately associated with the comic; Calamatus later does the same. Abel is clear-sighted enough to recognize that though he is "the writer in this family, after all," he lacks the ability to "write a more interesting diary, that's for sure. They made their journals readable, Pa and Calama." For him, this is because they wrote "with their blood," while he would prefer to "live a boring 80 years than write an interesting journal that ends in a blaze" (loc. 1555). However, the readability of the first two sections has to do with more than matters of blood and fire; it hinges on its brazenly humorous style. Besides, Meme's diary fulfills the additional task of providing exposition for the trickster. The physical dangers Abel is confronted with, in the end, are no less intense than those faced by Meme and Calamatus, but he maintains a duller tone throughout his diary. In fact, despite his fervent wish to live longer than "both of them combined" and to die in his bed, Abel sees more violent action than either of the others. The foil of Abel's diary shows that the narration is largely responsible for the humor in his father and brother's sections. It also confirms Sareil's point that comedy does not have its own domain and that it is the treatment of material that makes it funny (11).

HUNGER AND HUMOR

Ẹsẹ̀ gìrì nílé à ń jọfẹ́, goes the Yoruba proverb, meaning there is merriment in the house with a lot of food. The saying mirrors the Irish proverb "Laughter is brightest where food is best" and confirms Abraham Maslow's theory that people are more inclined to fulfill their other needs after their primary physiological needs are met. Laughter is potentially discomfiting for the reader of the *Diaries of a Dead African*, who may find himself laughing with a full belly at a famished man. How does laughter not become strained when it is directed at an embodiment of the trope of the poor, starving African?

Many funny things, when held to a certain light, take on a dubious quality. In general, the reader of a comic text must take advantage of its accompanying comic atmosphere and cues in order to enjoy it. Unfettered humor both implies and depends on detachment, in the situation Bergson colorfully terms the "momentary anesthesia of the heart" (11): Though it may at first seem counterintuitive, indifference constitutes the natural milieu of humor and the unruffled soul appreciates it best. Emotion is laughter's greatest enemy (10–11).[5] Therefore, in order to enter the state Carroll calls "comic amusement," the reader must be ready to "switch off" whatever pity he might initially assume is appropriate for such literatures and give full rein to pure intelligence. The *Diaries* encourage this in that it is Meme's own words that allow the reader the requisite distance from his otherwise pathetic life. For Meme, who finds himself "studying [his] remaining yams the way witchdoctors study the position of kola nuts," and wondering whether he "died years ago and forgot his body in Ikerre by mistake," it is the quantity of food, and not whether it is of "best" quality, that is a problem (loc. 60). "Permission" to laugh, if we need it, is granted by the sufferer himself, who hardly ever loses his dry tone and, indeed, refuses pity by actively cultivating an ambience where laughter is not a guilty pleasure.

Another reason Meme's story is important to this chapter is that traditional trickster tales often begin with hunger or some other lack. It is usually the case that once upon a time, there was a famine in the land and all the animals were hungry. Then, Spider (or Tortoise, Hare, or another trickster animal) went a-scheming. Many times, the setting is characterized by hopelessness before the trickster appears and transforms it for better or for worse. It is not surprising, then, if famine provides the impetus for the action in Nwokolo's novel and if Meme provides valuable exposition on it. He reveals Ikerre-Oti as a poor village where hunger is pervasive and the milk of human kindness has long dried up. The community is characterized by incredible stinginess and rampant greed. Calamatus, who holds all of his neighbors in contempt, calls them "hungry people" many times.

---

5. Translations are from Bergson, *Laughter: An Essay on the Meaning of the Comic*.

Yet hunger is paradoxically tied to humor. The humor of hunger might not necessarily be the "brightest" (in fact, it is quite dark) or always intentional, but it is present. Meme finds himself in an absurd situation when his wife, after physically "dragging around my loincloth, with me inside," abandons him to move to another town with her latest lover. She takes the bulk of his yam harvest with her, leaving Meme with only three tubers to last him two weeks. The inflexibility of the two-week fast overcomes him (in contrast with Calamatus, who has little respect for the long-suffering).

This situation denotes the oft-cited observation that laughter is closely tied to tears. For Obadare, humor is even "paradoxically bound up with social suffering in Africa" (*Humor* 64). He proposes an "aesthetics of misery" and suggests that "subaltern humor directly correlates to the material abjection and psychological humiliation in which millions of people across the continent are caught up" (65). Another more general reflection is that comedy is best described in relation to tragedy: humor can be present in "surprisingly serious contexts," like death (Ross 2).[6] Meme's situation, therefore, mirrors the tragic dilemma facing Ezeulu in Achebe's *Arrow of God*. Ezeulu, a chief priest, must declare the yam harvest before the people can gather and consume the crops. But the ritual depends on the whims of the god Ulu, who withholds authorization even as the people's need grows. The situation eventually turns catastrophic for Ezeulu and many others. Though Meme's salvation must likewise come from the village gods, *he* recounts his circumstances with comic irreverence. According to "Ikerre criminology," as he sarcastically puts it, he may not uproot any of his tubers until the official harvest date two weeks hence, and even then, only after the village idols have eaten the first fruits (loc. 143). Contrary to the veneration that Ezeulu has for his god, Meme mockingly uses terms like "Ikerre criminology" and "Ikerre-Oti's monstrous taboos" to dismiss the rites the same way he dismisses the people ("people who have jealousy and witchcraft running in their veins and they think it is blood" [loc. 38]). Even the village catechist bluntly confirms that Meme's is an extremely earthy situation outweighing any mystical or religious interpretation: "Is that not how I went to meet Catechist just before Easter," reports Meme, "and he said he won't waste his time and mine by praying, that my

---

6. Plato observes in *Philebus*: "There are also mixed pleasures which are in the mind only. For are not love and sorrow as well as anger 'sweeter than honey,' and also full of pain? Is there not a mixture of feelings in the spectator of tragedy? and of comedy also? . . . These mixed feelings are the rationale of tragedy and comedy, and equally the rationale of the greater drama of human life." (23).

32 • TYPOLOGIES OF HUMOR IN AFRICAN LITERATURES

problems had surpassed the kind that prayer and fasting solve" (loc. 38). That is just as well, since, as he clarifies later, "If there's one gift we didn't discuss on the day God made me, it was the gift of fasting" (loc. 274). To be sure, fasting would be the very worst of solutions.

Understandably, the immediacy of his problem means that Meme's language is peppered with images of food so that, for instance, food is portrayed in relation to yet more food: "If my yams of '95 were chickens, these tubers of today resemble the eggs they could have laid! Everything's so stingy nowadays, the rains, the soil,—and now, even my kitchen pot!" (loc. 117). Eventually, he is "dizzy with anger and hunger" (loc. 172). His faintness merges with his senses, so Nwozuai the gossip is described on two occasions as having a "melon head." It is not shocking, then, that when Nwozuai gets too infuriating, Meme's method of attack is to bite him. Walking home after the failure of the long-awaited harvest, Meme uses the description of "a full gourd of palm wine that must not spill" to represent the bleak thoughts swirling through his head (loc. 443). Inversely, food is elevated to a near-sexualized prominence as he finds himself contemplating the uprooting of a tuber, "all the while looking lustfully at the lush yam bushes on their poles" (loc. 311). Yam, described as the "king" of crops in *Things Fall Apart*, has taken on even more value than one might have imagined. And so, by the time he has "one tuber left and seven days to go!" (loc. 224), Meme has resorted to a solution as scientifically practical as it is ridiculous—measuring and boiling pieces of his precious yam by the inch and recalling a scene where a starving cartoon character slices a loaf of bread into transparent slivers.[7] Even now, while he despairs in the face of a grim reality, there is very little of the boringly factual in the way he recounts events.

As Meme deteriorates, he says about himself, "I was thinking all those evil thoughts that make a man's inside bitter even when he is drinking sweet palm wine" (loc. 165); "The sun slowly roasted my back as bitterness grilled my insides" (loc. 198). Given this conflation of self with meat, it is not surprising that Meme mourns the burial of his only goat's carcass with a rare solemnity.[8] Thinking that it died of a snake bite, he disposes of the goat but discovers later that it was still edible. He describes his grief at the "funeral" in these terms: "The crying that I cried when I buried my goat was nothing compared with

---

7. *Mickey and the Beanstalk* (1947).

8. Inevitably, then, after Meme is lynched, Calamatus describes his father's remains as a "dog's dinner" and as *suya*, or grilled meat (loc. 499).

the one I cried when I buried the pieces of my goat" (loc. 251). Furthermore, when Meme ponders his family's avoidance "as though I'm the village wizard whose favourite delicacy is the content of a swelling womb" (loc. 361), he reminds the reader that the desperation and astounding inventiveness generated by hunger have inspired great comedic moments, some of which go as far as to borrow from cannibalism. For instance, like Meme, who anthropomorphizes his goat, Big Jim, in *The Gold Rush*, turns to zoomorphism for comic effect. In one scene, Charlie Chaplin's character metamorphoses into a giant chicken before the eyes of his starving companion, who eventually, and quite logically, decides that "chicken or no chicken," he looks appetizing enough to eat. Cannibalism is equally a vehicle for humor in other movies, like *Sweeney Todd* and *Delicatessen*, where the main characters encourage and enjoy the consumption of human flesh.

These examples have in common a farcical reduction of humanity to its crassest form. Whereas tragedy or drama invite identification, empathy, or pity, farce, though close to horror, puts a distance between the audience and what is on display. Consequently, Jessica Milner Davis notes that while farce is the most violent of performed comedy, it is also the least offensive:

> The fundamental jokes in any farce plot are first, the inescapable fact that all human dignity is at the mercy of the human body and its appetites and needs; and second, an acknowledgment that the human body itself is imprisoned by the space-time continuum. If there is any moral message, it is simply that our common humanity levels all of us down. (*Encyclopedia of Humor Studies*)

Meme reminds his readers that people are, after all, just meat. But his narration creates the requisite distance—itself barely safe, otherwise would it be funny?—required for the reader to appreciate the humor. In so doing, he is indirectly confirming the trickster's belief that social status and title have no intrinsic value.

As though aware that his son will continue writing in his diary, one of Meme's last thoughts concerns Calamatus's birth and the absurd circumstances under which he gained his unwieldy name (to keep it short, he was supposed to be given the highly inappropriate name Clement). Calamatus himself is aware of continuing a tradition, at least on the level of diary keeping, and his first entry begins, "Okay, I'll keep Pa's diary. Let that be my inheritance from him" (loc. 446). He is Meme's successor in that he writes in much the same style as his father before him, constantly incorporating humor into the narrative. He shows his father's direct influence—for example, when he echoes Meme's dictum "Food is good, and anyone who disagrees with me should just step aside for me" (loc. 345) in this way: "Life is good, and anyone who disagrees should feel free to jump inside River Niger" (loc. 1034). Even though he never worries about what he will eat, he still exhibits something reminiscent of Meme—the craving that drives the trickster to provoke chaos. "Trickster's intelligence springs from appetite," as Hyde reminds us (22). Calamatus is in firm possession of a self-confidence, an economic stability, and a wiliness that Meme sorely lacks. These are manifest in his modification of his father's statement—for the trickster, life itself is good. Calamatus enters the scene hungry in a different way—he wants to be rich and to avenge the death of his father. In fact, having been used to set the stage for the trickster's entrance, bodily hunger ceases to be a concern. Calamatus instead creates humor out of *his* obsession: excessive amounts of money.

He uses writing to this end, taking the talent bequeathed him by his father and making a profit out of it. The resulting financial stability grants him social standing and superiority the likes of which Meme could have never dreamed. The chief and the village's other influential men, who never deigned to set foot in Meme's house, now come courting his son: they "were in my house, giggling like small girls looking [for] money to perm their hair. Money is a wonderful thing" (loc. 700). Calamatus clearly sees money as a measure of worth: "All those things rich people do, you can't blame them. As I'm sitting now, I'm feeling like fifteen human beings put together" (loc. 724). The contrast between fifteen people and a handful of small girls is clear.

To Helen Harrison, in her study of Oyono's *Une Vie de boy*, references to food "underscore the shared humanity." She agrees with Bakhtin, who says that bodily functions like eating serve to "emphasize the commonality of the human condition and to undermine social distinctions" (924–925). This observation may apply to Meme, who at various points seeks food from those better off. For Calamatus, it is money that serves that function. If money can increase his worth to that of fifteen people or turn men into small girls, it is because money has the power to reduce everything—people, their positions, and their authority—to a single material equivalent. And as can be deduced from the Ikerre elders' sudden affinity for girlish giggling, they are now open to finding the trickster and his actions amusing. They laugh *with* the trickster to signal their desired affiliation with him and even their subordination to him. The trickster, of course, laughs *at* them.

LANGUAGE AND "VERY LIGHT BRUSH STROKES"

Meme and Calamatus make stylistic and linguistic choices that make their writing amusing. First is the glaring divergence between serious situations and often lighthearted tone. This sort of contrast tends to invite analyses like those by Roger Mehl, for whom the "humorous man" (contrary to the "serious man") hastens to laugh about the gravity of his existence in order to avoid being overwhelmed by it (qtd. in Sareil, *L'Écriture* 22). While this may be true, it makes sense to look beyond the narrative style as a sort of "pleasure transmuted out of pain" (Schaeffer 121). Reichl and Stein are right to point out that "laughter occurs in a variety of functions [and should not be reduced] to a one-dimensional function" in postcolonial literature (12).[9] While the act of writing may well be therapeutic, Meme's face, which on a good day resembles a block of ironwood (loc. 478), currently remains devoid of smiles, no matter how much he imparts to his diary.

The "clash," or superposition, of two such contradicting judgments or series is termed by Bergson as the "interference of series." Even though Bergson, as is often the case, limits his study to French theatre, and in this instance the comedy of situation, he rightly recognizes that this phenomenon exists under different forms:

> C'est un effet comique dont il est difficile de dégager la formule, à cause de l'extraordinaire variété des formes sous lesquelles il se présente ... Voici peut-être comme il faudrait le définir: Une situation est toujours comique quand elle appartient en même temps à deux séries d'événements absolument indépendantes, et qu'elle peut s'interpréter à la fois dans deux sens tout différents. (45)

> [This is a comic effect, the precise formula of which is very difficult to disentangle, by reason of the extraordinary variety of forms in which it appears ... Perhaps it might be defined as follows: A situation is invariably comic when it belongs simultaneously to two altogether independent series of events and is capable of being interpreted in two entirely different meanings at the same time (31).]

The clash between form and content also evokes the theories that see laughter as the result of incongruity or incompatibility between things that

---

9. So, too, as debates in the area show, postcolonial literature is far from being one thing.

36 • TYPOLOGIES OF HUMOR IN AFRICAN LITERATURES

do not go together. Incongruity theories revolve around the fact that we learn and work with patterns. Sometimes the parts of a thing we encounter in our experience or imagination transgress those patterns and make us laugh (Morreall 10–11). In other words, a reader might expect a text that dedicates a substantial space to death, from title to content, would use correspondingly solemn language, in line with Genette's statement that in terms of our reception of a dramatic action, it is normal for the serious to come first (437). Nwokolo's diaries often do not follow that pattern.

This is perhaps best illustrated by Calamatus commentating on the dead herdsman he and Abel once stumbled upon as children: "He had died there overnight," he reports, "and his flock of ten white cows was standing around him like a football team waiting for their captain to recover from injury" (loc. 766). By downgrading the dead man to a sportsman about to bounce back from injury, and by elevating his silent cattle to supportive teammates, a "ludicrous context" is born; this cues the reader to ready a humorous frame of mind (Schaeffer 18). It is also worth noting that Nwokolo himself qualifies the disparity between content and treatment as intentional—the desire to "treat a very heavy subject matter in very light brush strokes." He adds that the *Diaries* are a "novel about a very human response to failure" (loc. 2436). And one very human response is laughter.

The Jumais' style is remarkable on a linguistic level. From time to time, the narrators give the impression that their writing is a word-for-word transcription of oral speech, and they include constructions that people do not often intentionally write down. "*Kai*, but I'm hungry!" (loc. 274) is, unsurprisingly, one of Meme's statements. Calamatus's entries include "So Pa just crazed like that eh?" (loc. 508); "Pa used to say that a man with madness in his family line should be careful how he laughs in public, before people move away and say: aha, his own has started" (loc. 548). "Crazed like that" is a sign of carefreeness in speech, while "eh?" and "aha" are markers of oral interjection—of interrogation and recognition.

Diaries of a Dead African expertly straddles a line between written discourse and a more insouciant speech pattern reminiscent of oral storytelling and everyday speech. Meme and Calamatus transcribe an English that borrows heavily from a West African source language in terms of syntax and semantics.[10] Utterances like "eating his money," "the whole villagers,"

---

10. In *Oxford Street*, Ato Quayson demonstrates how urban signs and inscriptions in Accra force the English language to jostle with local languages on the signs and in readers' minds.

"the kind of shout that they shouted," "my stomach was doing like a cement mixer," and many others have their place in the often-informal settings that privilege pidgins or varieties like Nigerian English. Many of them, in fact, mirror word construction in Kwa languages. The often-abrupt intrusion of structures alien to Standard English ("The crying that I cried when I buried my goat") add a delightful twist to the telling and create the surprise that is occasionally central to laughter. They may be unexpected because formal settings in West African countries often place emphasis on "correctness" and standard grammatical English in print texts. The Jumais' examples might be assumed to signal incapacities on the part of a writer who cannot distinguish between registers and the contexts that demand them. However, Calamatus and Meme may not be translators in the strictest sense, but their language hints at a strong context that has no problem surging onto the page and making a place for itself. So, unlike what are sometimes called mistranslations, the text is not oblivious; furthermore, it gets its message across impeccably. The novel thus displays unapologetically in print what is often discouraged and qualified as a lack of education or as errors.[11]

In the *Diaries*, Standard English is not given preferential or hegemonic status. This is in line with the development of a "youth" language in places like Ghana, where some write Pidgin English without a care or use words like *distin* or *somtin* in humorous contexts such as texting or creating memes. Abel complains, "Calama's handwriting is lousy. To worsen matters, he spells things the way they sound, which is the way to get into trouble with a language like English" (loc. 1555–1556). Calamatus hardly cares about being in good standing with the English language, nor is he intimidated by its status. Though "good" English is often a sign of status, the trickster is not taken in by the anxiety to speak it well, nor is he impressed by "the modern authority conferred by English," as Jesse Weaver Shipley terms it (532).

In a study of stationary and mobile inscriptions in public spaces in Accra, Ato Quayson describes mottoes, sayings, slogans, and proverbs (some of which sound like they come straight from the pen of a Jumai) as installing writing between oral performativity and literacy. Reading these texts

---

These texts, he remarks, "extend from a domain of oral performativity and into the domain of writing, such that the process of reading them requires an innovative understanding of their mixed genres and the orality/literary spectrum from which they draw their meaning(s)" (130). A similar practice appears to be bleeding into the Jumais' style.

11. Many of Meme's and Calamatus's passages could complement the examples Cecilia Folasade Ojetunde provides in her article about lexico-grammatical errors in Nigerian English.

"requires an innovative understanding of their mixed genres and the orality/literacy spectrum from which they draw their meanings" (*Oxford Street* 130). Similarly, to fully grasp the Jumais' diary entries requires a certain knowledge and understanding of the cultural context. This points to another Bergsonian observation about the sources of laughter—to understand them, they must be placed in the society that produces them (12). Though the *Diaries* are not aimed solely at a Nigerian readership (assuming such an aim were even feasible) and can be appreciated by others, putting into play one's "innovative understanding" while recognizing and laughing at the nuggets sprinkled throughout the entries reinforces the fact that humor implies community. The trickster, even at his worst, is a creature of community.

CALAMATUS: WHEN A TRICKSTER WRITES

While Meme and Calamatus employ similar humorous techniques, it is less evident that they are on the same page in terms of intent. Meme claims that he is telling the truth—"If I can't say the truth in my diary I don't know where else I can say it again"—and there is little reason to doubt him (loc. 287). Though mindful that the genre of diary writing does not automatically exclude external readers, he easily and unflatteringly dismisses them (and us by extension): "There're too many idiots that go around, reading other people's diaries" (loc. 108). For Meme, therefore, writing to his diary is, primarily, writing to himself. Acutely aware of his lack of friends and his outcaste status in the village, it is most likely the diary (and himself by extension) whom he addresses in the second person: "If you see how my chest was doing!" he exclaims in one instance. "That my heart did not cut was a miracle" (loc. 31).

Meme's humor is often produced in spite of himself. It is doubtful, after all, that he has set out to entertain the "idiots" who are going through his diary and who, to add insult to injury, may be reading it to digest a meal they could not bother to share with him. Instead, Meme points to the humor Genette qualifies as intentional on the part of the author but involuntary on the part of an unwittingly comic character. For Genette, involuntary comedy is comedy par excellence. It procures pleasure without trying and is nearly infallible, since its humor lies solely in the ear of its hearer. The character himself does not find the affair amusing. That is certainly the case for Meme, whose humor is a by-product of his style and personality. Involuntary comedy confirms that the idea of the innately comic situation makes little sense (439).[12]

Contrasted with this is voluntary humor, intentionally created for laughs (438). This suits Calamatus; he has already boasted about his inventiveness to his apprentice. Calamatus is a manipulator to the core, and this should be taken into consideration when considering his narration. He embodies Françoise Sagan's reflections on the writer: *"Le jour où l'équilibre s'établira entre ce qu'il est et ce qu'il dit, l'écrivain n'écrira plus. L'écrivain est un menteur forcené, un imaginatif, un mythomane, un fou, il n'y a pas d'écrivains équilibrés"* [The day balance is established between what he is and what he says, the writer will write no more. The writer is a manic liar, inventive, a compulsive liar, a madman . . . There are no stable writers] (qtd. in Migeot and Baverey 105). Michael Chabon, speaking of the link between tricksters and writers, affirms that a great book "is in part an act of deception, a tissue of lies: a trick . . . stories are only lies, and that lies are all we have" (qtd. in Hyde 2). Sagan's label of persistent liar affixes especially well to Calamatus, whose very existence is tied to falsehood.[13]

Like his father, Calamatus is aware of potential readers, but he takes us much more seriously, and to some degree, that affects how he writes. He is, for instance, worried that he could get into trouble should the diary—in which he has recorded his criminal activities and murderous intentions—fall into the hands of the police. For this reason, Calamatus from time to time returns to a previous, volatile entry and diminishes its importance—often with the excuse that he wrote it in anger. "My head was very hot," he excuses himself after one such instance. "But it is cooling down now. When I read what I wrote yesterday, I just shake my head" (loc. 508). He also looks back on the rash actions he has recorded—such as the infamous wine bath—and blames them on factors beyond his control, like the "demon" of money.

It is possible that Calamatus means every word. Perhaps he is simply boasting within the privacy of his diary. Yet, as a devout student of human nature who has undergone and "graduated" from scam training under teachers, it is not a stretch to imagine that he manipulates language in a strategic bid to

---

12. Genette provides the rather Bergson-esque example of someone slipping on a banana peel.

13. Having been passed off as Meme's biological son all his life, Calamatus is, in fact, the product of one of his mother's numerous affairs.

disarm any potential reader. Beyond making him more likable as a character, laughter also serves to make any event look less serious. Sareil shows that laughter always has a diminishing effect on dramatic events. It minimizes their reach and effects in the same way that drama tends to amplify them (*L'Écriture* 22). For the reader of Meme's diary, this reducing effect dilutes the writer's suffering. In Calamatus's case, it rather helps the trickster to shine the least-dramatic light possible on his activities, concretizing his ability to wield laughter as a tool. Indeed, the other writing exercise he takes part in—the faxes he sends his victims—"fishes" or "*mugus*"—casts an even more suspicious light on his sincerity as a writer. In the following extract, he quickly overcomes his regret of a lack of formal education and Abel's absence, and with good reason:

> I am a writer myself. He [Abel] can be writing his animal stories and other nonsense[;] me, I will specialize in writing con letters and writing fat cheques. Besides, it's even good that my English is using walking stick: when the *mugus* read my letters they think they have seen an illiterate that they can cheat; and they'll keep thinking like that till I have finished shaving their heads for them. Idiots. (loc. 964)

"I am a writer myself" says more than the fact of putting pen to personal journal; Calamatus is also a skilled fictionist and comic writer. "How," asks Pype in her study of pastors as new tricksters in modern-day Kinshasa, "are present-day tricksters and culture heroes represented in technologically mediated narratives, and what do they tell us about [the] current social universe?" (119). Calamatus, for his part, adapts to new media and incorporates his narrative style into it, using naïve-sounding faxes to land his "fish"—the biggest is one especially hapless American victim named Billy Barber. Calamatus successfully appropriates the stereotype of the uneducated, guileless African to instill a false sense of security in his victim. And to further answer Pype's question, what Calamatus as a trickster says about his social universe is that, using modern media, he can cross frontiers by refashioning himself and creating a new persona on a global platform. This leads to another difference between himself and his father, who seems to have no ties outside of Ikerre-Oti. The closest Meme comes to interacting with the wider world is, in his own words, "slapping a thirty-year-old television in a mud-hut masquerading as a sandcrete house, watching programmes from the other side of the universe" (loc. 52). Meme's lack of agency comes partly from the fact that he is a *passive* recipient of global media.

Calamatus, on the other hand, actively uses global media to appropriate the value the *Diaries* attributes to writing for his scams. He does this, specifically, by honing the terms most likely to pique interest. A study of his written correspondence with his target shows an astounding comprehension of human nature, transcending cultures he has no direct contact with. He simply disregards cultural differences and any claim that Western cultures might have to superiority because he does not believe it. In his verbal proficiency, he is at his most obvious as a successor to the traditional trickster. In many folktales, Ananse the spider approaches other creatures who have lived with him and who know him intimately and yet who allow themselves to be taken in once more. As a modern-day confidence man, Calamatus offers the tried-and-tested lure of easy money. Then he mostly lets human nature do the rest. The technique is simple, but the implementation shows finesse.

After Billy Barber "eats" the hook and begins corresponding with Calamatus, he reveals that he was intrigued by promises of an in-and-out transaction that would only entail providing bank account details. Over the course of their interactions, Calamatus keeps informing Barber of unexpected expenses cropping up. So Barber finds himself paying to set up a dummy company, paying for a dummy auditor's report, paying to cover the "Reserve Bank's" 1 percent charge, and so on. Each amount acts as an incentive and part of a sunk cost fallacy that completely ruins Barber. According to the situation, Calamatus cajoles or chastises Barber. For instance, when Calamatus pleads for an additional fifteen thousand dollars, the "walking stick" is very visible in the punctuation, the onomatopoeia, the unsophisticated metaphors, and the grammar:

> My dearest brother, Billy, I thank Almighty God who joined us together for this business that our millions have reached the front gate and is knocking gbam-gbam on the door of opportunity . . . Please don't disappoint me, and the two both of our future generations. Your obedient servant. (loc. 868)

It is easy to imagine Barber chuckling as he reads correspondence from the painfully earnest, innocuous sounding "Dr. Amechi," his Nigerian partner. Given the success of this technique, any reader who laughs at Calamatus for his "incorrect" English may well ask himself if the trickster is not more justified to laugh at *him*. Instead of the text simply inviting us to laugh at writers who it seems cannot write, it suggests through the trickster's sharp intelligence and incontestable results that the writer revels in his transgression.

MORALITY AND LAUGHTER

Calamatus is unapologetically himself. His role as the storyteller reveals his ethos, which is one that brushes aside absolute concepts of right and wrong. Such concepts are associated with formal spaces such as courts, schools, and churches. Monotheistic religions like Christianity differentiate sharply between good and evil. The trickster blurs those lines but, as Hyde confirms, is amoral and not immoral. He is not evil; he is simply not as preoccupied with moral sensibility as he is with seeing concrete results: "Trickster will appear to suggest an amoral action, something right/wrong that will get life going again" (7). The lack of remorse reminds us that the trickster, as is often mentioned, is on the margins of his community. He is characterized as liminal, and this plays out in different ways depending on the text. Hyde calls the trickster "the spirit of the doorway leading out, and of the crossroad at the edge of town (the one where a little market springs up)" (6). Calamatus manifests his liminality by residing in his village but "on the geographical margins" (de Souza 105). On his return to Ikerre-Oti, he is immediately ostracized and lives alone in his father's house. This is because Meme went on a suicide mission to kill as many of the people who had made him miserable as he could. People regularly throw rubbish into the yard of Calamatus's house, while Calamatus himself becomes the object of malicious gossip (at least until he becomes rich). This geographical removal from the public space is replicated in the distinctive code by which he lives and that he has explained to his apprentice. Yet, eloquent as he may be, Calamatus glosses over one point: for all that there is no regulatory Chartered Institute of Fraud, the 419 con artists *do* have a unique—albeit loose—code of conduct, including a section on ethics and morals.

Under this vision of right and wrong, FazO, under whom Calamatus apprenticed, has what he considers to be an ironclad defense of 419 scams. Whatever effect they have on their victims, indiscriminately tagged as "white men," is justified and even necessary: "That war they started five hundred years ago, when they carried our forefathers into slavery and raped our country, we're still fighting it today, and we shall win! Amen! We shouted" (loc. 1408).[14] Scamming, then, is a way for balance to be restored and might even

---

14. They sound remarkably like another confidence trickster, Soyinka's Brother Jeroboam, when he reconverts his former assistant Chume: "And you know yourself he's a hypocrite. All white men are hypocrites" (*Metamorphosis* 68).

contain an element of altruism. Yet, for all that slavery and colonization have ravaged the continent, this argument is wobbly. It is further devaluated by the grievous lack of racial profiling in the actual process of choosing a *mugu*. The thin excuse of vigilantism is subsequently demolished when Abel dramatically reveals Billy Barber's race:

> Calama had swung a fishing rod over a river teeming with a hundred and ninety million White Americans only to hook another African like himself. Billy Barber was darker than I was, with classic Bantu features . . . He sat there in the corner of my room as black and sarcastic as Meme Jumai himself. He was African alright. (loc. 2320)

It is doubtful that Calamatus or FazO would have cared either way about what, in the end, are just details. The trickster uncaringly distorts binary divisions; he troubles waters without necessarily providing a solution to the problem he has created.

As someone who starts out indigent and rises primarily by his wits, the trickster views society as a meritocracy founded on neither race nor morals. Social mobility, rather, has to do with cleverness and taking advantage of those who refuse to see the world for what it is. His position at the summit of society allows him to interpret the rules of survival and living as what best profits him. This explains Calamatus's genuine irritation at Barber for making a feeble attempt to trick him and, indeed, for getting caught up in his scam in the first place! "I don't like greedy people," Calamatus declares indignantly and without irony. "For a man to think he can get eighty-five million dollars just because he has a bank account! He should be punished for his greed! He should be flogged and sent to a psychiatric hospital!" (loc. 1145–1147). If the victim deserves his punishment, it is because he lacks the innate qualities that separate the trickster from the rest of society. Neither has he made a serious attempt to understand the rules of the game. He has received his just desserts, which should serve as a lesson to him to be more watchful.

The lack of sympathy points to the idea that the object of laughter deserves to be mocked for not displaying the requisite alertness to his environment (Bergson 13). For Calamatus, the punishment of fools ties in to his interpretation of social logic, itself linked to the idea that "laughter, while based on superiority, serves as a social corrective" (Morreall 8). Laughter makes its object much more aware of his surroundings, an especially necessary lesson for Barber. Barber, the distant correspondent, serves as a perfect automaton à la Bergson, a person who refuses to pay attention to his environment and who makes onlookers laugh. Calamatus obligingly feeds enough slivers of fuel into him to keep him going until he falls into an open trap. It is therefore thanks to Calamatus that at his meeting with Abel, Barber states that Calamatus has "killed his greed quite dead" (loc. 2270). When resources are limited, becoming the object of the trickster's mockery serves as a wake-up call for one to keep his wits about him. This, more than the excuse of righting the wrongs of a five-hundred-year-old war, serves as justification for the trickster's actions.

BROTHER JERO—THE TRICKSTER'S PLAY ON COMPLICITY

The Trials of Brother Jero (hereafter, *Trials*, first produced in 1960 and published in 1963) and *Jero's Metamorphosis* (hereafter, *Metamorphosis*, 1971) are comedies by Wole Soyinka, winner of the Nobel Prize for Literature in 1986. *Trials* was published the same year Nigeria gained independence from British colonial rule; the backdrop is that of a new nation adjusting to many challenges, including political transitions, social tensions, and a general crisis of identity. *Metamorphosis* was published shortly after the bloody Nigerian Civil War (1967–1970). With a clever, irreverent kind of humor, the plays explore themes like the abuse of power and social inequalities.

"Brother" Jero is much like Calamatus in that he is unapologetically amoral and aims to be superior. Jero is a clever charlatan passing as a miracle worker. He seeks to "stand out, to be distinctive," which proves a constant challenge given the multitude of preachers out to beguile converts: "Inevitably they must begin to call me . . . the Velvet-hearted Jeroboam . . . I have not breathed it to a single soul," he confides, "but that has been my ambition" (*Trials* 19). This information is disclosed to the audience, who are privy to his real opinions throughout the play. While Sareil notes that "*au theatre . . . le spectateur a un contact plus étroit avec les personnages*" [in the theatre . . . the spectator has closer contact with the characters], he attributes this intimacy to the actors' convincing interpretation of their characters (*L'Écriture* 92). However, beyond the standard conventions of theatre, closer interactions between a trickster and his audience can also be deliberate on the trickster's part, with the aim of eventually laughing together at a common target.

"He knew very well that I had one weakness—women," Jero chattily confesses in his exposition. "Not my fault, mind you. You must admit that I am rather good-looking" (*Trials* 11). Mabel Evwierhoma reads this as a testament to Jero's "fixation on good looks and visual performance," which is tied to "parsimony, philistinism and mercenary traits." Jero, she posits, "directs our attention to his physical stature, which in turn redirects our attention to his ethical conduct. This boast is to make him attractive, and links his thirst for prestige with maleness as well as patriarchy in the Church. Jero therefore exhibits patriarchal excesses" (496). While it is, of course, an option to read the trickster's character through a lens of strong disapproval—it is easy to agree with Evwierhoma that "ethically, [Jero's] verbal performance is foul" (494)—another reading invites us to look beyond condemnation and allow that the way he engages with his audience and followers is honestly funny. For instance, "mercenary traits" finds an echo in our description of the trickster, while lust is one of the ways his burgeoning appetite reveals itself (Hyde 8). Furthermore, comedy does make even the "foulest" of pills easier to swallow. Given that in a comedy, seriousness is extinguished—or at least muted—Jero has the advantage that his spectators are predisposed to laugh. Evwierhoma's point that Jero means to make himself attractive is valid. However, it goes beyond using his physical features or his velvet cape to appeal to churchgoers. Attractiveness appeals equally to the audience and ensures that they laugh with him and not *at* him.

Addressing them familiarly with "Mind yous" and "You must admits," all the while painting others in an unflattering light, Jero indicates that *he* is the one to watch as both protagonist and occasional narrator. And as the narrator, Jero naturally tells the audience what he wants them to hear. He opens the *Trials of Brother Jero* with exposition—his past apprenticeship, the struggle for beach land, his campaign for said land by way of dancing francophone girls dressed as Jehovah's Witnesses, his success at usurping his former master. Within these first few lines, he establishes himself as a clever victor, inviting the audience to see things from his perspective. Whereas Calamatus personifies Sagan's writer who lies to his reader, Jero profits from Ernest Lunel's observation that theatre impacts promptly and intensely on the mind of an audience (14). What is more, a reader or audience is more likely to side with whomever is crafting the story (Sareil, *L'Écriture* 94). Bergson comments, with his colorful imagery, that in a comedy, the audience will through "natural instinct" align themselves with the duper because it is better to be duper than dupe. He likens the spectator to a child who has borrowed a friend's doll (the dupe) and who joins with the duper to maneuver the new string puppet all over the stage (38). This shows audience and trickster merged into one or, at least, bleeding into each other and sharing sensations tightly linked to laughter and pleasure. This sort of emotional osmosis recalls Elizabeth Block's comment about the narrator of Homeric poems: "In the oral context . . . his emotions can be shared without question by the listener" (156). The genres are different, but Jero actively searches for a similar closeness; though Bergson does not mention this, the desire for communion can work both ways.

By partaking in the pleasure of puppeteering with the audience, Jero accords himself another status that is usually the domain of the theatre audience—judge of the action. Jero's manner of "judging" is twofold: First, he directs other characters into scenes and behaviors as he sees fit. For instance, after first refusing him permission, Jero finally allows his assistant, Chume, to beat his wife, Amope. This is after Jero discovers that Amope is the very creditor who has camped obstinately in front of his house and is demanding payment for the velvet cape she sold him on credit. The second form of judgment takes place as he watches the scene he has set in motion unfold. In this regard, he is like Molière's Scapin, who acts like a theatre director in the middle of the play.[15] Jero gives his own interpretation of Bergson's absorbed spectator—he "observes," "grimaces," "gasps," and "tut-tuts" alongside other commentary as he gets caught up in Chume's comically pathetic attempt at wife beating (*Trials* 34–35). By ingratiating himself to the audience, Jero confirms that laughter implies recognition and complicity.[16] His audience give him immediate feedback within the intimate setting of the theatre. They are then directed to laugh at the expense of others—Chume, Amope, the nameless congregation, politicians, his fellow preachers, and others.

Intimacy aside, the question of narrator reliability is as relevant with Jero as it is with Calamatus. Jero, let us not forget, is invested in painting himself as the superior party. As theatre director, he can decide who speaks and who is not heard simply by showing interest (or not). During his exposition, for instance, Jero lets the Old Prophet speak only long enough to illustrate his own story. Jero listens indifferently for a short while and then dismisses his former master with ease even as he is roundly cursed. He renders the man's words irrelevant just by turning his attention back to his audience:

He continues to mouth curses, but inaudibly.

JERO (*ignoring him*). He didn't move me one bit (*Trials* 11).

Hoisting himself above more foolish characters is not an aimless objective when read in light of the superiority theory. "In our competition with each other," as Morreall explains, "we relish events that show ourselves to be win-

---

15. Scapin gives some characters lines to repeat and actions to execute. Then he scrutinizes and criticizes their performances with comments that would be at home in the mouth of a seasoned theatre director.

16. "*Le comique . . . s'adresse à l'intelligence pure. Seulement, cette intelligence doit rester en contact avec d'autres intelligences. . . . On ne goûterait pas le comique si l'on se sentait isolé. Il semble que le rire ait besoin d'un écho . . . Si franc qu'on le suppose, le rire cache une arrière-pensée d'entente, je dirais presque de complicité, avec d'autres rieurs*" (11). ["Its appeal is to intelligence, pure and simple. This intelligence, however, must always remain in touch with other intelligences. . . . You would hardly appreciate the comic if you felt yourself isolated from others. Laughter appears to stand in need of an echo . . . However spontaneous it seems, laughter always implies a kind of secret freemasonry, or even complicity, with other laughers, real or imaginary" (Bergson 4–5).]

ning, or others losing, and if our perception of our superiority comes over us quickly, we are likely to laugh" (6). For Jero, whose philosophy is closely tied to getting one over on others, feelings of superiority can account for his attitude toward other characters. For example, in *Metamorphosis*, Chume is once again firmly caught in his master's plans, despite his initial stubborn refusal and despite the fact that at the end of *The Trials*, he had furiously attacked Jero with a weapon. Jero notes quite condescendingly to the audience that although he "had [his] doubts for a while [about his hold over Chume, he] should have known better" (*Metamorphosis* 71). His asides show that the pride he takes in his trickery is often proportional to the foolishness he manages to reveal in others. Most of the time, as happens when he reconverts Chume, he reveals others' shortcomings by talking circles around them.

VERBIAGE AND NOMENCLATURE

Jero is especially adroit at tuning language to suit whatever environment he finds himself in. He is at his most candid in asides or addressing the audience directly. For example, speaking of his nemesis and creditor Amope: "It was a sad day indeed when I woke up one morning and the first thing to meet my eyes was a daughter of Eve. You may compare that feeling with waking up and finding a vulture crouched on your bedpost" (*Trials* 11). However, when interacting with other characters, he will immediately switch to a language more befitting not only in terms of content—there is little mention of vultures—but also in terms of form. Brother Jero turns into a paragon of Christian virtue, "something of an ascetic" to borrow his own term. Fed and clothed by providence, this version sleeps on the beach, if indeed he sleeps at all (*Trials* 22). Naturally, he speaks only in Christ-like tones. The contrast between his honest impressions and his smarmy speech to the same Amope is striking: "Sister . . . my dear sister in Christ . . . (*Hems and coughs.*) I—er—I hope you have not come to stand in the way of Christ and his work" (*Trials* 15–16).

That same sanctimoniousness permeates his mannerisms as well, so that switching from describing his "customers" (to the audience) to commanding Chume to rise in the name of the Lord demands "*altering his manner*" (*Trials* 25). In the next play, Jero reconverts Chume in part because he segues "*progressively into a 'sermonic' chanting style*" (*Metamorphosis* 69). Chume is duly ensnared by the sermon, which borrows stock phrases and imagery from Christian discourse: Jero's acquisition of wings on his feet, his would-be martyrdom on the beach, Chume as a "dark soul lost and howling in the knowledge of eternal damnation" with his mind "turned away from the light of reason and [his] judgement clouded," and other such descriptors (*Metamorphosis* 69).

The humor in that last example is ironic and the scene alternates perspectives: On the one hand, Jero is inviting judgment of events through a divine filter. However, with a trickster posing as the face of divinity, the audience cannot help but regard the "holy" events through an awareness of humanity's vulgar tendencies. Jero did not grow divine wings when he was attacked on the beach—fear propelled his feet; at his death, he could not seriously be considered a Christian martyr; and Chume may well howl after burying his cutlass in Jero's skull, but it would likely be out of intense satisfaction.

The contrast between Jero's candid discourse and its "pastoral" counterpart is best amplified when he is among other members of his profession. Here, with fellow pastors who know each other to be crooks and yet feel the absurd need to keep up appearances, there is the most curious overlap of styles. The "pious nonsense," as Brother Ananaias calls it (*Metamorphosis* 51), mixes with squabbling and insults. When Brother Isaac asks how an illegally sourced government file was procured, Jero responds, quite devoutly, "The Lord moves in mysterious ways," to which Ananaias adds mockingly, "His wonders to perform. Amen" (*Metamorphosis* 78). Then, there is Shadrach, the overly hallowed, who refers to himself in the royal "we." He is brought down to earth by Ananaias, who calls him a "fatuous old hypocrite" (*Metamorphosis* 74). The latter, caught lifting a wallet, turns immediately to biblical admonishment: "Verily verily I say unto you, it is easier for a camel," he begins, only to lose steam and end "and so on and so forth." Ananaias's quote, along with the pastors' general self-satisfaction, is an eloquent testament to the fact that they do not do much besides rehashing the same old lines. At the same time, their reliance on biblical texts shows the texts' incredible elasticity.

Additionally, Jero specializes in comic renditions of prayer, his unique take on *parodia sacra*, where baser discourse caricatures the repetitive nature of liturgy. For example, while praying against his "one weakness," Jero squeezes his face "in agony" and exhorts his brother in Christ to pray with and pray for him. He repetitively calls on David, Samuel, and "Je-e-esu" as the situation quickly approaches religious trance. Chume chimes in with the refrain "Help him, Lord. Help him, Lord," which, as he gets more worked up, transforms into a more natural sounding pidgin: "Help 'am God. Help 'am God. I say make you help 'am. Help 'am quick quick." The next stage is falling

50 • TYPOLOGIES OF HUMOR IN AFRICAN LITERATURES

into gibberish and speaking in "tongues": "Abraka, Abraka, Abraka . . . Hebra, Hebra, Hebra." (*Trials* 20–21). Later, Jero leads Chume into a similar state, this time punctuated with numerous cries of "Sing his praise" and "Hallelujah! Hallelujah, praise the Lord" (*Metamorphosis* 70–71). Then he steps aside and coolly watches Chume get even more carried away. These scenes are orchestrated as a reminder that Jero is above his congregation and at least on par with the audience.

All this accumulation might appear excessive. However, it bears noting that Jero is operating in an atmosphere and in a wider context where manipulating words, all the while piling them up extravagantly, is of supreme importance. This is particularly relevant when it comes to finding a name. In his bid to stand out from the other "charlatans" and "scum," one of his preoccupations is finding a title to encompass all the divine attributes he wishes to be associated with. This is keeping with a larger pattern in literature where churches headed by dubious characters are baptized with the most impressive names. In Ken Saro-Wiwa's *A Forest of Flowers*, the village of Dukana witnesses the birth of the Holy Spiritual Church of Mount Zion in Israel, which comes to join the likes of the Brotherhood of the Cross and Star. In Zakes Mda's *Ways of Dying*, Archbishop, B.A., M. Div., D. Theol. (U.S.A.), Prophet Extraordinaire, heads the Apostolic Blessed Church of Holly Zion on the Mountain Top. In Kwaw Ansah's film *Praising the Lord Plus One*, a charlatan founds and leads the Miracle Temple of the Supreme Tabernacle International. Another pastor in José Agualusa's *My Father's Wives* oversees the Evangelical Church Hideaway of the Most High . . . Jero's own church is in keen competition with the "Brotherhood of Jehu, the Cherubims and Seraphims, the Sisters of Judgement Day, the Heavenly Cowboys, not to mention the Jehovah's Witnesses" (*Trials* 4). Yet another competitor heads the Shadrach-Medrach-Abednego Apostolic Trinity. Jero, then, must shine especially bright. This results in the birth of the Church of the Apostolic Salvation Army of the Lord, complete with flag and uniform.[17] But this is not enough. Within the collective of the army, which would regroup his fame-hungry brothers, he must burn yet brighter. Titles like "the Velvet-hearted Jeroboam" (*Trials* 19) and "the Immaculate Jero, Articulate Hero of Christ's

---

17. In the fantastically titled "Mark Christian Hayford: A Non-Success Story," G. M. Haliburton notes that Mark, brother to J. E. Casely Hayford, named his church the Baptist Church Mission and Christian Army of the Gold Coast (24).

Crusade" (*Metamorphosis* 32) help in that endeavor. From atop his perch, he is free to manipulate his flock, politicians, and even his formerly reluctant subordinates. Jero confirms that he really *could* teach them all "a trick or two about speech-making" (*Metamorphosis* 39).

CHURCH AND CARNIVAL

Decidedly, the trickster uses the gift of gab to illustrate Bakhtin's observation that a "new type of communication always creates new forms of speech or a new meaning given to the old forms" (16). For his part, Calamatus is fully engaged in the creation of newer forms of speech, which will hereafter be utilized and modified by internet scammers.[18] Brother Jero has the advantage of a religious lexicon that he can borrow from; the openness of biblical exegesis allows him to give new, irreverent meaning to the older form of the Bible. Thus, through the preachers and their parodic language, Soyinka evokes the tradition of Rabelais's carnival atmosphere, which, among other things, is responsible for creating ridicule out of ecclesiastical texts. The carnival "marked the suspension of all hierarchical rank, privileges, norms, and prohibitions" (Bakhtin 10). The laughter incited under this atmosphere often targeted institutions, particularly the Christian Church and its image as a bastion of seriousness and of morality.

This may explain why certain expressions of humor have long been a source of ire in some influential schools of Western thought. Pelton mentions in passing how "greatly estranged the comic and the holy have become, since the Renaissance and the Reformation" (11), and one might remark that this disaffection is even older. *The Republic* famously condemns Homer's representation of the gods laughing in the *Iliad*: Whatever makes a man "laugh mightily" must be expunged from literature, especially if it causes mirth in the gods: "When a man lets himself go and laughs mightily, he also seeks a mighty change to accompany his condition . . . If, then, someone makes noteworthy human beings overpowered by laughter, it mustn't be accepted" (*The Republic* 66). In a similar fashion, Christian tradition is aware of the debasing potential of laughter and sometimes expresses disapproval akin to Pla-

---

18. Calamatus (also) works with four-part typologies: "the oil letter, the contract letter, the ammunition letter, and the human rights letter" (loc. 984)

to's. Building from Umberto Eco's *Name of the Rose*, Andrew James Johnston states that to certain thinkers, humor is considered "a danger to authority because laughter has a levelling effect which threatens to rob matters divine of their dignity" (17).

That is not surprising, as Jero has no qualms equating the body of a nubile bather to the heavenly: "Every morning, every day I witness this divine transformation, O Lord" (*Trials* 20). Similarly, Christian music is ridiculed when it passes the lips of characters who are obviously dishonest or especially half-witted, like Sister Rebecca singing the hymn "Are you washed in the Blood of the Lamb" "lustily, deaf to the world" (*Metamorphosis* 82). Considering the potential for parody, the Church sometimes pits morality against "foolish" laughter. Baudelaire's discourse on laughter reviews some of these moralistic diatribes against laughter, itself qualified as damnable and of satanic origins. Some of them buttress the "officially Christian" statement that a wise man only laughs while trembling by pointing to the popular "fact" that the wisest of men, the Incarnate Word, never laughed (5).[19] In any case, in these writings, the spirit animating laughter is perceived as having the sort of concrete consequences described by Bakhtin, wherein freedom triumphs, if for a short while, over the dominance exercised by the Church.

In that light, and given that colonialism was intertwined with proselytization and education from the Christian Church, it makes sense to view the African trickster as a figure against domination. The colonial exercise brought "to heel" productive agents to "extract the maximum use possible" out of them, while state power creates an official master code to be integrated into the people's consciousness (Mbembe 28, 103).[20] Officialdom, according to Bakhtin, reaffirmed a predominant truth "put forward as eternal and indisputable." For that reason, it was "monolithically serious" and "the element of laughter was alien to it" (9). Concerning the texts made available to the public of the Gold Coast (now Ghana), for instance, Stephanie Newell makes mention of the tight limits set by Christian educators (*Literary Culture* 9).

---

19. Bossuet makes the same claim, to which Genette points out that following this line of reasoning, it could be claimed that Jesus never sneezed, coughed, or even breathed (Genette 413). Critchley, for his part, states that if, as many theorists hold, laughter is the preserve of human beings, "then the question of whether Jesus laughed assumes rather obvious theological pertinence to the doctrine of incarnation." Some medieval scholars, presumably with a sense of humor, would "trawl the Evangelists for evidence of levity" (25–26).

20. Homi Bhabha likewise explains how in India, Christianity, "a form of social control," was used to encourage caste divisiveness to prevent "dangerous" political alliances (*Location*, 87).

Ngũgĩ wa Thiong'o presents the missionaries and the colonial administration as one organism with control over printing presses, publishing houses, and education. He goes on to categorically condemn this education as a "cultural bomb" that had the effect that the early African novel, influenced by the Bible and by *Pilgrim's Progress*, tended to produce "a subservient non-violent African christian Uncle Tom" as hero (69). This form of education, he concludes, was used by "the master armed with the bible and the sword" (4) to subjugate the minds of the colonized in a process he labels as the psychological violence of the classroom (9).

Nevertheless, even according to Ngũgĩ, all is not bleak. His narrative introduces a culture hero to counter the culture bomb. Hyde notes that as a culture hero, the trickster brings about fundamental change (189); Ngũgĩ certainly sees him as a catalyst for revolution among the colonized. The trickster, "being small, weak but full of innovative wit and cunning, was our hero. We identified with him as he struggled against the brutes of prey like lion, leopard, hyena. His victories were our victories and we learnt that the apparently weak can outwit the strong" (10). This conforms with Ruth Finnegan's description of the mythic trickster—"small, wily, and tricky animals who cheat and outdo the larger and more powerful beasts" (335). Lynn agrees with the idea of tricksters as champions: "their defiance of arbitrary or unjust rules and customs may offer . . . a sense of liberation to their audiences. In their drive for freedom, then, tricksters routinely resist the forces of domination" (153–154). The trickster is sometimes responsible for the creation of the world or else, finds a way to give men a gift that is fundamental to their survival and development—whether fire or fish traps (Hyde 158) or, as Ngũgĩ insists, self-affirmation.

CARNIVAL AND HYPOCRISY

While the trickster's unfettered innovation and wit mock authority and substantiate some fears of the leveling effect of laughter, there is also more to the trickster than his ability to laugh at domination. Inasmuch as an interventionist analysis may appropriate him as a weapon against hegemony, he is at best a double-edged one. The audience may well laugh at his antics; they can as easily find themselves laughing at him. To complicate matters further, especially if he is the hero of his community, people may find that while laughing at him, they "laugh at themselves" (Pelton 10). Furthermore, a trickster character does not inevitably descend from the oppressed. Hyde observes that many Native Americans connected the arrival of Europeans with the trickster ethos—shamelessness, opportunism, and a disregard for community—"surely trickster was at hand" (11). "Here," he adds, "was a race and a way of life that took as central many things which aboriginally belonged at the periphery" (12).

For different reasons, then, there is more to the trickster than simply laughing at the dominant religion and culture. If Jero calls attention to the carnival tradition, it is principally because he appropriates some practices, like reworking Christian texts, for comedic purposes. However, Soyinka does not fully conform to the subversive paradigm. Even though the Christian Church is an essential backdrop in the *Jero* plays, it cannot be said that the aim of the plays is a respite from the "official," long-term hold it has over society. Bakhtin stresses that in Rabelais's France, the carnival, like the olden feasts of fools, is a temporary break from an otherwise far-reaching ecclesiastical influence. There, the Church is an institution that is established differently from how it is in Jero's community. In that atmosphere, when the "entire world is seen in its droll aspect, in its gay relativity," people become less respectful of authority (12). In Jero's Nigeria, Christianity represents a comparatively newer religion and belief system that are jostling with what was previously there for space—different ideologies, different customs, or a different take on morals. It is questionable to what extent native pastors have "The Church," such as it is, backing them. Besides, in the unlikely event that it presents a unified front reminiscent of the French Catholic Church, one wonders how much authority it commands anyway; besides politicians and other pastors who insult him to his face, Jero is constantly confronted with Amope's brazenness. Unfazed by the threat of Jero's celestial powers, she proposes not to stand in the way of Christ and his work "if Christ doesn't stand in the way of me and my work" (*Trials* 16).

The trickster is an ancient phenomenon. Jung studies the trickster's place in Native American mythology and counts him as one of his famous archetypes. To establish the trickster's continuity in modern society, Hyde offers two routes. On the one hand, "If the trickster stirs to life on the open road, if he embodies ambiguity, if he 'steals fire' to invent new technologies, if he plays with all boundaries both inner and outer, and so on—then he must still be among us, for none of these has disappeared from the world" (11). In that case, the confidence man is a likely candidate. Still, the trickster, who, after all, cannot be present everywhere there is dishonesty or ambiguity in modern society, needs a sacred context. That is to say, the story must have a ritual setting—what

Hyde calls "moral or medicinal motives." The trickster, he concludes, belongs to polytheistic societies. This seems to be the case in Ikerre-Oti; to justify his refusal to give Meme credit, a shopkeeper tells the story of Tortoise, who tricks the hyena into giving him his pottage for the hand of a nonexistent daughter. This is also suggestive of Achebe's Umuofia, where stories featuring trickster characters are regularly told. These societies are either organized into small-scale, segmented communities or are feeling their way through a modern state and education system that have been imposed from above.

Sareil notes that laughter "desacralizes"—it opposes libertinage to religion (*L'Écriture* 22)—and he uses texts by Molière to illustrate this. It must be noted, however, that Molière often presents a sincere moralizer as a foil, as though to remind the audience that underneath the mockery, the place of state institutions is immutable.[21] The *Jero* plays, on the other hand, do not suggest that characters any wiser or more sanctified than Jero exist. The ridiculous characters in Molière's *Les Femmes savantes*, or the religious men who felt targeted by his *Tartuffe*, may confirm Bergson's central thesis that funny characters are stiff machines who lack self-awareness. Jero, in contrast, is acutely self-aware. He never doubts his lack of godliness, nor does he seem to believe in godliness at all; his asides are enough proof of this. For Sareil, Bakhtin, and Bergson, comedy strives to "remind" men of what they really are—that is, not divine; laughter reminds Church officials and people in high positions that they are physical creatures with bodily functions. This is not news to the trickster nor, indeed, to the society he caters to. Rather than the gratuitous mocking of religion, the trickster represents an aspect of society that questions the attempts of some to set themselves apart as élite. This belief is seen in Calamatus's disdain of doctors and lawyers and in the lack of a voice of morality in the *Jero* plays. Thus, the ridicule in these plays, though similar to Bakhtin's concept of carnival laughter, focuses more on human hypocrisy than on institutions essentially. It is about making a case for the trickster's worldview: those who make special claims to elevated status or anointing by God are dissemblers. And he is the first of them. What, then, does this say about those who follow him?

---

21. In later versions of *Tartuffe*, the king himself is on the side of this intervention. *Le Tartuffe* caused such an uproar that Molière was forced to modify the text and "clarify" in the preface of subsequent versions that his intentions were not to mock the Church. The first two, more scandalous versions are no longer available today after Louis XIV, instructed by the archbishop of Paris, banned them. The "Affaire Tartuffe" is considered the biggest controversy in the history of French theatre (Prest 2). The hullaballoo underscores the political reach of the Church.

COMPLICITY AND REVERSAL

R.S. Rattray notes, and Pelton echoes him in this, that African trickster tales "contrast sharply" with the morals normally taught to children (Pelton 31). Generally, too, we may associate laughter with aggression or lack of feeling, since it is often produced at the expense of another party. To Sareil, laughter is born of an accident, awkwardness, the observation of failure—in other words, under negative circumstances for a "victim" (*L'Écriture* 21). In which case, adds Morreall, "the pleasure is mixed with malice towards those being laughed at" (4). For his part, Bergson invites his reader to take a step back and observe life as in indifferent spectator, upon which the people tripping and falling over in the streets turn into comedic actors.[22] In short, laughing at others, as Jero does and invites us to do, means targeting them. But that is not all there is to it. For all that trickster stories recount what children are explicitly told not to do, it is mostly the adults who tell the stories to the children, who "re-tell the stories the following day to other children" (Ngũgĩ 10); folktales serve to socialize (Quayson, *Strategic Transformations* 54). These comments suggest that the trickster fulfills other understated but important roles and that here, too, his relationship with his community is not so clearcut. Hyde notes that the modern-day trickster in America embodies things that are true about the country but that cannot be said openly (11). Likewise, Jero represents an aspect of society that is not necessarily worthy of boasting but still exists and for which he alone cannot be held responsible.

Jero's congregation, for instance, displays more awareness of their environment than Bergson and Sareil might give them credit for. It is possible that they are using the trickster as much as he is using them. The plays suggest a kind of partnership between trickster and worshippers that requires the latter to actively sustain the trickster or at least be compliant in their situation. Jero says of his congregation, "I am glad I got here before any customers—I mean worshippers—well, customers if you like." He adds that he feels like "a shop-keeper waiting for customers" (*Trials* 20). They are indeed his customers in that their dealings smack of permissiveness and reciprocity. While Jero is not helping them out of the goodness of his heart, he can use his congregation only as much as they permit him to. He may display greater intelligence than his flock on any given day, but they are the ones who tolerate and even

---

22. A quote attributed to Mel Brooks goes: "Tragedy is when I stub my toe. Comedy is when you fall into an open manhole and die."

encourage the trickster's continued existence. Why they would do this may be linked to Pelton's remark about the trickster's "essentially comic nature" (11). Hyde, too, notes why the trickster tale makes its audience laugh: "The entertainment derives from his self-indulgent refusal of such commands [about how to behave], of course, for there is vicarious pleasure in watching him break the rules, and a potentially fruitful fantasizing, too, for listeners are invited, if only in imagination, to scout the territory that lies beyond the local constraints" (12). The congregation's laxity echoes the appeal the trickster continues to represent to audiences.

To illustrate, there is a fantastic scene where Jero, handing his rod to Chume, briefly leaves his church service with Chume in charge. After a fleeting disquiet at his new and sudden duties, Chume acquits himself of the task quite admirably:

> CHUME *is obviously bewildered by the new responsibility. He fiddles around with the rod and eventually uses it to conduct the singing, which has gone on all this time, flagging when the two contestants came in view, and reviving again after they had passed. CHUME has hardly begun to conduct his band when a woman detaches herself from the crowd in the expected penitent's paroxysm.*
>
> PENITENT Echa, echa, echa, echa, echa . . . eei, eei, eei, eei.
> CHUME (*taken aback*). Ngh? What's the matter?
> PENITENT Efie, efie, efie, efie, enh, enh, enh, enh . . .
> CHUME (*dashing off*). Brother Jeroboam, Brother Jeroboam . . .
>
> CHUME *shouts in all directions, returning confusedly each time in an attempt to minister to the PENITENT. As JEROBOAM is not forthcoming, he begins, very uncertainly, to sprinkle some of the water on the PENITENT, crossing her on the forehead . . .*
>
> CHUME (*stammering*). Father . . . forgive her.
> CONGREGATION (*strongly*). Amen.
>
> *The unexpectedness of the response nearly throws CHUME, but then it also serves to bolster him up, receiving such support.*
>
> CHUME. Father, forgive her.
> CONGREGATION. Amen (*Trials* 27–28)

As Chume continues to receive an "amen" to every statement, his enthusiasm grows proportionate to the responses, which themselves spike from "more and more ecstatic" to "overpowering." His timidity discarded, he easily glides into the sorts of prayers and prosperity doctrine that a seasoned prophet might make: "I say those who dey push bicycle, give them big car tomorrow. Give them big car tomorrow. Give them big car tomorrow, give them big car tomorrow" (29). In truth, though he is later to be promoted to the status of prophet in *Jero's Metamorphosis*, Chume does not appear to need this formal recognition.

Besides its hilarity, the scene illustrates several points. First, if Jero's disingenuousness were ever in question, it cannot be so now. The ease with which Chume takes up the mantle shows that in these plays, one need neither calling nor serious training to succeed as a prophet; a known (or "expected") pattern of words and actions will suffice. In addition, it is interesting to note that the "victims" are about as complicit in keeping the game going as the trickster. They perform a seamless dance, providing a crescendo of "amens" when required. Jero believes that they keep coming back because they are "strange, dissatisfied people" (*Trials* 20), but he may not have read them well. Perhaps they are coming back neither for his empty promises nor his plethora of titles—the attraction might be an argument for maintaining the trickster role, which appears to be tolerated and even indulged. There is, for example, a woman whom Jero describes as his "most faithful penitent; . . . even in the midst of her most self-abasing convulsions, she manages to notice everything that goes on around her . . . She is always the one to tell me that my mind is not on the service" (*Trials* 25).

The congregation, eagle-eyed when they choose to be and yet adamant about keeping the trickster in place, can be read as more than blinded characters being led by the nose. This is not to say they are fully cognizant of Jero's lies. The audience is indeed laughing at them and not with them; in part, at least, they illustrate the assertions that laughing implies a sad or unpleasant event. But at the same time, they hint that "sad," "unpleasant," and "victim" can themselves be hazy in ways comparable to "humorous" and "trickster." Their eagerness to keep the well-oiled wheel going—whether with Jero or with Chume at the helm—shows the congregation is making a case for the trickster not as a mere rascal or as an individual function (the audience is never given the impression that the congregation deplores Jero's absence any more than they mourn the disappearance of his old master) but as a social role that fills some vital purpose tied to the need for entertainment and laughter.

The moral ambiguity of the trickster does not imply that there are no lessons to be learned; they are simply "extraecclesiastical," to borrow Bakhtin's term. The trickster thrives in a situation of penury. This can be an outright famine, as is the case in Ikerre-Oti. It can also be the less dire but no less dramatic economic hardship hinted at in Jero's society. When he succeeds, especially when he uses verbal talent against great odds, the result is covert or overt approval. Calamatus, though called a fat "flea," is hailed as a hero when he swindles enough to become the richest man ever seen in his village. Provided he keeps "spraying" them with money, few care that his riches are ill-gotten. Similarly, Jero's quick thinking sees him at the head of the Church of the Apostolic Salvation Army of the Lord, with both politicians and his fellow pastors bowing to his superiority. Overall, tricksters, as "outlaws and survivors" (Lynn 161), tell their audience that in a world "characterized above all by scarcity" (Mbembe 131), the real champion is the one who can use his wits to survive and even thrive.

In this way, Bakhtin's liberating carnival atmosphere becomes more relevant to instances of the trickster, since both suppose an alternative view of the world, perhaps another "social logic" sanctioned by laughter. Therefore, without feeling any contradiction, the audience can be amused by Jero, who merrily shares divine visions of promotions to Chief Clerk or Minister for War. In fact, as a comic hero, the trickster often embodies what Ronald de Sousa calls the phthonic quality of laughter—the aspect that is "particularly susceptible to moral condemnation" (289) but no less enjoyable for it. That this quality sparks laughter confirms that even within the ecclesiastical setting, it would be extremely reductive to judge the trickster as bad.[23]

• • •

Jung observes that there is "something of the trickster in the character of the shaman and medicine man, for he, too, often plays malicious jokes on people" (256).[24] Living on the razor edge of discovery sets the trickster up to "fall victim in his turn to the vengeance of those whom he has injured. For this reason, his profession sometimes puts him in peril of his life" (Jung 256).[25] The

---

23. Hyde affirms that "if the spiritual world is dominated by a single high god opposed by a single embodiment of evil, then the ancient trickster disappears . . . The Devil and the trickster are not the same thing, though they have regularly been confused . . . He embodies and enacts that large portion of our experience where good and evil are hopelessly intertwined. He represents the paradoxical category of sacred amorality" (10).

24. To give an example: in Ahmadou Kourouma's 1968 novel, *Les Soleils des indépendances*, there is a medicine man whose mystique is based on harsh authority, which hides actual his lack of spiritual power.

25. If the medicine man is a charlatan, then texts can and do mock other forms of spirituality besides Christianity.

trickster operates in a mechanism that is not foolproof and that can suddenly humble him. This impermanence requires him to remain alert to stay above the competition. That Jero's first scene involves a forcible "handing-over" is an important statement on this precariousness. It also explains Jero's constant preoccupation with distinguishing himself from others. If the audience sides and laughs with the trickster because of his superior intelligence, they are not obligated to be loyal to him should he slip up. They will just as freely laugh at the trickster should he ever find himself getting a taste of his own medicine. So Jero himself becomes an object of derision when we witness him legging it upon being confronted by an irate Chume:

> CHUME rushes in, brandishing a cutlass.

> CHUME. Adulterer! Woman-thief! Na today a go finish you!

> JERO looks around.

> JERO. God save us! (*Flees.*) (*Trials* 42).

Just now discovering what the audience already knows—that his plans have backfired spectacularly—Jero can, in a rather ironic twist, count only on God and not the cool superiority he has up until now proudly displayed.

It is often said that the trickster thrives in liminal spaces. Calamatus lives on what might be called the "periphery" of the world while engaging with occupants of its "center." Jero, for his part, is exploiting and mangling a religion whose tenets his followers have not yet grasped for themselves. Consequently, this kind of humor comes from a search for balance within a setting that is uneven. A larger observation is that the trickster's humor inhabits societies where traditional principles and institutions must work side by side with more modern ones. Most of the latter were imposed and are still taking root alongside older ones that are either evolving or dying out. This can result in characters having to navigate within an awkward amalgam comprising the ways of the global world and the African village, the Christian Church and their own take of philosophy, and so forth. These characters often find it hard to harmonize the two series; this creates a special kind of working chaos that is propitious to the comic.

CHAPTER 2

Mimic

Mutton dressed as lamb; wolf in sheep's clothing; pearl before swine; silk purses out of sows' ears; square pegs in round holes; *apɔnkye mpɛ* cake.[1] Two things may be comparable in some ways but so mismatched in others that one occupying the space of the other seems laughable. The previous chapter showed the humor of unrepentant crooks professing to be choirboys. This chapter reads characters who also try to slingshot themselves into an exclusive group but do so with little of the trickster's panache and fall on their faces. They are flatter characters whose unabashedly Manichean worldview demonstrates an enduring theme in African literatures, that of clumsy cultural mimicry. Iterations of this typology have appeared in texts from century-old articles through stage theatre to online sketches—and remain easily recognizable.[2] This chapter reads a classic example of that theme, *The Blinkards*. Comic mimicry happens when an obsession with status leads characters to

---

1. An Akan saying: "Goats don't like cake."

2. From Casely Hayford's *Ethiopia Unbound* (1911): "Gradually it had come to dawn upon educationists that the error of blindly imitating western methods must give place to original lines of racial intellectual development; and for that reason centres of learning were eager for information as to where mistakes had been made in the past, and how they might be remedied in the future." (161).

The Ghanaian comedian KSM addresses culture shock and transitions in his famous 1990s "Saga of the returnee": "Ghanaian Returnees." *YouTube*, uploaded by Thetgifshow, 13 October 2009, https://www.youtube.com/watch?v=wdgalisFKuc&t=134s&ab_channel=Thetgifshow.

In a 2023 skit, the Ghanaian comedian TooMuch Pampii plays the part of a man who has spent three days abroad and now introduces himself as "Ray from United Kingdom" to an old friend on the phone. "Ray" pretends to have never heard of Ghana, Mfantse, or his friend until she dryly informs him that his mother has died. His old accent, mannerisms, and language make a sudden return: "Can you imagine if man get like 3 years for UK, how far?" *Facebook Reels*, uploaded by Toomuch Pampii Gh, October 2023, https://www.facebook.com/reel/21832391457697.

blunder their way through the sociocultural, historical, and political categories used to separate people.

The resulting humor may at first appear disconcerting because it sanitizes otherwise uncomfortable themes, such as segregation. In point of fact, an African in a suit and tie or trying to speak English was once considered amusingly incongruous for attempting to master foreign norms. It was not too long ago that race was a common justification for classifying and ranking peoples in English colonies—generally speaking, free Europeans on one side and African labor on the other.[3] A well-known defense of colonialism and the infamous partition of Africa was that white men had been burdened with the task of bettering Africans. According to the popular polygenist narrative propagated by theoreticians, adventurers, and anthropologists alike, one's character, behavior, and even worth emanated from one's race. Whites were intelligent and civilized, while blacks were lazy and had no history.[4] Colonies "were increasingly persuaded to know themselves: that is, as subordinate to Europe" (Ashcroft et al. 1). This meant that even as, ideally, a native person was "normalized" in an exercise of "subject formation," he remained in his own "single, specific category."[5]

As is often the case when attempts are made to herd human beings, practice was messier than theory, and a narrative this simplistic is made brittle by the very stereotypes on which it depends. Miscegenation was one example of the resulting ambiguities and spillover, even though mixed marriages were criminalized in places like South Africa and denounced in places like the Gold Coast.[6] To complicate matters, the colonized inexorably displayed some of the attributes that supposedly inhered to the colonizers: Africans quickly learned to speak European languages, which allowed them to reason with Europeans according to their own terms. Gold Coast thinkers like J. E. Casely Hayford, the lawyer and statesman, became quite toothy about attempts to pass bills into law and weaponized their Western education and familiarity with the relevant literature.[7] Parallel to the produc-

---

3. "The History of the Idea of Race." *Encyclopædia Britannica*, Encyclopædia Britannica, inc., www.britannica.com/topic/race-human/The-history-of-the-idea-of-race.

4. For more on this, see *European and African Stereotypes in Twentieth-Century Fiction* by Sarah Milbury-Steen.

5. Bhabha, *Location of Culture* 86–87, Mbembe 28.

6. Carina Ray, *Crossing the Color Line*, 2.

7. See *The Truth about the West African Land Question*, in which Casely Hayford systematically dismantles the assumptions about the British government's "proprietary rights" over Gold Coast lands.

tion of meticulous treatises by such intellectuals, associations such as the Aborigines' Rights Protection Society, founded in 1897, sent delegations to Downing Street with petitions, publicly reminding the British government that, according to treaties *they* had introduced, policies must meet certain requirements before they could be passed.[8] The rise of the "educated native" was the cause of some headaches for the administrators of colonial territories. Still, the differences between the white and black races continued to be trumpeted well into the twentieth century.

Given the constant declaration of the superiority of the "center" to the inferiority of the "periphery," it is not surprising that carving out an identity and affirming pride in it were early goals of both African nationalism and modern African literature. In "The Novelist as Teacher," Achebe famously announces his literary revolution: "To help my society regain belief in itself and put away the complexes of the years of denigration and self-abasement" (44). While literature plays a role in this important effort, self-affirmation sometimes fell into familiar Manichean perspectives: The colonized was independent *of* the colonizer and his culture commensurate *to* the latter's culture;[9] "emancipation and recognition," as Achille Mbembe says, focused on "the essence, the distinctive genius, of the black 'race'" (12). This produced a discourse that, he continues, smacks of naïveté and reductionism.[10] Consequently, such arguments are sometimes criticized for reproducing "outmoded binaries that reinforce the colonial domination [it seeks] to undermine" (Ball 3) and for forming an essentializing discourse that opposes the Western self to black humanity.

BLACK AND WHITE: THE "GOOD OLD" DISPARITIES

Colonialism was legitimated by the argument that Europeans were bringing a transformative civilization to those who did not have it. But even though colonization proclaimed that it sought its own obsolescence, the annexation of Africa was not meant to be a short-term project; the economic and political benefits meant, paradoxically, that Africans were not expected to be-

---

8. See Rebecca Shumway in Belmessous's *Empire by Treaty*.

9. As Ashcroft et al. note, "Eurocentric assumptions about race, nationality and literature return time and again to haunt the production of post-colonial writing" (7).

10. "The uncompromising nature of the Western self and its active negation of anything not itself had the countereffect of reducing African discourse to a simple polemical reaffirmation of black humanity" (Mbembe12).

64   •   TYPOLOGIES OF HUMOR IN AFRICAN LITERATURES

come fully civilized within the foreseeable future. What prevented them was precisely their Africanness. Colonialism was thus built on a contradiction: Africans needed civilizing; Africans could not be civilized.[11] In light of what we consider to be scientific and factual today, we might find a trace of humor in the imposition of racial superiority as fact; power dynamics of that nature invite satire and beg to be disparaged. A more interesting venture, however, would be to hold that rickety binarization up against our earlier premise: the tendency of African literatures to grow humor in spaces of ambivalence and uncertainties. In spite of (and sometimes because of) itself, colonialism created a wealth of those. Colonialism had to reckon with people, whose overwhelming characteristic is less some stringent racial quality than the tendency to trip over air and smudge the lines in the sand.

In this chapter, the mimic's highest ambition is to impress unrealistic and mostly disjointed European standards onto African characters, starting with herself. In the process, she inadvertently creates a caricatural "culture" that ridicules the demarcations (such as they may be) between white and black, center and periphery, Europe and Africa, modernity and tradition, conservative and subversive, piano and drums, and other such labels. Mimics educe the aspect of Incongruity theory that highlights "two or more inconsistent, unsuitable, or incongruous parts or circumstances, considered as united in one complex object or assemblage" and violating mental patterns (Morreall 12). Clumsy and over-the-top, mimics unite incongruities between "black" and "white" elements; these incongruities stem less from natural traits than historically established patterns.

Modern African literature has long had ways of reworking established patterns to create absurdities. This is particularly true of the literature pro-

---

11. As Neil ten Kortenaar says, "Pacification by the British meant everyone was treated equally and rationally, *except* those the empire deemed primitive and irrational, which is to say, the colonized" ("Modern African Tragedy" 91).

The colonized were aware of this contradiction. Casely Hayford muses in *Ethiopia Unbound*: "There was a theoretical policy and a practical one, the latter having as its aim such a shaping of circumstances as would for ever make the Ethiopian in his own country a hewer of wood and a drawer of water unto his Caucasian protector and so-called friend" (98–99). And "With the gin bottle in the one hand, and the Bible in the other, he urges moral excellence, which, in his heart of hearts, he knows to be impossible of attainment by the African under the circumstances; and when the latter fails, his benevolent protector makes such failure a cause for dismembering his tribe, alienating his lands, appropriating his goods, and sapping the foundations of his authority and institutions" (69).

duced during and soon after the colonial period. The cleavages imposed by colonialism left impressions on literature; comic writers, in turn, appropriate those for their own ends, opposing white to black and exaggerating cultural differences to underscore the illogicality of crude binaries. To borrow E. M. Forster's terms in *Aspects of the Novel*, they perceive how pattern and rhythm shape our expectations for the people in the story and then use incongruities in the pattern and rhythm to make the people and their story comical. In other words, characters refusing to stay in their designated lane is a great plot device. The Cameroonian comedian Valéry Ndongo illustrates that in the following tale: An African, newly arrived in Paris, dialogues with an older compatriot who has lived in France for thirty-five years. The older man disapproves of the trends he has observed in recent migrants.

> *Ici à Paris, il faut t'intégrer. Mais quand tu t'intègres, il ne faut pas t'intégrer n'importe comment. Ton intégration doit suivre un processus. Il ne faut pas faire comme certains de ces petits Noirs que je vois souvent ici à Paris, à peine arrivés ils s'intègrent déjà. Vraiment je ne vous comprends pas vous les petits Africains d'aujourd'hui, la mondialisation vous tourne la tête. Étant en Afrique, ils téléchargent le plan métro sur Google Map, connaissent les us et coutumes des Parigots, maîtrisent les noms des fromages, la différence entre vin blanc, vin rouge, vin rosé, grand cru, millésime, etc. Des choses que même certains bons Français de France ne connaissent pas . . . Tu arrives là avec ton doctorat Lettres modernes françaises, tu parles le français du dictionnaire, ce n'est pas bon.*

[You need to integrate, here in Paris. But when you do, don't go about it any old way. Your integration needs to follow a process. Don't be like many of those young blacks I see, who integrate as soon as they get here! I truly can't fathom you young Africans of today—globalization has turned your head. They haven't even left Africa, but they've downloaded the subway plan on Google Maps; they know Parisian customs; they've mastered the different cheeses; the difference between white wine, red wine, rosé, grand cru, vintage, etc. Things that even some real French people from France don't know . . . You arrive here with your PhD in French Modern Languages, speaking dictionary French. It's not right.] (qtd. in Astruc 7–8)[12]

---

12. Rémi Astruc, "Transformations de l'Afrique, transformations du rire," *Humoresques* 38 (2013): 5–13.

66 • TYPOLOGIES OF HUMOR IN AFRICAN LITERATURES

The *Canard enchaîné* periodical is referring to something similar in a review of Oyono's *Le Vieux nègre*, when they say that the novel addresses the "*bon vieux contraste noir et blanc*," the good old black/white dichotomy that insinuates that behavior, circumstances, and "essence" are congruous with origins.

MIMICS ACROSS LITERATURES

Early in the twentieth century, Gold Coast nationalist, lawyer, and writer Kobina Sekyi wrote and produced a play called *The Blinkards*. In the following passage, Mr. Tsiba, a rich Cape Coast farmer whose answer to life's challenges is his "many cocoa land," has brought his daughter to Mrs. Borɔfosɛm's house for an education. He details his expectations:[13]

> MR TSIBA Thank you, sir—er—ma'am. (*Gets up*) I have bring my girl for English education.
> MRS B Don't stand up when you are talking to me.
> MR TSIBA Beg pardon, sir—er—ma'am. (*Gets up, then sits*) You make her behave like white lady. Teach her all the things you have learn at London. By the grace of the big one in the sky, I get some money. I have many cocoa land. I want you to make her English. She don't like stays: she don't like boots; she want to go out in native dress. She like *fufu* too much. She like *dokun* too much. I know white ladies can't chop *fufu* or *dokun*, because their middle is too small with stays: then she will eat nice European things. Thank you sir—er—ma'am. Ta! Ta! (*Gets up and shakes Mrs Borɔfosɛm's hand. Then says to Miss Tsiba*) Obey your new English missis. She will make you fine lady like herself (21).

Mr. Tsiba has high hopes in Mrs. Borɔfosɛm's powers of transformation; he wants her to make Miss Tsiba English. In fact, before taking his leave, he

---

13. The play is performed in English and Mfantse. Ayo Langley, who published it in 1974, transcribes Mfantse speech on pages parallel to the English text, using the Akan alphabet. The [ɔ] and [ɛ] sounds are the same as those found on the IPA (International Phonetic Alphabet) chart. "Fanti" is an older, anglicized spelling of "Mfantse" and is spelled as such in the play. "Fante" is another accepted spelling. When I use "Fanti" in this chapter, it is to reflect what is employed in the primary text.

expresses the desire that his daughter learn to blush like English ladies do in the books he has read. Mr. Tsiba opposes what he sees as his daughter's crude, African nature—aversion to stays and boots, love for the heavier local dishes—to his conception of white daintiness and finery: sow's ears on the one hand, silk purses on the other. This dialogue displays something that a significant portion of the humor of the play reposes on: the gap between the "African" and the "European." By confidently saying he knows that white ladies are incapable of eating African foods, Mr. Tsiba shows that knowledge across those groups is not always reliable. Though he is clearly not to be taken seriously, Mr. Tsiba's anxiety for his daughter's transformation points to the wider social phenomenon he is trying to integrate his family into. Cape Coast is home to a large population of Mfantse people ("Fanti" in the print version of Sekyi's play). It was also a colonial seat of government. At the time, the town's coastal location and administrative role meant increased contact with Europeans, which sparked a fever for all things "white" among some sections of the populace (Mfantses have a lingering reputation for being entertainingly wedded to pretentious, foreign mannerisms [*"aborɔfosɛm"*]).

The late-nineteenth and early twentieth centuries saw intensifying incursions by missionaries, administrators, and traders into West Africa, signaling the definitive shift to formal colonialism. This greatly transformed the social fabric. The period saw the rise of a distinctive social class situated mainly among the coastal towns of West African countries like Ghana, Sierra Leone, and Nigeria. The members of this class found themselves between the representatives of European powers and their fellow Africans in the hinterland. In *Self-Assertion and Brokerage*, Farias de Moraes and Karin Barber label this group a "pioneering élite." They were naturally familiar with their home cultures but had also integrated European cultural elements: "This two-sided allegiance made them, almost despite themselves, into brokers. They mediated in politics, trade, and in cultural activities, representing the Africans to the Europeans and the Europeans to the Africans" (1). This geographical and social position created ambiguities for the new social class. They spoke flawless Victorian English, followed English clothing fashion, partook in church marriages, and embraced London finishing schools for the daughters. At the same time, however, they married polygamously and campaigned for education based on African languages. The contest between identities generated some measure of unease, since every aspect of their lives boiled down to mediation (1). The contrasting conceptions about marriage or the appropriateness or otherwise of their clothing give the impression that while it may

68 • TYPOLOGIES OF HUMOR IN AFRICAN LITERATURES

have been possible to create a happy union between African and European identities, it was not an easy or obvious undertaking.

Indeed, with their anxious social reaching, Seyki's Mr. Tsiba and Mrs. Borɔfosɛm show that it is much easier to tell when a healthy cultural balance has *not* been found. Mrs. Borɔfosɛm is a mimic character who wants one culture to efface the other. The mimic disowns her local traditions but does injustice to English ones in the process. She is a self-appointed (and largely failed) intermediary between the two groups, a figure of unease and laughter. The vacillations between these traits are why some mimic characters play a more ambivalent or tragic role. In texts like V.S Naipaul's *The Mimic Men* and Jean Rhys's *Wide Sargasso Sea*, mimicry emphasizes the gravity of themes like displacement, disillusionment, and shame. Furthermore, Homi Bhabha theorizes extensively on mimicry, positing that it reveals the ambivalence of colonial discourse and is even insidious to colonial power.[14]

For their part, the mimics in Sekyi's play are supremely unconcerned with tragic tropes or intricate interpretations. Miss Tsiba has cultivated tastes that are diametrically opposed to her father's desires. Mr. Tsiba seems happy to ignore the fact that an African woman living in colonial Africa cannot truly become a white English lady, either by force of will or even by the grace of God and "many cocoa land." The scene underlines the foolishness of his expectations by couching his fancies in ridiculous language; *he* certainly does not speak flowing Victorian prose. Mr. Tsiba proclaims his rejection of "native" customs but struggles with English, continuously referring to Mrs. Borɔfosɛm as "sir." Mrs. Borɔfosɛm, the "English missis," has similar difficulties. To set her up as a teacher is to underscore her role as a privileged insider doling out knowledge and social cachet—such as they may be—to those who cannot access them directly. As a misfit to both cultures, she is an object of derision both to her creator and his audience; a lot of the humor relies on the contrast between how she trumpets an ideal but mangles it in practice.

Bergson, using the stubborn miser Harpagon from Molière's *L'Avare* as an example, confirms the one-track mind-set that many comic characters exhibit unawares. Were they mindful of their own ridiculousness, Bergson says, they would be shamed into hiding their more questionable traits (15).[15]

---

14. See Bhabha, Homi. The Location of Culture. Routledge, 2012, and Bhabha, Homi. "Signs Taken for Wonders: Questions of Ambivalence and Authority under a Tree outside Delhi, May 1817." Critical Inquiry 12, no. 1 (1985): 144–165.

15. "*Un défaut ridicule, dès qu'il se sent ridicule, cherche à se modifier, au moins extérieure-*

Mrs. Borɔfosɛm mindlessly flaunts her worldview—that there are two worlds, England and the rest, and that she belongs to the former. Given the political weight backing the English culture, she is confident that the audience can only be on her side.

It is worth noting that mimicry is a charge that can be laid by both imperialists and nationalists.[16] Colonizers may regard the "assimilated" African with suspicion or scorn. Stephanie Newell refers to a conversation reported by the future governor, Gordon Guggisberg, and his wife in the Gold Coast. The absurd and theatrical dialogue takes place between two "partly educated natives" who are "airing their newly-found language," to the supposed admiration of their peers and the hilarity of the Guggisbergs ("Local Cosmopolitans" 108–109).

Africans, as well, were hardly more impressed by the mimic. The nineteenth-century "Gone Fantee" movement, also known as the "Doctrine of Return to Things Native," was a response to the erosion of Mfantse culture. This was a Cape Coast cultural renaissance that encouraged indigenous traditions and expressed dissatisfaction with missionary education (Tenkorang 165). The spirit behind the movement is expressed several times in Casely Hayford's *Ethiopia Unbound*; one scene mocks a schoolmaster "whose [Western-inspired] attire certainly invited attention." The narrator paints an unforgiving portrait before concluding that "he certainly looked a veritable 'swell,' but he also did look a veritable fool" (73–74). In the same vein, readers of late nineteenth-century Gold Coast newspapers would write in to complain about the loss of traditional language and dress in favor of colonial culture.[17] Today, internet comedians offer a similar criticism of the blind adop-

---

ment. *Si Harpagon nous voyait rire de son avarice, je ne dis pas qu'il s'en corrigerait, mais il nous la montrerait moins, ou il nous la montrerait autrement*" (15). ["But a defect that is ridiculous, as soon as it feels itself to be so, endeavours to modify itself, or at least to appear as though it did. Were Harpagon to see us laugh at his miserliness, I do not say that he would get rid of it, but he would either show it less or show it differently" (8)].

16. "Without deviating from their stunted language," writes Newell, "the two men have a misunderstanding and a full-scale argument, followed by a public reconciliation scene" ("Local Cosmopolitans" 109).

In "The Enduring Relevance of Kobina Sekyi's *The Blinkards* in Twenty-First-Century Ghana," Awo Mana Asiedu addresses the continuing "folly of trying to be something we are not. This play is still performed in Ghana today, because of its continuing relevance for twenty-first-century Ghanaians, many of whom have yet to learn the lessons of the drama" (52).

17. In September 1897, the *Gold Coast Methodist Times* published an article titled "Reasons for the Resumption of Native Names."

tion of Western culture. The erasure of African ways of life has consistently been seen as a problem to be tackled and even as a moral issue.

Thus, wherever Western cultures are mindlessly associated with modernity and progress, the thoughtless copycat becomes easy prey for commentators. It is therefore not surprising if fifty years after *The Blinkards*, Wole Soyinka's *The Interpreters* (1965), with its different genre, background, and style, showcases a lofty Lagosian mimic who could be descended from one of Sekyi's Cape Coast characters. Ayo Faseyi is excessively respectful of public image and cultural signs to the point of berating his English wife for not wearing gloves to an embassy reception. He is himself wearing a bowtie to attend this function that he had to "wangle" his way into in order to be "presented." For that to happen satisfactorily, his wife must wear gloves because, regardless of location, it is a formal function. Unfortunately, she gave her gloves away when she moved to Nigeria and does not understand the fuss. "Who do you see wearing gloves in Nigeria?" she asks, coming across as a sensible foil. Faseyi, on the other hand, expects her to exercise the same level of English decorum at an event in Nigeria as at a garden party attended by the queen of England and is adamant that these are "simple requirements of society which any intelligent person will know" (39–41). One of those requirements, apparently, is calling his mother "Mummy," but only in front of other people, which underlines the performative aspect of his persona.

Though the figure of the "prototypical mimic-man" is a "popular, pan-imperial stereotype,"[18] a clumsy character trying to cross over from a social group to a superior one is not specific to African or postcolonial literature. In *Le Bourgeois gentilhomme*, Molière exploits the image of a bourgeois parvenu breaking social conventions in order to be recognized as an aristocrat. He similarly mocks the would-be intellectual in *Les Femmes savantes*. Likewise, Hyacinth Bucket ("It's pronounced boo-KAY"), the pretentious heroine of the BBC series "Keeping Up Appearances" sees her attempts to rub shoulders with members of the gentry repeatedly fall short. Characters who make observers laugh through their affectations and social climbing seem to be a universal theme; writers use exaggeration to appeal to the audience's barometer of common sense. The most obvious differences between the European and African texts are racial and sociopolitical. Some of the conceptions of race, however, can still be tied to old European views on class. Class often

---

18. They feature in texts by Rudyard Kipling, Joyce Cary, and E. M. Forster (Newell, "Local Cosmopolitans" 105–106).

bars entry into the grander social group. This is true for Monsieur Jourdain, whose efforts to improve his dressing, speech, and overall education only serve to underscore his bourgeois state. A similar thing happens to Stephano the drunken butler and aspiring king in Shakespeare's *The Tempest*. When mimicry across class lines is the object of satire, the lower classes seem to reveal their own boorish nature when they fail to pass as anything other than members of their class. These examples therefore reinforce social distinctions and social hierarchy.

That explains why the colonizers mock mimic men—they think that social hierarchies represent something immutable—but not why African nationalist authors mock them. Sekyi mocks his blinkards not because he thinks that social hierarchies cannot be transgressed but because he thinks that social hierarchies of this nature are ridiculous and should be rejected. There may be some mockery here even of English habits shown by the English—in other words, English habits (like gloves) are absurd for everyone in the heat of the tropics.

THE BLINKARDS: COMIC MIMICRY AND EXCESS

Kobina Sekyi, or Esuman-Gwira Sekyi (1892–1956), was a lawyer and early Gold Coast nationalist. He was educated in Cape Coast's Mfantisipim school and the University of London. After being called to the bar at the Inner Temple, he returned to practice in Cape Coast, where he was a prominent face in early nationalist organizations like the Aborigines' Rights Protection Society and the National Congress of British West Africa. He was also a prolific writer, best known for *The Blinkards*, which premiered in 1916 and was the Gold Coast's first stage play in English. Set in Cape Coast, it follows Mrs. Borofosem, who, having spent all of three months in London, returns home an English lady, complete with dress, food, speech, and mannerisms. This means that she forces her reluctant husband to greet her with a kiss, to smoke cigars, and to sprinkle the ashes on the carpet for its upkeep. She takes to wearing woolen clothes, a lorgnette, and a pair of gloves. Her language is just as ostentatious as her appearance. In fact, her ease with Fanti is matched only by her desire not to speak it, and she expresses herself in broken English as often as possible: "Call me 'duckie,'" she tells her hapless husband. "Dear is too much common. Even some of the clerks call their wives 'dear.' Mrs Gush my friend from Seabourne, on the East Coast, always addressed by her husband as 'duckie . . . Say 'duckie,' and I will call you 'darling' as Mrs Gush do" (9–11).

72 • TYPOLOGIES OF HUMOR IN AFRICAN LITERATURES

The aptly named and often-cited Mrs. Gush is described by Elaine Utud-jian as one of the "very poorly-educated members of the British lower-classes" (26). Writers like Sekyi and readers like Utudjian can look down on her for her lack of status and education, but it is also true that her mere existence stands for power and prestige in the colonies. This means that for Mrs. Borɔfosɛm, who does not understand gradations or subtlety, Mrs. Gush represents the epitome of Englishness. If she cannot change her name, Mrs. Borɔfosɛm can at least badger her husband for English terms of endearment.

Abu S. Abarry states that "any critical understanding" of the play reposes on the meanings of the characters' Akan names (158). Sekyi's Cape Coast audience was indeed aware that Mrs. Borɔfosɛm translates loosely as "Mrs. Foreign Mannerisms" (in this case, English ones). Still, Sekyi is so unsubtle with his nomenclature and characterization that non-native speakers can guess quite accurately what the names, which are his unique creations, mean. Besides the emblematic Mr. and Mrs. Borɔfosɛm, there are other characters, like the long-winded Mr. Kyerɛwfo (Mr. Writer). Mrs. Borɔfosɛm encourages Mr. Tsiba (Mr. Small Head) to marry his daughter Miss Barbara Ermyntrude "Erimintrude" Tsiba to Mr. Okadu (Mr. Follower). When wedding invitations are sent out, it comes to light that, phonetically, Mr. Tsiba's full name contains a hint of Greek or possibly French influence: Mr. Aldiborontiphoscophornio Chrononhontonthologos Tsiba. It is safe to say that Mr. Tsiba holds roughly the same place as Mr. Kwasia (Mr. Idiot) in the playwright's esteem.

Sekyi's text addresses the eradication of African traditions—in particular, the growing practice of adopting European courtship-style marriages, to the detriment of traditional marriages. Miss Tsiba, mentored by Mrs. Borɔfosɛm, rushes into a church marriage even after her mother dies from shock at the news. Eventually, Miss Tsiba must be saved from imprisonment for bigamy after she is wed to another (her extended family refuses to recognize her church marriage). The young lawyer Onyimdze wins her case in court, and the play ends with the sudden reconversion of Mrs. Borɔfosɛm to the more "sensible" way of doing things. Before this happens, though, the audience is treated to many scenes that pile up ridiculous behaviors and situations because of an underlying anxiety to do things the English way.

The culmination of the foolishness is the Cosmopolitan Club. Interestingly enough, as Catherine Cole points out, the play was first performed in Cape Coast's own Cosmopolitan Club. In the play, the club represents a wider phenomenon of clubs and societies established by young men along the West African coast in the nineteenth century. Members socialized at meetings and social events like formal dances. The clubs were places for learning and adopting European cultural practices like ballroom dances or debates. Newell says of their reading habits, "Often labeled 'mimics', this group of readers consisted of newly educated but otherwise non-status-holding youths, often young men, who banded together in the southern 'anglophone' belt of the region and, with increasing frequency as the twentieth century progressed, formed their own 'literary and social clubs' in order to debate moral issues and 'study the higher problems with the aid of good books'" (Newell, *Literary Culture* 29).

In *The Blinkards*, they fail at this spectacularly. They are ill at ease with European cultural elements and in their interactions with those they feel adhere too closely to "tradition." Sekyi is merciless in his portrayal. Other associations of the period provide a foil, such as the more political Aborigines' Rights Protection Society, which was formed in 1897. This society was also in favor of tackling higher problems but did so in more impactful ways. They are, for instance, responsible for petitions protesting some elements of colonial rule, including a highly inequitable land bill, and famously sent a delegation to England to meet with British officials about conditions at home. Though they were more of a proto-nationalist movement than a decolonial one, they still paved the way for more vehement protestation later. Therefore, with regard to the much more milksop members of the Cosmopolitan Club, Sekyi agrees with Newell that they would have "debates" but presents a peculiar version of the word:

READER (*Drinking some water, and reading*) "In conclusion of this treatise on 'How to be a Gentleman', I must embrace opportunity to impress force on you to say that without tailors and hatters and shoemakers, gentlemen, we are nothing"

1ST MEM Well said!

2ND MEM Praise God

3RD MEM A Daniel come to judgement!

VICE-PR Amen!

PRES (*Gavelling sharply*) Order! Silence in court! Continue, brother.

READ (*Bowing to President, then to Members*) I must express to you my thanks and gratitude, gentlemen, for your most vociferous ovation. (*Reading*) "To continue my dissertation, I say, without tailors and hatters and shoemakers, we will be savages."

1ST MEM God forbid!

2ND MEM Heaven forfend!

3RD MEM *Deo* not being *volente*! . . .

READ "Without these people, we will walk barefoot. We will wear native dress. Our feet and arms would be naked, and indecent. But with the help of these useful workmen we have mentioned, and, I must add, with the help of European merchants, who have given us ham and bacon and milk and sugar and--"

1ST MEM Marmalade

READ "—and marmalade and jam and lemonade and beer and stout and champagne—ripe, mellifluous, elevating champagne, and--"

2ND MEM Good old fizz!

READ "—brandy and whiskey—"

TREAS And soda.

READ "—and gin and rum."

3RD MEM And vermouth.

The verbose speechifying continues in the next scene, the reception after Miss Tsiba is wedded to Mr. Okadu. Present among the revelers are the members of the Cosmopolitan Club:

MR KYE (*Shouting above the din*) I have great pleasure for proposing the health of the bride and the bridegroom today. The manifestations of incredible merrimentations has displayed in this capacious hall due to wedding matrimonial jollification. Long live the bride and bridegroom!

Loud applause. Mr Kyerɛwfo sits, wiping his face.

MR KYE (*To neighbour*) What did I say? Did I speak well?

NEIGH Very nice: almost like a European. (103–115)

The president takes himself for a judge, calling for silence in his court with all gravitas. His brothers, vice president, treasurer, and the rest, affect similarly pompous manners—bowing, applauding, voicing their outrage with a "God forbid" here and a "Heaven forfend" there. They approve of the Reader's dissertation and Mr. Kyerɛwfo's toast through Latin interjections and malapropos quotes. All of these express their understanding of cosmopolitanism—loud external signs borrowed from British courts of law, debates and readings, institutes of higher learning, and European wedding receptions. They make emphatic distinctions between European and "native," good and bad, "useful" and "savage" or "nothing," but their arguments for and against are shaky. It appears that most of what they seek in European culture is hedonistic, if not strictly tied to the stomach: clothing and foods that they itemize with childlike glee. What is more, the alternatives making the native end of the spectrum so horrific are not justified as such. They do not bother to explain why locally sourced food and drink or clothes exposing their arms and feet make no sense. Rather, by vociferously supporting ideas they cannot defend, the members of the club make European cultural elements look foolish by association. The food and drink, ripe and fizzy as it is, seems to have intoxicated and stultified them.

In terms of vocabulary, Mrs. Borɔfosɛm at least seems aware of some of her limits. The club members have a predilection for repetition; "embracing the opportunity to impress force on you to say that" European things are good. Mr. Kyerɛwfo and the Reader think that the length and complexity of the sounds they make outweigh their sense. It helps that they are acclaimed by an audience who may or may not understand the content of their speech but who are clearly impressed by its sounds. In the end, their love for pretentious and polysyllabic words makes Fanti, which they forbid, appear almost noble simply by virtue of not being spoken.[19]

Soyinka plays on a similar phenomenon in *The Interpreters* (1965) when he cleverly transcribes the Professor's pronunciations to great comic effect: "Oh der," the Professor says earnestly when he cannot find his wife, "end the ledies are wetting for her." There is no need for the narrative to comment on how unfortunate he sounds. When Caroline appears, the Professor reiterates his statement, and even her name is not spared anxious attempts to Westernize, or maybe to de-Africanize, his English.[20] He transforms his vowels to differentiate them from how a Nigerian would normally pronounce them: "Ceroline der, the ledies herv been wetting for you." He then tells her to "cem en," as they "mesn't keep the ledies wetting" (142–143). It might be that the ladies are simply waiting; whatever it is, though, "wetting" does not sound like something they should be doing at the moment. Illustrating further still the persistent capacity of linguistic mimicry to generate humor, Chi-

---

19. Showing that the satiric scene is "disorderly and crowded," "choked with things," and dominated by "idiocy, foolishness, depravity, and dirt" (qtd. in Ball 14).

20. Jo Shoba and Kari Dako study "slanging," a popular phenomenon that in Ghana is also termed as using a Locally Acquired Foreign Accent, or LAFA.

mamanda Adichie's protagonist in her 2013 novel *Americanah* describes yet another mimic thriving across the decades: "Bisi, a girl in the form below them, who had come back from a short trip to America with odd affectations, pretending she no longer understood Yoruba, adding a slurred *r* to every English word she spoke" (78). The redundant *r* in Bisi's speech and in the Professor's "herv," is explained by the fact that such speakers often overcompensate for their normal accents to hide untoward influence from African languages. This means that "rhoticity is often overextended to occur where it would not be expected, as in *cash* [karʃ], a 'hyper-correction' phenomenon" (Shoba and Dako 232). The idea that one must be transformed by setting foot abroad, or even in a local space that is considered Westernized, is one that writers continue to harvest humor from.

READING

What is the source of the repetitive, nearly overwhelming spew of words, especially from the Cosmopolitan Club? From the look of things, alcohol is one potential cause. The text suggests several times that another cause is reading—at least, the wrong kind of reading. It is not for nothing that the audience's introduction to the club is through a Reader who does everything to live up to his title. Later, at the end of his own speech, Mr. Kyerεwfo (Mr. Writer) revealingly asks, "What did I say?" as though he were simply a conduit for words learned by heart. And in fact, after the best man at the wedding gives a similar-sounding speech and is also acclaimed for his "fine speechification," done "like a European," Mr. Kyerεwfo jealously says, "I don't think much of it: he read from memory" (117). These men are the extreme illustration of a common experience in colonial educational systems across the world, which relied greatly on rote learning and recital.[21] V. S. Naipaul's *A House for Mr. Biswas* illustrates a similar phenomenon in a Caribbean context when the young Mr. Biswas learns, without much conviction, "to say the Lord's Prayer in Hindi from the *King George V Hindi Reader*, and he learned many English poems by heart from the *Royal Reader*" (44). At their own meeting, the president of Sekyi's Cosmopolitan Club itemizes their relatively modest library but reassures his members that they "will make further additions to [their] bibliotheca" *after* they "have learned all by heart (109).

---

21. For insight into British attitudes to colonial education, see, for example, the British politician Thomas Babington Macaulay's *Minutes on Education in India*.

Mimic • 77

The Blinkards has a peculiar relationship toward European-style education, particularly uncritical learning through books. Given that colonialism relied on texts to validate and propagate itself, Sekyi is wary about embracing them wholeheartedly. Cole notes that:

> Sekyi defined "modernization" as a process of critical evaluation and selective appropriation. He contrasted modernization with "civilization," which he defined as the compulsive tendency to adopt anything associated with British and/or white culture and categorically denigrate and reject all aspects of African/Akan culture. Sekyi advocated modernization with a critical, African-centered difference: a deliberate consideration of what was useful and detrimental about ideas and practices adopted from abroad, and a circumspect integration of those ideas with local Fante culture. (loc. 752–754)

This meant there was a right way to imbibe books. A model to follow might be Sekyi himself, who read mindfully: "K.A.B. Jones-Quartey contends that the more European philosophy Sekyi read at school abroad, 'the more African he became'" (Cole loc. 833–834).[22] Therefore, books are not all bad. The agency of Sekyi's culture hero Onyimdze sets him apart from other characters because he knows the European court system intimately. Without his education and extensive reading, he would not have been able to interpret the law, defend Miss Tsiba in court, and save her from imprisonment. This is partly why his name can be translated as "Knowledge." Indeed, he believes that winning the case will have the wider consequence of "knocking" sense into the community about respecting traditional values. The subsequent change in Mrs. Borofosɛm confirms that this is true, and Mr. Borofosɛm admits, "You say I am following Onyimdze? Of course, I am: he has more brains than I" (159).

During the colonial period, books held an ambivalent status. On the one hand, readers like Ngũgĩ were suspicious of the sort of moralizing, Christian texts made available to Africans. On the other hand, European literacy had obvious advantages, including allowing the thinkers who became

---

22. Suspicion and ambivalence toward books are not an exclusively African response. The famous inquisition scene in Cervantes's Don Quixote puts the hero's books on trial for their influence on him. The text even suggests from the beginning that books are to blame for turning his mind. Don Quixote is worth noting because, for Bergson, he is a comic character par excellence due to his blinkered fixation on an ideal. The fact that his books are found guilty and burned for being behind Don Quixote's fixation on chivalry implies that literature has the power to bring life-changing and dangerous acts to life.

nationalists to articulate and disseminate their ideas to a wide audience.[23] Modern African literature itself "was, of course, created in the crucible of colonial modernity" (Gikandi 173). Albert S. Gérard has shown that modern African literature was written in what he calls the "third wave of African literacy"; Sekyi produced his play amid that wave. This period was characterized by increased literacy and greater cultural production by African subjects, some of whom became "more outspoken about the abuses of white power" (150). De Moraes and Barber also note that, initially, the culture brokers' literary activism was turned toward proving their competence. They wanted to be sufficiently Westernized while being competent in their home cultures to be better brokers. They thus favored the use of petitions and delegations to make their concerns heard by the colonial government. But the late-nineteenth and early twentieth centuries saw a growing disillusionment as they realized that access to the top levels of their fields was barred to them. This period precedes a more agitated surge in nationalism and the demand for full self-determination. Written texts played an important role in that agitation.

Ambivalence permeated the political atmosphere in which African subjects sought a balance that did not yet involve overthrowing the political system but still maintained dignity within it. It is, however, worth noting that the colonizers tended to feel ambivalent as well. Through the dialogue between the two dandies as reported by Guggisberg, Newell demonstrates that Europeans held semi-educated Africans in contempt for their inability to assimilate their lessons "properly." However, they also mistrusted the more Western-educated subjects. Partly by virtue of their training, through which they "imbibed radical thought" (Utudjian 23), these Africans regarded the whole colonial enterprise with varying degrees of suspicion. On the whole, then, the British preferred to deal with "illiterate" rulers. In the Gold Coast, they employed the so-called policy of Indirect Rule and favored "the 'authentic' African set over against the cultural fraud" (Newell, *Literary Culture* 162). The government took advantage of and transformed preexisting institutions—for example, exploiting the framework that allowed it to appoint its own traditional chiefs to ensure that its economic and political interests were taken care of. Inevi-

---

23. Gikandi affirms that "one of the most attractive aspects of colonial culture, from the perspective of the colonized, was what came to be universally conceived as the gift of literacy. Even though many African subjects may have been ambivalent about many aspects of colonial modernity, they seemed unanimous about the power and enchantment of literacy and the culture of print that enabled it" (383). He is referring specifically to Western letters.

tably, in the name of respecting tradition, the British also invented tradition and altered its meaning.

Nevertheless, literacy eventually became one of the markers of leaders and the rising social classes. Its importance to the social fabric is illustrated in many African texts, including Achebe's *Things Fall Apart*, where the missionary Mr. Brown "begged and argued and prophesied. He said that the leaders of the land in the future would be men and women who had learned to read and write. If Umuofia failed to send her children to the school, strangers would come from other places to rule them" (118). While Mr. Brown's very presence in Umuofia shows the disingenuousness of his statement (literacy was not going to stave off foreign rule; the British were already there), Achebe illustrates a fact restated by Kwasi Konadu and Clifford Campbell: "The missionary and colonial classroom and its book depots were the laboratories in which both elite and nonelite (and their children) encountered the 'colonial package' and through which socioeconomic aspirations were shaped in colonial society" (11).

REALITY VS. FICTION

In *The Blinkards*, the wrong kind of reading is partly responsible for the alarming indoctrination of the population. The significance of books is hinted at when Nyamekyε the servant, the first character on scene and who is to be instrumental in "curing" Mrs. Borɔfosεm, exclaims, "What a beautiful book," (4) as he cleans. Nyamekyε admires the cover of the book and perhaps the prestige it represents. The audience is made to believe that he cannot read English, since he expresses himself almost exclusively in Fanti. The book belongs to Mrs. Borɔfosεm, who explains one of its purposes: "Haven't I told you that, in England, leaves are placed in books to dry, the books when the leaves are dry, being placed in the drawing rooms?" (4).

Like her, the other blinkards are often associated with some form of written text that also serves as a prop. It can be a cookbook or a dictionary, as is the case with Mrs. Borɔfosεm herself, who confounds her cook with demands for English food and consults her dictionary to find the proper pronunciation of the word "petal." Mr. Tsiba faithfully carries his pocket "dickhendry" with him so that he can speedily look up words (one gets the impression that this is often). He confides to Mrs. Borɔfosεm that he named his daughter "Erimintrude" because "I see it in a book the day she is brought forth: so I call her

80 • TYPOLOGIES OF HUMOR IN AFRICAN LITERATURES

so." He also clarifies that it is "some book I have reading" that told him that "All modest young ladies blush at certain times" and that Miss Tsiba therefore needs to learn this act posthaste (21). Mr. Tsiba is staunchly obeisant to English texts and the cultural authority they represent, even giving in to the repulsive act of kissing Mr. Okadu on the forehead to signal his consent to the engagement. Members of the Cosmopolitan Club and Mrs. Borɔfosɛm's twittering lady admirers regularly refer (and defer) to how-to texts. The club members even state their intention to order more copies of How to Dance and Don't.[24] The Cape Coast ladies assert themselves by saying, "We know how to behave: we have read 'Don't'" (61). Books, therefore, are a status symbol and a guide to daily comportment.

They fulfill the latter objective more, especially when we consider that even fictional genres set in Europe are taken as prescriptive. Mr. Okadu and Miss Tsiba, it turns out, are prepared to meet and fall in love as dictated by specific reading material.[25] According to the formulaic romance books they have read, the first encounter must involve chance; failing that, the semblance of fortune will do. At the garden party chosen as a romantic setting, Miss Tsiba proactively says, "I will drop my handkerchief when he gets near; then he pick it up, and we can talk without being introduction. That's what the girl has done in the book I read last night till morning." Mr. Okadu, who fortuitously read the very same book the night before, decides to go one better and topple over:

> MR OK (*Walking slyly towards Miss Tsiba*) Oh, I feel nervous! I wonder if I can be able to manage it. Ah—h! I will fall down (*Slips intentionally behind Miss Tsiba's chair, and then clutches the top of her parasol as if to save himself*)
>
> MISS TSI (*Jumping up*) Whatever is that? (*Turns round*) Oh, I hope you don't hurt yourself.
>
> MR OK (*Jumping up with alacrity, and raising his hat with a flourish*) Please pardon my clumsiness: I just slipped behind your chair. Allow me to restore to you your umbrella (*Brushing sunshade and handing it* [TO HER])

---

24. *Don't: A Manual of Mistakes and Improprieties More or Less Prevalent in Conduct and Speech*, published in 1912 (Newell, *Literary Culture* 167).

25. Their encounter is like a parody of Francesca and Paolo from Dante's *Inferno*. Dante's characters largely blame their illicit romance and downfall on the act of reading.

MISS TSI (*Receiving sunshade*) Thank you very much. You are kind. I
hope you have not hurt.

MR OK I am all right, thank you; but I am glad I fell down.

MISS TSI What do you mean?

MR OK I mean to say that I am glad I have fell, because it has introduced
us. (47–49)

The dialogue ends with Mr. Okadu asking Miss Tsiba to "walk" with him. They exit, and not too long after, things come full circle when a pregnant Miss Tsiba walks into a doctor's office to her father's great shock and shame. Miss Tsiba and her fiancé are judged for having read "last night till the morning." They are absurd because neither can produce the language to elevate the situation: "Ah—h! I will fall down," with the accompanying tumble, is hardly romantic material. While they are enthusiastic enough about the format of the romance text, they do not trust in Providence to set the action into motion. Their subsequent heavy-handedness ridicules the scenario. Such characters parody a genre that might already be considered vapid for its extravagant language and cringeworthy sentimentality. Miss Tsiba and Mr. Okadu thus seem to have trouble separating fiction from reality. They exemplify one of Jean Price-Mars's observations of Haitian society: borrowing Jules de Gaultier's term *bovarysme collectif* (inspired by Flaubert's heroine), he describes a shame of one's history and a conception of self that is based on fantasy (11). Price-Mars's ambition in *Ainsi parla l'Oncle* is to show the Haitian people that their own literature is valuable, a lesson that Sekyi also wants to share with his audience.

The fact that writing can wield such a strong influence means that in *The Blinkards*, religious characters who believe firmly in the Bible are even more intractable. A pompous reverend minister comes to warn Mr. Onyimdze about the supernatural punishments he has brought upon his head by winning the court case. Another champion of memorization, the pastor recklessly throws about biblical verse, comparing Mr. Onyimdze to Nebuchadnezzar and himself to an avenging angel: "By the authority of the most high God, and of his son, Jesus Christ, I warn you that the vials of godly wrath will be poured on your devoted head for winning the bigamy case, and helping to make of no avail the holy sacrament of Matrimony. 'And I heard a great voice out of the Temple saying to the seven angels, Go your way, and pour out the vials of wrath upon the earth'" (147). His rant goes on in like manner before he finally makes his exit.

82 • TYPOLOGIES OF HUMOR IN AFRICAN LITERATURES

The playwright seems to be saying: here is another case where a book, taken in without moderation, has driven a character mad. In that way, then, the text is scornful of the semi-educated mimic like Mr. Okadu. The mimic has not cultivated good reading habits to help him develop the mental acuity to parse good from bad reading. At the same time, the play mocks those who have been "overly" educated by their reading material, such as the members of the Cosmopolitan Club and the reverend minister.

CULTURE AS PERFORMANCE: "SHOWY TOMFOOLERY"

If, as Mbembe reminds us, the object of colonization was to "shape the face of a new humanity" (28), then the mimic is an instance when the influencing force shaped a deformed character who speaks as much to Bhabha's mimic— "not quite" the same (86)—as to Bergson's image of the caricature. The art of the caricaturist, for Bergson, is about taking advantage of some distortion by blowing it up and making it visible. Caricature takes what nature may have begun and pushes it to its paroxysm (10). Here, the writer over-imbues the mimic with certain airs and habits to turn him into "an imperfect English clone" (Kwaku Larbi Korang, qtd. in Asiedu 45).

What does it mean, then, to be "perfectly English" in *The Blinkards*, whether by nature or even as a clone? Neither Mrs. Borɔfosɛm nor any of the other mimic characters is particularly reminiscent of an English person, except as the distorted version of an idea. Mr. Onyimdze explains that there are certain "things English people do just because they have unconsciously got into the way of doing them. Such things, among each people, are never capable of being learnt" (63). Mr. Onyimdze does not say what these things that can never be learnt are. Perhaps the essence that he believes makes a "genuine" Fanti man has its English counterpart. Surprisingly, he does not refer to colonial might as a distinguisher. He does imply that the things, whatever they may be, have little to do with external signs.

The mimic's overreliance on objects—whether Mrs. Borɔfosɛm's lorgnette or Mr. Okadu's hat that he brandishes "with a flourish"—reinforces the fact that each culture as presented in *The Blinkards* can be reduced to performance. As though nodding to the theatre setting Sekyi has placed them in, props and costumes are used to signal one's real or imagined affiliation with a nationality. For instance, according to stage directions, during a garden party at Victoria Park in Cape Coast, "Ladies and Gentlemen, in European clothes,

Mimic • 83

[are] parading up and down" (41) in a display of what Mr. Borɔfosɛm has called "showy tomfoolery" (17). At that same party, Mr. Okadu, in a fit of poetic inspiration, declaims, "I'm clad in coat and trousers, with boots upon my feet; And *atamfurafo* and Hausas I seldom deign to greet: For I despise the native that wears the native dress—The badge that marks the bushman" (45).

Given the sociohistorical events of the period, it is not entirely his fault if the mimic over-imbues objects with importance. In "The Invention of Tradition in Colonial Africa," Terence Ranger observes that the incursion of Europeans into African territories in the late-nineteenth and early twentieth centuries coincided with a flowering of traditions invented by European settlers who wanted to add a sheen of respectability to their activities. Some administrators oversaw their districts like "lordly prefects" and created their own traditions in the process (216). Inspired by the signs displayed, such as fancy dress, some local chiefs created their own tribal traditions; nationalists became involved in the creation of traditions as well (243). The traditions that influenced the mimic characters were those inspired by gentlemen and professional men. These neo-traditions, Ranger reports, had the greatest impact on Africans. Their creators were preoccupied with questions of glamour, respectability, and order, thus according importance to signs and rituals (including clothing) that were considered overdone and even "deplored" in England (217).

Sekyi identifies his characters according to their attire, making them engage with clothes as more than routine stage costumes. The *ahyentarfo*, who wear European clothes, are pitted against the *atamfurafo*, who wear "native" cloth.[26] At first it seems that the clothes are an indication of the person's substance. Therefore, Mr. Okadu despises the nature of *atamfurafo* that is intimated by their "badge"; Mr. Borɔfosɛm has told others that he thinks Mr. Onyimdze "is a fool because he wears cloth" (159). When Mrs. Borɔfosɛm receives visitors, she divines (correctly) from the way they knock that they must be in native dress; in another scene, one of the *ahyentarfo* insults her friend by telling her "*w[']atar mmfato wo*" (your clothes do not suit you), to which her friend retorts "*w[']abrabɔ mmfata atar*" (your lifestyle is not suited to European clothes).

These occasions notwithstanding, it is a difficult business to graft the culture represented by the clothes onto oneself. Using external signs as removable as clothes to classify characters' nature creates a challenge. For one thing,

---

26. This is the literal translation.

it seems that in Mrs. Borɔfosɛm's Cape Coast, cultures can be abandoned or taken up by putting on or taking off certain items of clothing. Mimics even claim to have forgotten how to speak Fanti when fully decked in woolen suits and gloves. At the end of the play, Mrs. Borɔfosɛm (who has presumably already switched once) signals her about-face by appearing onstage "*in native dress*" and declaring, "It suits me, isn't it?" Now that this performance is over––or as she puts it, "it is all finished"—she admits that she feels "so comfy" (157). Her husband follows suit and is also free to dress more comfortably.

The couple's change of heart is only one, if the biggest, instance where the play hints that adopting (and so, discarding) cultures is a superficial act. On other occasions, the characters slip up and "reveal" themselves and the shallowness of their performance. Mrs. Borɔfosɛm catches herself speaking Fanti and hastily declares that she has "forget" herself. Bame observes the continued success of this trope: "This is the humor that follows when the conceit of self-deception is exposed to ridicule. It is a theme that has long been popular among actors seeking to amuse Fante audiences" (39). In the same vein, Mr. Tsiba is halfway through a meal before he remembers that he should be eating it with a *faka* (a fork); he then reprimands his houseboy for not putting the cutlery out, because without the external signs to act as a prompt, he falls back into old habits. He slips up again when he has to greet visitors before he remembers to say "good afternoon" in English. Cole is right to state that "in *The Blinkards*, clothing is the ultimate symbol of a person's identity and cultural affiliation" (791). More than that, the play suggests a game of props and behaviors, some of which have no real purchase because of their superficiality. Humor comes from the fact that what some characters are claiming to reject—language, food, even behavior—is affixed to them.

Another notable instance of cultural switching is Nyamekyɛ, the servant who puts Mrs. Borɔfosɛm to "rights" after he tries to kiss her as the English do. From the beginning, he clearly does not belong with the mimic crowd. He views his mistress with a mix of befuddlement and wariness. "English" things, as prescribed by Mrs. Borɔfosɛm but not computing with his own logic, do not appear to take: she reprimands him for not leaving dry leaves in books and for sweeping up the ashes from the carpet. But even Nyamekyɛ, intoxicated and armed with a few props, shows how easy it is to "become" a white man when he enters the infamous scene and declares in English, "I whi' man toray." Like any mimic worth his salt, he is now "in straw hat, an old frock coat, white trousers, brown boots, smoking a cigar, and holding a withered branch." He calls Mrs. Borɔfosɛm "duckie" and tries to kiss her as she has often encouraged her husband to do. The shame catalyzes the halt to her "English" performance. According to Mr. Borɔfosɛm, who comes to Nyamekyɛ's defense and likely echoes Sekyi's thoughts, the "white lady" has been "hoist with her own petard" (153).[27] Newell justifiably disapproves of Sekyi's method: "The male servant defeats the impudent mistress, enacting the ultimate authority and cultural legitimacy of the male" ("Local Cosmopolitans" 112). Nyamekyɛ was previously described by Mr. Borɔfosɛm as "a Fanti among Fantis," who "does not understand kissing" and might think that it involved biting or worse (Sekyi 11).[28] Dressed as he is in his final scene, and declaring his whiteness, it is obvious that he has, in fact, been paying attention.

For his part, Mr. Onyimdze disturbs the unwritten societal code that demands dress match training and comportment. He announces his own colors: "The court has risen, I have no case tomorrow. I have taken off the European sacks and the Inns-of-court gown which are my working-clothes. I have put on the native garb, I have withdrawn my feet from boots, I have put on sandals" (24). He then spends the rest of the play defending native values. Mrs. Borɔfosɛm's fan club, scandalized, declare that his having an English education and wearing native dress is tantamount to "misbehaving" (61). Mr. Tsiba, who likes for things to follow simple patterns, complains bitterly that, until he opens his mouth, one has no way of knowing that Mr. Onyimdze has been to England. It is perhaps not so surprising if Mr. Onyimdze is less caricature and more stick-in-the-mud. He sees through the crude mechanism that the comedy is built on and refuses to play by those rules.

THE "ENGLISH"

Englishmen and women, for all that they are so central to *The Blinkards*, are mostly absent from the play. They are primarily filtered through the mimics' interpretation of their culture. Other than a reference to an "Ipay" and a "Chutney" who run a store (27), the most prominent is the infamous and physically absent Mrs. Gush of Seabourne and the sacrosanct words and actions: "That is how Mrs Gush has done it" (19). The Cosmopolitan Club mem-

---

27. In this case, Shakespeare is not (just) a sign of mimicry but is also the most effective way to sum up events. This is a complicated case of mimicry marking the mistake of mimicry.

28. Charles Larson uses kissing as an example to counter the assumption that European cultural elements are necessarily natural or universal (63).

bers do remind each other to "prepare well" because some white men will be present at some of their activities (109). This admonition shows that while Newell is right to state that the mimics' intended audience is not primarily Western ("Local Cosmopolitans" 109), and while the groups may not have the opportunity to mingle much, the specter of the white men's authority and approval hangs over the black characters.

The mimic's obsession with Englishmen and women ties in further to Ranger's observations about the forming of neo-traditions. On the one hand, neo-traditions became reality over time; on the other, they distorted the past in order to come into being (212). If, as Ranger states, the English created these traditions with the intention of impressing African subjects and deepening the divide between white and black, then the mimic becomes doubly absurd for attempting to copy something that lacks a significant degree of authenticity. He reproduces an invented iconography of Englishness. It is possible that the substance of the blinkard's mimicry is an artifact devised to reinforce colonial hegemony. While the mimic showcases cultural contamination, the literature simultaneously makes a mockery of the idealized European culture. There is an implicit statement about a culture that forces people to wear stays and keep their arms and feet covered, that produces inane romantic literature to rot young people's minds, and that forcefully transposes a foreign religion and law onto cultures that were managing quite well without. If the mimic is aware that English culture is a performance that may be discarded when the moment calls for it, it is not certain that the Englishman who produces and follows all of his own social conventions is in the know.

At one point, the stage is given to a lone white man who is presented as the lover of an unknown character. Their relationship is interpreted as a sign of moral decay in the commentary of an Old Man, who declares, "The world has gone wrong! These are they who sell our country to white men . . . all for the sake of money . . . Just fancy that she has so much finery on her person" (128). The white man thus stands for degeneration but also inescapable economic clout. More important, there is not much ostentatious about his clothing or speech. But as Mrs. Borɔfosɛm reminds Mr. Onyimdze, "it doesn't matter" that they are *not* in England (139). At the end of the day, whatever the community decides is English is what it means to be English. "Their efforts at anglicisation are shown to have failed on every count," writes Newell (*Literary Culture* 161). This is undoubtedly true, but their definition of anglicization is more elastic than it might seem at first.

The play, then, defines Englishness more by what it is *not* than what it is.

Time spent in England has little to do with it. Race apparently has only so much to do with it. Mrs. Borɔfosɛm is revered for staying in England for three months, while Mr. Onyimdze was there long enough to complete law school. He even says that he was more anglicized in Cape Coast than he was after six months in England; his trip to England rather converted him into "Fanti man" (63).[29] In terms of using signs to signify one's belonging, it appears that Fantis who have never set foot outside of the country or possibly interacted with a European have somehow ended up more "English" than the English. The contradictions and confusions become even more complicated when the term "white" is used even to characterize blacks. The term it is often translating, ɔborɔnyi, here, too, indicates foreign ideas more than skin tone. This means that while Mrs. Borɔfosɛm acknowledges that Miss Tsiba cannot realistically be expected to blush, she still states that her husband's voice is like that of a white man. Also, she carelessly bandies statements like "Mr. Okadu is almost a white man," upon which Mr. Okadu obligingly "tries to look white" (75).

Otherwise, what does it mean to be Fanti in the beginning of the twentieth century, when Mr. Onyimdze and Mr. Borɔfosɛm acknowledge that they were first and thoroughly anglicized at home? Those characters who might be qualified as the "noble savages" belong to the old guard. Nana Katawerwa, Na Sompa, and Grandfather Akodee, who represent tradition as conceived of by Sekyi, belong to an older generation that, no matter how romanticized and venerated, is not equipped to thrive in the current space. They are the representatives of what Newell calls "an idealised but lost African past" (*Literary Culture* 157). Nana Katawerwa, Miss Tsiba's grandmother, acknowledges that without Mr. Onyimdze, she would not have been able to help her granddaughter. The agency of this group is mostly oral, using well-placed words to arouse pathos or influence other characters and the audience.

The fact that mediator-type characters are being given center stage indicates the extent to which the society is undergoing change. Traditions are suffering erasure; this becomes clearer when the text is compared to *Things Fall Apart*, for instance. The atmosphere and worldview of Achebe's text relies on proverbs, religious rites, and ancient social practices. While the novel certainly does not suggest that cultural elements are immutable, there is a facet of dependability and perhaps even timelessness to these traditions. It is mostly

---

29. Becoming aware of oneself as black or African or Nigerian when in England or America is a common theme. It plays out in *No Longer at Ease* in Chimamanda Adichie's *Americanah*.

in the latter parts of the novel that it becomes apparent that a great social revolution, embodied by the British, is about to take place. In *The Blinkards*, that change is proceeding with full vigor so that harking back to tradition may not be a likely or even feasible outcome.

"What I cannot understand," Mrs. Borofosem admits in a rare and candid moment, "is that, in spite of all which makes our lives so enjoyable, our ancestors, whose lives seem so hard to us, lived longer and were happier than we can live or be" (6). By referring to "the ancestors," her speech indicates that the play is preoccupied with an idealized past. As Ball says, "A remarkably enduring commonplace of satire theories is the notion that satire, even at its most revolutionary, gazes nostalgically and conservatively back upon a privileged golden age . . . If there is a golden age implied by postcolonial satire it will be located before colonial intervention" (9–11). The colonial enterprise believed that the black man could not and should not be a white man; he had a "nature" that could not be erased. Nationalist agenda also believed the same but for different reasons: Sekyi's writing was aimed at inventing a "golden age of Africanness . . . to indict the local effects of colonialism with the full weight of the 'past' at his fingertips" (Newell, *Literary Culture* 157). The fact that both colonialists and nationalists are conservative in their view of the mimic figure hints at his surprisingly political valence.

Sekyi's intention is to make his audience return to a culture he presents in an idealized light. *The Blinkards* supposes that it is easy to get beyond mimicry and that the traditional culture can yet be retrieved. The play is therefore optimistic at heart. It also shows a certain naïveté, since it does not fully probe the fast-changing sociopolitical realities or the agency that European culture represents. In addition, the emphasis on performance and change supposes the possibility, however minuscule, that the mimic is more self-aware than critics have previously given him credit for. The switching of clothes and attitudes implies a certain adaptability that is usually not considered in relation to this character.

DRAWING THE LINE: MESSRS. ONYIMDZE AND SEKYI

For all that it promotes preserving traditions, *The Blinkards* makes it clear that not every character displaying a mix of different cultural elements is absurd. One fair criticism of theories of humor is that stating the necessary conditions for humor is not always sufficient to account for it. In this case, characters who break cultural "patterns" are not necessarily a trigger for laughter. In fact, it happens that certain combinations of cultural elements are quite congruous and if not idealized, then at the very least excused. One very serious cultural broker is the young barrister Mr. Onyimdze, who admits that sometimes he expresses himself better in English than in Fanti (35). His speech patterns can be quite argotic and drawn out. Utudjian says that, on occasion, he uses the "most incongruous phrases and obsolete exclamations borrowed from a student's pseudo-learned jargon." Sekyi himself, she contends, is not always aware of the subtleties of his borrowed language (25). The statements that she objects to include "It's the old Gorgon and a victim. Poor devil-ess! I wonder what's the game." As "high-flown" as Utudjian finds his language, Onyimdze is one of the play's most humorless characters. Sekyi also trained as a barrister and famously refused to wear English dress outside of court.[30] It is not surprising that critics usually tout Onyimdze as virtually inseparable from Sekyi himself. In fact, some of his proclamations come verbatim from the playwright's tracts.[31] The lawyer regularly interrupts the absurdity to share what must be Sekyi's own convictions—for example, that "our genuine Fanti old men who are proud in every way of their nationality are wiser, healthier and infinitely more respectable and dignified than those who are anglicised" (59). H.V.H. Sekyi, his son, believes that Kobina Sekyi "was Mr. Onyimdze" ("Foreword to *The Blinkards*" x).

Another text by Sekyi, a short story titled *The Anglo-Fanti*, is printed alongside *The Blinkards* in the Heinemann edition. Here, too, Sekyi's characters utter his own ideas. The story is about a boy whose "development is not at all normal. Possibly he is not as strong as he might have been, because his people have become more or less Europeanised" (178). Kwesi Onyidzin ("Nameless") also believes in European superiority before leaving to study in England. There, he experiences a rude awakening and returns home, "confirming his rejection of European pretensions to superiority." Onyidzin's end is tragic—thoroughly disillusioned by his society's unending love of European lifestyles, he wastes away and, on his deathbed, admonishes his family not to stray from "the narrower to the wider duty" (255). Whether Onyidzin or Onyimdze, this sensible character is not without fault, as Utudjian shows. Abarry is even more trenchant. For him, Onyimdze "hardly seems

---

30. See Asiedu, Langley's introduction to the 1974 edition, or Gibbs.

31. Langley notes that Onyimdze is reciting sections from Sekyi's own *The Meaning of the Expression "Thinking in English"* (35).

emancipated"—perhaps an unfair critique, given the general lack of political emancipation in the Gold Coast at the time. Abarry contends that "his life is a pathetic dramatization of what happens to the 'civilized' anglicized African who tries to tiptoe back to his ancestral roots" (160).

Tiptoeing may be the best he can do. Mr. Onyimdze cannot fully identify with his ancestral roots, such as they may be. Yet he would obviously prefer to be viewed through the rosy light that shines over the *atamfurafo*. The old *atamfurafo* have moral right, which makes the judgment they pronounce on others weighty: Miss Tsiba's grandmother asserts, "If this is English, then the English are barbarians" (124). For Mr. Onyimdze, they are unspoiled and truthful—"genuine"—and he is conscious of their gaze. He is very embarrassed by the Okadu-Tsiba affair because people consider Mr. Okadu to be his protégé. The worst thing for the thinker would be to be painted with the same brush as the mimics. It stands to reason, then, that his motives are not purely altruistic, even when he appears on stage to admonish foolish behavior. Sareil makes a similar observation about the thinker in Molière's theatre, stressing how much Molière's reasoners intervene inappropriately and offer their services at the least-convenient moments. The awkwardness that travels with them shows that their main function, like that of other dramatic secondary characters, is to emphasize the hero's aberrations. Mr. Onyimdze, by underlining the mimics' faults, serves to highlight his own attractiveness. There is, therefore, an inherent anxiety implied in writers who must distance themselves—or their avatars—from the figure of the mimic who so often generates repulsion.

Things are more complicated for Sekyi, given the ongoing cultural brokerage. He "operates in a binary model in which—with the exception of members of his own highly educated class—the only alternative to being a 'noble savage' is to be a fraud, a denationalised mimic of English culture" (Newell, *Literary Culture* 162). So by painting Mrs. Borɔfosɛm so unappealingly and even appallingly, the playwright is making it plain that despite being an "anglicized" Fanti, he, and others like him, hold no love for her beliefs. Sekyi found the expectation that those who sojourned abroad would adopt "English" habits repellent. At the same time, nicknamed the "Sage of Cape Coast," he himself was not fully integrated into life in Cape Coast upon his return home—Newell even states that he was "isolated" (159). In the foreword, his son reminisces about his father's sartorial choices, statement pieces in their own way: "Except in the cool month of August, or in the highest courts of law where wigs and gowns were de rigueur, he wore his native togas at all times, whether attending a meeting of the Paramount Chiefs council . . . whether appearing before the lower courts (where his garb is said to have irritated some magistrates)" (x). If we consider that Mr. Onyimdze "is" Sekyi, as much of criticism would have it, then the mimic may reflect the Europhone writer's own possible unease with his anglicization and serve to deflect attention from it.

BEYOND *THE BLINKARDS*—CULTURAL MEDIATION IN *LE VIEUX NÈGRE ET LA MÉDAILLE*

H.V.H. Sekyi sums up his father's motivations: "[Society] never abruptly replaces whole limbs with borrowed ones . . . To substitute the tail of a lizard for that of a fish is a false reaction—not a natural adaptation to any change in the environment but an absurd and monstrous innovation, resulting not in some healthier new creature, but in a mere abortion" (viii). "If *The Blinkards*, then, seems to be more moral than art, it is because the dramatist intends it to be so," Abarry writes (160). Certainly, both Sekyis propose a reading of the text as a moral map. As Newell puts it, the entire play can be equated to a kind of instruction manual on avoiding the vice of mimicry (*Literary Culture* 167). Comic vice, for Bergson, acts as a framework for a character to step into. A ready-made framework explains why mimicry is so recognizable. Contrary to tragic vice, comic vice is simple, inflexible, and ossifies a character; that, for Bergson, is a main difference between a comedy and a drama.[32] No matter how well integrated into the character's personality, comic vice ends up as the central character of such comedies. It is for this reason that many comedies have a proper noun for a title: *L'Avare, Le Joueur*, and others (14–15). To that list we can add *The Blinkards*. Sekyi even names his characters in direct relation to it. As much an idea as a character, it makes sense that very soon after her change of heart, and when Mrs. Borɔfosɛm can no longer be accurately called Mrs. Borɔfosɛm, the play ends.

---

32. "*Un drame, même quand il nous peint des passions ou des vices qui portent un nom, les incorpore si bien au personnage que leurs noms s'oublient, que leurs caractères généraux s'effacent, et que nous ne pensons plus du tout à eux, mais à la personne qui les absorbe*" (14) ["A drama, even when portraying passions or vices that bear a name, so completely incorporates them in the person that their names are forgotten, their general characteristics effaced, and we no longer think of them at all, but rather of the person in whom they are assimilated" (7)].

92 • TYPOLOGIES OF HUMOR IN AFRICAN LITERATURES

Like comic vice, Kobina Sekyi is himself practically a character.[33] Even during the sillier moments, the lessons interfere with the action. *The Blinkards* is a classic, one of the earliest-written texts to address a frequent complaint. Since then, other farcical characters have followed a similar trajectory. However, transparently "mimic" literature is not terribly creative, as Abarry has noted. For Bhabha, too, mimicry translates "the low mimetic literary effects" of the colonial imagination (85). Still, comic literature continues to be inspired by the imbalance between African and Western cultures as well as their mutual strangeness, even if writers do not always resort to characters as unpolished as the mimic.

As Sekyi does with the Bɔrɔfosɛms, Oyono ends *Le Vieux nègre et la médaille* [*The Old Man and the Medal*] on a note of homecoming after Meka, the hero, goes through a startling number of misadventures over a short period. *Le Vieux*, which I touched on in the introduction, is a brilliantly subtle novel published in 1956 (English translation in 1967). In it, a small African community contends with its cultural practices and adapts as well as it can to incursions from the French colonial government, education, and church. At the beginning of the novel, Meka and his entire community are thrilled at the news that he is going to be honored by the French colonial officers in an elaborate ceremony. Yet, just a few hours after he receives the medal, Meka loses his way and is arrested for trespassing in the *quartier blanc*, the section of the town restricted to whites. Meka, refreshingly, is not a one-dimensional character; he plays the part of an intermediary very differently from the mimic. It is true that, initially, Meka is proud to be recognized and appreciated for the sacrifices he has been encouraged to make for the colonial culture. But for all that Meka shows a frank admiration of the French, the narration continuously betrays an undercurrent of lucidity about his situation that culminates in an outright rejection of French culture. In reality, Meka is aware of the fact that his show of support for France has come at great personal sacrifice. He has lost his two sons to the world war; what is more, his land was "donated" to the Catholic mission after God, through the white priest, announced that it pleased him one fine morning to seize it (16).

The much-vaunted medal is supposed to be "*celle de l'amitié, de l'amour et du respect que les Blancs voulaient témoigner à Meka*" (70) ["the medal of the friendship and love and respect that the whites wanted to show for Meka" (61)]. The statement is certainly taken at face value: when the award

---

33. Asiedu, citing Gibbs, notes that Sekyi acted in the 1916 production (47).

Mimic • 93

is announced, the narrator reports that the ecstatic screams emitted by the community could easily be mistaken for a warning siren by a freshly debarked white man. This single-minded delight and pleasure gesture to the conviction felt by the African characters that Meka has crossed over, so to speak, and is now a "brother" to the white men. The community is equally convinced that his wife is "a white woman" and that Meka now wields concrete agency to ensure, for example, that roads are built at his say-so. While they consider that Meka is one of theirs, he also has access to the white men's clout.

At the same time, Meka himself is aware on some level that this cannot be true. His awareness comes to a head during the fourteenth of July celebrations, which also double as the award ceremony. For Meka, this occasion highlights his position between his African culture and his adoptive French culture, which seems to have adopted him back:

> *Tête nue, bras collés au corps, Meka se tenait immobile dans le cercle dessiné à la chaux où on l'avait placé pour attendre l'arrivée du Chef des Blancs. Des gardes maintenaient à grand-peine ses congénères massés derrière lui. Des blancs . . . étaient en face, dans l'ombre de la véranda de M. Fouconi . . .]il réalisa qu'il était dans une situation étrange. Ni son grand-père, ni son père, ni aucun membre de son immense famille ne s'étaient trouvés placés, comme lui, dans un cercle de chaux, entre deux mondes, le sien et celui de ceux qu'on avait d'abord appelés les « fantômes » quand ils étaient arrivés au pays. Lui, il ne se trouvait ni avec les siens ni avec les autres. (95)*

> [Meka stood bareheaded and quite still, his arms to his sides, inside the circle painted with whitewash where he had been placed to wait for the arrival of the White Chief. The guards were having difficulty keeping back the crowd of his fellow Africans massed behind him. In front under the shade of M. Fouconi's veranda were the white men . . . He realized what a strange situation he was in. Neither his grandfather nor his father nor any member of his huge family had ever been placed as he was inside a whitewash circle, between two worlds, his own world and the world of those others who had been called ghosts when they first came to the land. He was not with his own people, and he was not with the others. (85)]

Meka feels his uniqueness keenly, as the sole participant in the ceremony who can attest to being between two worlds. He does not quite belong to the mass of blacks being kept at a distance and is waiting to integrate the French

94 • TYPOLOGIES OF HUMOR IN AFRICAN LITERATURES

waiting in the shaded veranda. The whitewashed circle in which he has been placed takes on all its heavy symbolism. Standing at attention, dressed in a brand-new outfit, and wanting to believe that the medal testifies to all the virtuous feelings the French have toward him, Meka even begins to despise some of his fellow blacks. He refuses to even glance at the chiefs, who, he is convinced, must be envious of him. Here, there is an important convergence from anglophone places like the Gold Coast. Whereas the British took advantage of existing structures, for instance, appointing their own chiefs and ruling the people indirectly, the French preferred a different approach, the most famous of which is the Policy of Assimilation. Assimilation encouraged the systematic erasure of African cultural practices in favor of French culture. The aim was to make colonized Africans as "French" as possible.

Obviously, Meka never attains the circle of "ghosts"; for all the sacrifices he has made for France, he and his peers have imbued the medal with far more meaning than it has. He understands very little of the French code, whether the language or some of those mysterious cultural features that Onyimdze refers to; he even admits that it is virtually impossible for him to tell white men apart: they are like antelopes in that regard (95). In comparison, Mrs. Bərəfosɛm is an expert on European culture. As is the case with Mrs. Bərəfosɛm, toward the end of the narrative, Meka undergoes an epiphany and realizes that there is an insurmountable breach between the colonized and the colonizing culture. The narrator, on the other hand, who has amused himself with this knowledge throughout the novel, does not change his tone but carries on with the same tongue-in-cheek mood and humor.

Even though the moment within the white circle is meant to be poignant and elevating, the award ceremony is constantly overshadowed by Meka's own impudent inner voice and the narrator's even more irreverent storytelling. Oyono's favored technique involves diminishing things that are supposed to be solemn and rarefied by associating them with the failings of the human body. This translates into the ceremony, so that slowly but surely it is taken over by bodily functions. Not too long after haughtily taking his place in the circle and offering his self-congratulatory observations, Meka's body begins to betray him as he stands under the hot sun waiting for the governor to arrive. Oyono brilliantly describes it: "*Ce fit d'abord son cou raide qui se fatigua*" (96) ["His tiredness had started first in his stiff neck" (86)], and things go downhill from there. Soon after his neck begins to misbehave, Meka's feet, unaccustomed to shoes, feel as though they were being pierced clean through by a needle. The heat is stifling. Then, from "afar," the climax: the pressing and mounting urge to urinate. Eventually, Meka would give anything to be crouched behind his hut relieving himself as he does every mundane morning, medal be damned. By the time the governor arrives, the overwhelming presence of the physical has thoroughly frustrated Meka and his anticipation of transcendence. As a result, he ends up morbidly fixated on the enormous governor.

The Frenchman's body is not spared either—partly because we are not distracted by whatever he is saying (Meka does not understand him; by extension, neither do we), our focus is oriented to his voluminous lower chin, which is likened to an old breast the color of laterite. Furthermore, he is so sweaty that Meka stews in anguish as he wonders whether the white Chief is going to stick his sopping wet "craw" against his shoulders as he is doing with his fellow white men. Oyono's narrative technique recalls what Bakhtin calls "grotesque realism," where "the material bodily principle, that is, images of the human body with its food, drink, defecation, and sexual life, plays a predominant role. Images of the body are offered, moreover, in an extremely exaggerated form" (18). The narration also recalls Mbembe's references to the postcolony, those societies marked by the violence of colonialism. With Meka so engrossed by the trembling of the white man's voluminous chin, the inflation and deflation of the skin under that chin, the movement of the white man's jaw as he speaks, as well as his hot breath, Mbembe might say that Oyono's narrator is using grotesque imagery to highlight the regime of violence:

The body is the principal locale of the idioms and fantasies used in depicting power. If indeed it is the festivities and celebrations that are the vehicles for giving expression to the *commandement* and for staging its displays of magnificence and prodigality, then the body in question is first a body that eats and drinks, and second a body that is open—in both ways: hence the significance given to orifices, and the central part they play in people's political humor. (Mbembe 107)

The award ceremony is a vital turning point in Meka's overt disenchantment with colonialism. This comes to a head with his imprisonment for trespassing in an area reserved for his white "brothers." By the time he is released, he entertains very few illusions about the transformative powers of the medal or how he is regarded by the French. His discourse is now very different when next he addresses a statement to a Frenchman: *"Dis-lui que je suis le dernier des imbéciles, qui hier croyait encore à l'amitié des Blancs"* (150) ["Tell him I am a very great fool, who yesterday still believed in the white man's friendship" (134–135)].

96   •   TYPOLOGIES OF HUMOR IN AFRICAN LITERATURES

In *The Blinkards*, there are speeches at the end that reiterate the central message; they are mostly devoid of humor. Something similar happens in *Le Vieux nègre*: as though to make sure that the reader has imbibed the message about not promoting another culture to the detriment of one's own, there is a large reunion in Meka's village, Doum, toward the end of the novel. There, the black characters reexamine their relationship with the colonizers. There is little of the enthusiasm of before and far more bitterness at the way Meka and, by extension, all of them have been treated. Oyono's narrator, however, cannot seem to help being amusing even now and, consequently, does not allow the comic tone that has permeated the whole narrative to dissipate for the lesson to shine through. The characters are as entertaining now as they were before the revelation, and Meka himself continues to display comic traits. For instance, though he is hale and hearty, if a little shaken by his night in prison, he pretends to be on the verge of death in order to garner sympathy and admiration for his fortitude.

The increasingly comic atmosphere means that although they reaffirm their newfound pride in their traditions, these traditions are not presented in the same hallowed light as a Mr. Onyimdze, say, would shine on them. The men of Doum accordingly indulge in petty squabbling all through their conference. One of them, Engamba, highlights the enduring nature of their laughter when he likens the incapacity to recognize a joke to a "white" trait: "*Mvemas! Mvemas! vociféra-t-il. Êtes-vous devenus tous des Blancs? Vous ne connaissez plus la plaisanterie!*" (183) ["'Mvemas! Mvemas!' he shouted. 'Have you turned into white men? Can't you take a joke?'"]. At this, the company, we are told, "brightened" (165). Soon enough, the gathering makes fun of Meka, some "*farceurs*" going as far as to pantomime his imprisonment—the same experience that marks such an important narrative watershed. One of Meka's compatriots is asked to spare the others the dust from his balls: "'*Je porte les couilles d'un Blanc!*" he retorts, "*pas de danger. Tout le monde riait.*" (183) ["'I've got a white man's balls,' he said laughing. 'So that's no danger'" (164)]. Another, laughing uncontrollably, says that he would have loved to see the white commandant pin the medal on Meka's loincloth instead of his chest. "*Le rire*," the narrator informs the reader, "*éclata avec la violence d'une eau bouillonnante longtemps contenue qui rompt sa digue*" (185) ["The laughter burst with the violence of boiling water that has been held back breaking out" (166)].

The overall lesson of the story may well be on reclaiming pride in their culture and traditions; it puts at least as much stress on the hysterical laughter that takes over the entire group and that is difficult to contain or control. Oyono places less emphasis on categorically condemning one culture over the other: both are essentially reduced to their shared (and disgustingly humorous) humanity in the form of secretions, protrusions, and odors. In a way, then, the text gestures to the ethos of the trickster, who is suspicious of claims of superiority.

Le Vieux nègre deals with themes similar to *The Blinkards*, but the treatment is obviously different. And though he is speaking about a South African context, Njabulo Ndebele's thoughts on the usefulness of entertainment in African literature become relevant for affirming one of the greatest differences. Ndebele regrets the superficiality of many African writings whose sole and obvious purpose is to reflect binary symbols—"symbols of evil on the one hand, and symbols of the victims of evil on the other hand." The characters, he says, are presented as finished products without any real history (28). Though the character types he names are not particularly comic ones—"'sellouts,' 'baases,' 'madams,'" etc.—the mimic can be added to his list, for the same reasons of lack of development and surface symbolism. Positing that these characters are born of an ideology steeped in moral issues, Ndebele says that, in fact, the writer's objective is hardly met—for him, surface representations inform without bringing about any real change. As an alternative to the "attack-attack-attack method" (Newell, *Literary Culture* 160), Ndebele proposes another technique, one that seems to be taken by Oyono—the "timeless tradition of storytelling":

> A story is allowed to unfold by itself with a minimum of authorial intervention through which a storyteller might directly suggest how readers or listeners should understand his story. Two key effects result from the lack of such intervention. Firstly, the entertainment value of the story is enhanced, and the emotional involvement of the reader is thus assured. Secondly, such involvement does not necessarily lead to a lulling of the reader's critical consciousness. (20–21)

Without seeking to minimize the damage of colonialism, the subsequent cultural erosion or racism, the desire to amplify the entertainment value of literature is revealed in a more circumspect approach to the question of incongruities and intermediacy. The mimic becomes reflective of a wider quality of literature. Also, the mimic, however much disavowed, becomes a figure for the text's own intermediate position.

CHAPTER 3

Interpreter

In Amadou Hampaté Bâ's *L'Étrange destin de Wangrin* (hereafter, *Wangrin*), Jean-Jacques de Villermoz is the new deputy to the field administrator at Diagaramba, French Sudan.[1] A young Frenchman descended from aristocrats, he likes to joke that thanks to the French Revolution he is a count without a bank account. However, his relative destitution does not stop him from putting on airs—here in his colonial African post, he carries on much like his peered ancestors did—"*il se comportait en grand seigneur*" (63) ["always the fine gentleman" (39)]. Besides clumsy plays on words and a resolve to amass riches, his passion, as reported by himself, is "mounting" beautiful girls and stallions. His daily attire, riding boots with golden spurs, functions as a stylistic complement to his persona. Topping off the image is a monocle. To the people of Diagaramba, who have never encountered one before, the monocle is a source of mystery. Thankfully, things are elucidated by Villermoz's African steward, who lets it be known that a monocle is a rare item indeed, whose purpose is to identify the sons of the royal houses of France and Navarre, and that Villermoz would have only to present his at the French treasury (or at the cash registry of any business) to be given as much money as he desired.

Wangrin, published in 1973, is a fascinating narrative. Wangrin is an enigmatic adventurer in French West Africa at the beginning of the twentieth century. Biographical, traditional oral, and supernatural elements come together to create a series of fantastical events set in colonial West Africa.[2] While Antougoumo the steward is otherwise not very important to the advance-

---

1. Translations are from Hampâté Bâ, *The Fortunes of Wangrin* (1999).

2. French West Africa, as Jeanne Garane explains, comprised "Mauritania, Senegal, French Soudan (now The Republic of Mali), French Guinea (now The Republic of Guinea), Côte d'Ivoire, Upper Volta (Haute Volta—now Burkina Faso), Dahomey (now Benin), and Niger between 1895 and 1958, [and] covered 4, 689,000 square kilometers" (1).

ment of the plot, his interpretation of European objects and behaviors to an African audience gestures to Wangrin; like Wangrin, a professional interpreter, the steward finds himself mediating between two populations. While Antougoumo might believe his own questionable stories, it is likelier that he invents Villermoz's legend to acquire some of that reflected glory for himself. More important still, the reader is pulled up short by the contrast between his wildly imprecise information and its matter-of-fact narration. There is something amusingly engaging about the fact that the count's remarks about nonexistent bank accounts have not at all been considered. This episode is one of many from African literatures that suggest the humorous potential in cultural misunderstandings, even in complicated or difficult settings.

There is a basic mechanism in these encounters, which I refer to as "comic interpreting." Two groups are separated by a gulf, often linguistic. One side produces noises and actions that the other side does not understand but assumes fall under the ambit of foreign weirdness. The other side does things equally incomprehensible to the first. Then, a third, learned party places himself between the two groups, ostensibly to promote communication. Instead, he produces an entertainingly inaccurate text capable of taking on a life of its own. The resulting humor is evocative of trickster folktales but also of Molière plays—for example, dramatically ironic in the form of a wink from storyteller or character to audience, all over an ignorant party's head. The colonial setting means this humor is largely grounded in and complicated by power imbalances. While they have a high threshold for amusing misunderstandings, they always risk tipping the wrong way.

Wangrin is a perfectly multilingual and proficient interpreter whose cultural brokering still manages to be as imprecise as the steward's. He works directly under *commandants*, local colonial officers heading different posts.[3] However, he is not exactly working for them. When he returns from one special assignment, it is with a message from the Fulbe people, threatening war. The war will be long, savage, costly, and harmful to the French officer's personal comfort—or it would be, were it not made up. Wangrin frightens the Frenchman with phantasms of bloodthirsty locals, who, in truth, have no interest in taking up arms (but shrug resignedly at what *they* have diagnosed as the colonizers' simmering potential for madness). To the awe and gratitude of both sides, Wangrin, while touting his profound knowledge of Fulbe

---

3. In an endnote, Hampâté Bâ explains that colonial administrators of every rank were "commandants" (374).

culture to the French and the psychology of white men to the Fulbe, offers solutions to problems that never existed.

Given the many injustices in the colonial context, it is tempting to emphasize Wangrin's subversiveness and resistance. Still, an exclusive focus on subversion would ignore much of the comic interpreter's unpredictability. As Sathya Rao convincingly argues, in *Wangrin*, "Conflict as well as opposition are no longer a matter of brutal and inefficient oppositions" (224). Jeanne Garane similarly remarks on the interpreter's faithlessness to the colonial powers and his own people (2). Reading the story as an example of African comedic sensibility, with a focus on the interpreter's amorality and ambiguity, complicates the polarity between colonial power/colonial subject, tradition/ modernity, and other binaries addressed in chapter 2.

Using Achebe's *Things Fall Apart* to highlight the broader issue of cultural brokering, this chapter builds on different dimensions of the problems with interpreting. At the heart of the chosen scenes is a back-and-forth between cultures perceived as very different and whose relationships are defined by power asymmetries. Serving as a bridge is a character whose dishonesty or incompetence undermines mutual intelligibility and straightforwardness. They are public scenes between African and European interlocutors, with an African interpreter and a diegetic audience whose appreciation of humor may resonate with that of the reader.

INTERPRETING

The interpreter as a comic figure is more likely than not to fall spectacularly short of norms, including the basic parameters of translating and interpreting (which I discuss together in this chapter).[4] That is what makes him interesting. Thus, we can begin by looking at some common expectations and assumptions brought to a normal interpreting exercise. Or as Roderick Jones asks in *Conference Interpreting Explained*, "What is an interpreter?" He answers with a simple enough scenario: "Imagine two people sitting in a room.

---

4. Some of the questions the comic interpreter raises, such as accuracy and fidelity, are a mainstay of the scholarship on translation. The two practices are so intertwined that they are often theorized in relation to each other. It is not unusual to consider that an interpretation *is* a translation (Nicholson 42; or Pöchhacker 9). But even this may be an unnecessary distinction; for Alex Bühler, the argument that "a certain activity aiming at comprehension is an activity aiming at comprehension" is the epitome of triteness (56).

They may be politicians, businessmen or women, trades unionists or scientists. They wish to discuss their work but speak different languages, and neither speaks the other's language well enough for the discussion to be useful. So they call in someone else, who speaks both languages, to explain what each is saying in turn. That person is an interpreter" (3). Little of what he is saying can be disputed when applied to professional contexts. Jones acknowledges that while this image is "simplified to caricature," it still represents the essence of interpreting. As he mentions, the "basic techniques of interpreting, however, are the same . . . whichever geographical area one lives and works in" (1).

What is of particular interest here is what happens when some of the assumptions and foundations of the field are applied to different situations, especially those unapologetic about their deviancy. Jones's definition above is striking for the level playing field that it brings to life. The people in his chain of communication are from impressive disciplines; it is implied that they are equals who desire to hear each other's points of view, "sitting" together and constrained only by linguistic barriers. These obstacles are then removed by a person who is just as impressively proficient in his craft; the image supposes a horizontal meeting ground. In such a situation, the criteria for evaluating a good interpretation are scientific, qualitative, and quantitative.[5] This is not always the reality of the colonial interpreter. We can expect his practice to be even less grounded in objectivity and honesty when he is a comic figure, when his context is that of a story, and when his ethos is grounded in trickery or incompetence.

In *The African Imagination*, Abiola Irele contextualizes Wangrin's casual extraordinariness by pointing to the disarray created by colonialism: "Wangrin has grasped with remarkable intuition the truth of his situation: in a world of changing values, there can be no established code of conduct until the dust of history has settled" (90). Wangrin's behavior, besides highlighting the deleteriousness of colonialism, shows as well that an atmosphere influenced by anarchy is *also* propitious for the laws of humor. Humor, as Simon Critchley reminds us, produces a "world with its causal chains broken, its social practices turned inside out, and common sense rationality left in tatters." It does this by creating a disjunction "between expectation and actuality. Humour defeats our expectations by producing a novel actuality" markedly different from norms (1). This resonates with Irele's observation that Wangrin deviates from "the code of judgment we normally apply to instances of

---

5. See Farnoud.

human behavior." That is not to say that colonialism was an amusing enterprise. Rather, colonial law and ethics preach a straight, predictable trajectory for each subject. But as the narrator reminds us, their very conceptions of worth and justice depend on a person's origins. Hence, whether personally or professionally, Wangrin is too shrewd and unincentivized to conform to superficial notions of right or wrong that ultimately serve a spurious goal.[6] Besides, his astute detachment from norms, coupled with his predisposition to trickery, is echoed in the freedom and suspension of judgment that normally accompany the experience of humor.

Providing a foil to Wangrin are those who see injustice as all the more reason to be predictable and reliable. Also at the beginning of the twentieth century, but in South Africa, Sol Plaatje highlights the obstacles interpreters face when courts are multilingual and where justice cannot be the same as in a European country. The white men who interpret in native cases, as he observes, are so convinced of their superiority that they are often callous toward the "unfortunate wretches" on trial (58). Because he is so aware of his responsibilities, Plaatje's notions of interpreting are very serious. They are founded on knowledge, transparency, truth, and justice. In short, very little of his account lends itself to the elasticity of a Wangrin, who rather shows what goes missing when seriousness is privileged all the time.

"SWEETNESS" IN INTERPRETING

While colonial and settler contexts are significant, comic interpreting is not reducible to the colonial encounter. It is important to note other forms of cultural brokering, especially as comic interpreters hardly limit their sources of inspiration. In *Things Fall Apart*, when Ekwefi narrates the story of "Tortoise and the Birds" to her daughter Ezinma, she inscribes into it what this chapter is considering a form of comic interpreting:[7] Tortoise, the worse for wear during a famine ravaging the animal kingdom, ingratiates himself to the birds when he discovers that they have been invited to a feast in the sky.

---

6. "The law is not itself justice . . . The law of the colonizers has been a bulwark of slavery, colonization, apartheid, patriarchy, and racist oppression, but laws have also been overturned in the name of what the law should be." Neil ten Kortenaar, "Law and Literature" (2).

7. A take on intralingual translation: What Roman Jakobson terms "rewording . . . an interpretation of verbal signs by means of other signs of the same language" (233). Cronin also points out that orality has "specific psychodynamics" that have different effects on interpreting (388).

He convinces the birds to let him speak "for" them to their eminent hosts. Because he is also "full of cunning and . . . ungrateful," Tortoise informs the birds that the custom of the sky people is to choose new names for feasts (68). After the birds pick new names, Tortoise adopts the name "All of you." Assuming that there are cultural differences at work, the birds accept this strange custom and are pleased to avoid faux pas. At the feast, the sky people are led to think that Tortoise is an avian king. When they bring out the spread and declare that it is for "all of you," Tortoise gobbles it up under the eyes of the betrayed birds and their oblivious hosts. The birds remain silent while the sky people similarly make no comment. They assume the birds have a different cultural understanding of hospitality and priority and must let their leader and spokesperson eat first.

Tortoise's kind of interpreting is necessary but not because the sky people and the birds speak different languages. Rather, he has an important quality—he possesses a "sweet tongue" and is a "great orator" (68). His function is to pass on a message, as interpreters do; additionally, however, the message must be fine-tuned to sound "sweet" to the audience. The concept of "sweetness" in *Things Fall Apart* and other texts refers to the rhetorical apparatuses that make use of stylistic linguistic elements, notably proverbs. Besides underscoring the ingenuity of tricksters, an implication of "Tortoise and the Birds" is that on certain ceremonial occasions, one may address other parties only through a specially designated spokesperson.

Wangrin conforms to a very similar custom: on occasion, he lets a griot, a traditional bard, speak sweet things on his behalf and with full authority. The narrator even calls the practice "*la décence traditionnelle*" (121) ["the prescriptions of traditional demeanor" (81)]. In *Speaking for the Chief*, Kwesi Yankah studies the Akan *akyeame*, who play similar roles to griots. Yankah calls them "social mediators of speech or rather specialists in the artistic reporting or representation of speech" (8). An ɔkyeame (the singular form) transmits a chief's declarations to the public, and vice versa. However, verbatim repetition and self-effacement are not his aim. He embellishes the text, going as far as to "ratify," "supplement," or "complete" it (13, 109). Yankah reports that one ɔkyeame informed him that in a public setting, any message not routed through him was invalid. While Akan settings are different from those of folktales from Ekwefi's Igboland and Wangrin's Diagaramba, Yankah's analyses offer perspective. Wangrin's own embellishments recall those created by social mediators of speech like the *akyeame* or his own griot. Like any trickster worth his salt, the comic interpreter extends these functions beyond their

104 • TYPOLOGIES OF HUMOR IN AFRICAN LITERATURES

acceptable limits, magnifying his creativity and authority while projecting a dutiful, even boring professional interpreter. The comic interpreter, as Irele says of Wangrin, makes "his own rules as a means of self-fulfillment" (91). Interestingly, as the next sections show, the colonial context also encourages performance; in different ways, this translates into the production of messages whose primary function is to suit appearances while sounding "sweet."

"AND THE CROWD LAUGHED": THE COLONIAL INTERPRETER AS A COMIC FIGURE

In literature, the functions of the interpreter and the messenger frequently bleed into each other. This might be a result of preexisting cross-pollination and the similarity of certain professions. Yankah notes that ɔkyeame has often been translated as "linguist"; the functionaries "responsible for the conduct of foreign affairs in the colonial and precolonial life of West Africa have been variously described as 'ambassadors,' 'messengers,' and 'linguists'" (27). He adds that, given their mastery of language and verbal mediation, it is easy to mistake the interpreter and the ɔkyeame for each other (25). In any case, the colonial interpreter is often an African who has received varying degrees of training and produces results of varying accuracy. The various branches of the colonial apparatus employed interpreters in order to communicate with the local populations, if only to apprise them of the upcoming changes in regime and routine. That is the case with the white missionary in *Things Fall Apart*, who informs the people of Mbanta that their continued worship of "false gods, gods of wood and stone," will result in their being "thrown into a fire that burned like palm-oil" (102). For such contexts, Michael Cronin differentiates between what he calls an autonomous and a heteronomous system. In the autonomous system, the colonizers encouraged fellow Europeans to train in the local languages and used their own nationals as interpreters. Conversely, in the heteronomous system, colonial subjects were taught the imperial language and then recruited as interpreters "by force or through inducements" (393). The latter system is what is illustrated during the incursion into Mbanta.

During this first proselytizing exercise, which I touched on briefly in the introduction, the missionary tells the people of Mbanta to give up their own deities and attain the happy kingdom of the one true God who has a son (even though he has no wife). The message is convoluted enough without the interpreter briefly becoming the focus of the meeting. He speaks a different dialect from the people of Mbanta and makes rather unfortunate choices, such as substituting "my buttocks" for "myself." His errors introduce a risible turn into the conversation that the people of Mbanta, who are already puzzled by the odd encounter, cannot help taking advantage of: "'Your buttocks understand our language,' said someone light-heartedly and the crowd laughed" (Achebe, *Things Fall Apart* 102). The incident is a sign of the obstacles that badly trained interpreters risk meeting. In this example, what is supposed to be a solemn religious message and a warning that the tenets of the society will be shaken becomes tainted by corporeal, quasi-vulgar connotations. The protagonist, Okonkwo, even leaves the meeting convinced that the newcomers are mad.

Ineptitude is one thing; deliberate textual manipulation is another entirely. And it is understandable that the status of the interpreter can be a source of unease to those on the different ends of the communication line. If the danger in autonomous interpreting is that the European interpreter may "go native" and no longer promote the program of the colonizing power, then heteronomous interpreting is arguably even more hazardous (393).

FAITHFULNESS AND INTERPRETING AS PERFORMANCE

Fidelity is a major theme in translation and interpreting studies. Theorists consider that there are two main constraints facing a translator: the original text and the target language and culture. Choosing, therefore, to undertake the exercise as a "simple" translator (strictly following the letter of the message), or as a writer in one's own right, is a central issue. Saint Jerome's fifth-century designation "of two fundamentally different approaches to translation—sense for sense or word for word—remains firmly entrenched today in many institutions" (Angelelli and Baer 7). This reflects Cicero's own terms, *ut interpres* or *ut orator*. More recently, Jean-René Ladmiral proposed the neologisms *sourcier* and *cibliste* to distinguish between "faithfulness" to the original text and a focus on how the receiving culture will read the translated text.[8] Georges Mounin's equally colorful *verres transparents* and *verres colorés* distinguishes between a translation that acts as a "transparent glass" or a "stained glass" (74).

---

8. From "*source*" and "*cible*," a target.

106 • TYPOLOGIES OF HUMOR IN AFRICAN LITERATURES

If they firmly choose one camp over another, a *sourcier* risks a stilted, word-for-word translation, while a *cibliste* risks inaccuracies. For example, Nicolas Perrot d'Ablancourt, who translated Latin and Greek works into French, would not hesitate to modify a text to suit seventeenth-century French rules of propriety. It was reading his translations that Gilles Ménage coined yet another famous phrase, *"la belle infidèle"*—likening d'Ablancourt's texts to a former mistress, who was "beautiful but unfaithful" (Delisle and Woodsworth 43). An implication is that a translated text will reveal one bent or the other.[9]

The debate on fidelity exists because of fundamental uncertainties underscoring the translation and interpreting processes. However, it is also true that translation and interpretation studies can take a number of things for granted—that granting more importance to the source or target language is a question of choice or style,[10] that the source and target languages carry a more or less equal weight, and that there is a fundamental respect for the message and a care for how it is conveyed.[11] Now, while these are typically true, they suppose that interpreting takes place under relatively serious conditions.[12] Ideally, it builds on "1) command of the native language, 2) command of the source language, 3) command of relevant world and background knowledge, and 4) command of interpreting methodology" (Jungwha 1–2).

In *Things Fall Apart*, the interpreter's command of the first pillar is questionable. Antougoumo, Hampaté Bâ's houseboy, possesses the first pillar, vague hints of the third one, and may be lacking in the other two. However, his etiology of the monocle carries its own logic: clothing and accessories are representative of colonial power. For example, the pith helmet, worn by colonial officers, paints a picture that is laughable and "ridiculous" but that

---

9. *"On sera sourcier ou cibliste, mais pas les deux à la fois!"* ["one is either a *sourcier* or a *cibliste*, never both!"] (Ladmiral, qtd. in Basamalah 31).

10. Ladmiral, for example, prefers the *cibliste* method. Ngũgĩ, on the other hand, believes the only way to "effectively" use African philosophy, folklore, and imagery is to translate it "almost literally" into European languages (8).

11. For instance, according to the SICAL method, omitting a sentence in a translation counts as a *"faute grave,"* a serious error (Farnoud 277).

12. "Theoretically," states Jungwha, "interpreting requires a faultless command of both the source and target languages, a deep insight of the subject matter and mastery of the correct methodology needed to carry out the interpreting process" (1). He is expounding on a key concept by Danica Seleskovitch and Marianne Lederer—the Interpretive Theory of Sense. Ideally, an interpreter listens to the message and understands it, deverbalizes it to retain its sense, and then reformulates it (correctly) in the words of the target language.

induces fear (25). It thus makes more sense for the houseboy to conclude as he does and for his interpretation to be accepted. In the colonial context, power cannot be glossed over. At the same time, it is already the case that questions of power influence translation and interpreting. As Susan Bassnett and André Lefevere note in the *The Translator's Invisibility*, "Translation is, of course, a rewriting of an original text . . . Rewriting is manipulation, undertaken in the service of power" (vii). In literature set in colonial Africa, the issue of power inevitably takes on a significant dimension.

In instances that require that the interpreter transform a text to or from a colonial language, this language carries disproportionate importance and thus the potential to skew the process. Lawrence Venuti notes that even today, North America and the English language play a disproportionate role in the production and dissemination of translations. What happens when the hegemonic language is also an official colonial language, represents overt power and authority, and is accused of economic and "spiritual subjugation" (Ngũgĩ 9)? In addition to transmitting decrees and laws, French and English convey messages that require timely responses from the speakers of the other languages. We can note, for example, this message borne by the district commissioner's messenger to the men of Umuofia in *Things Fall Apart*: "The white man whose power you know too well has ordered this meeting to stop" (144).[13] Interlingual communication thus takes a more vertical direction. The political weight behind the official language can even render the *sourcier-cibliste* debate moot by introducing interferences and inadvertently encouraging misinterpreting.

The interpreter's goal can veer from ensuring a "transparent" or "beautiful" text to managing the *context* in which it is produced. The usual problems with producing material on the spot can be eclipsed by another material concern—the presence or threat of a representative of the official culture. Thus, the interpreter may become overly conscious of his subordination to the colonial sender/receiver. Under these circumstances, his concern with textual fidelity can be dismissed in favor of overt faithfulness to the person and the power he represents.

The interpreter may decide that his objective is to ensure that the text produces—or appears to produce—the results he thinks will satisfy the occasion. If necessary, he will not hesitate to break the "laws" of interpretation by fiddling with the sacrosanct content of the source text. In this way, his

---

13. The reference to power calls to a very recent memory of the community's humiliation.

108 • TYPOLOGIES OF HUMOR IN AFRICAN LITERATURES

aim is to produce a "sweet"-sounding message while appearing to produce an accurate text in order to preserve his own privileged position. Paradoxically, being hindered by power grants him a kind of freedom and elasticity that are not available to the interpreter, as conceived theoretically, who has often been required to be invisible or neutral during communication.[14]

LE VIEUX NÈGRE ET LA MÉDAILLE: DEFLATING THE TEXT TO SUIT THE CONTEXT

If he can get away with it, the comic interpreter might reduce the content of the text. In Oyono's novels, the French chief of police, whom the local people identify by the disparaging title Gosier d'Oiseau (trans. "Bird's Throat"), is widely feared for his brutality. In *Le Vieux nègre*, he discovers that an old black man was imprisoned and maltreated for wandering into the white district without papers. This should be a standard affair, except that it happened a few hours after the infamous award ceremony where the same old man was awarded a medal for faithful service to the French government and declared their brother. Feeling rather awkward, Gosier d'Oiseau quickly summons Meka, the recipient of the medal, before him. He does not speak Mvema, so he addresses his long message to Meka via his interpreter. After a long, dramatic night coming on the heels of an equally intense day, the reader might very well be curious to hear what the white man has to say. However, the interpreters in Oyono's novel are certainly consistent; here, too, the narrative is kept as unceremoniously short and dry as the one cited in the introduction to this book ("something like that"): "*L'interprète traduisit—Le Blanc a dit beaucoup de choses et si je me mettais à te traduire tout cela, nous passerions toute la nuit*" (153) ["The interpreter translated—'The white man has said a great many things and if I tried to translate them all we would be here all night'" (137)].

With his bluntness, this character prefigures Ladmiral, who admits that each translation exercise provokes some measure of exasperation in the translator. If this interpreter does not wish to spend "the whole night" on a text, it is partly because, as Ladmiral notes, translating provokes a certain frustration: "*ça ira comme ça, on ne va pas tout de même y passer sa vie.*" ["it's fine as is; surely we're not going to spend a lifetime on this" (138)]. Ladmiral

---

14. See Venuti, Rivera, or Angelelli.

is acknowledging that it is pointless to search for the perfect interpreted text. Oyono's interpreter, on the other hand, grants himself permission to deviate from and transform the message. Possibly he is worried not only about his own time (the day has been long for him as well) but also about the notoriously short temper of his employer, who might be annoyed if he felt uneasy at a long conversation he did not understand. Plaatje makes a similar comment about his own experiences, though he refuses to be swayed by the risk of remonstrations for delaying the court (56). With his lackluster attitude, Oyono's interpreter, on the other hand, might be in spiritual communication with those interpreters who, according to Plaatje, find it tiresome to render the full meaning of things: "They prefer to cut it short at the expense of the prisoner's information" (Plaatje 58).

"*Tout ce que je peux te dire*," continues the interpreter in *Le Vieux nègre* to the freshly released prisoner, "*c'est que tu vas retourner chez toi . . . et qu'on va te commander une autre médaille*" (153). He adds another line about Meka's luck and need for a lamp the next time he ventures into the city, before ending it all anticlimactically: "*C'est tout*" (153). ["All I can tell you, is that you can go back home . . . and they are going to get you another medal . . . That's all" (137–138). To him, the rest of Gosier d'Oiseau's message, which might even have contained the shadow of reconciliation, if not an outright apology, is not worth the time it would take to say it when Meka is the audience. Besides, what more could the old man want? As the interpreter has already explained, "*Ton cas est arrangé*" (152) ["Your case has all been fixed up" (137)]. The main objective here is that Gosier d'Oiseau see that his orders to Meka—go home and wait for another medal—are implemented. If that can be accomplished by shaving down the text he is given, the interpreter will do so without qualms. To an extent, the humor excludes the reader, who is not privy to the finer details of the message and never will be. The interpreter has decided that the information will not go beyond his ears, either to Meka or to us.

His agency colors the author's own methods of conveying the message to the reader. One source of the humor is the fact that Oyono's reader receives messages in French and thus has clear access to the Mvema that Meka speaks. Though Meka and Gosier d'Oiseau do not understand each other's statements, we do, and seemingly perfectly. This means that interpreting in the colonial setting is beset with problems of understanding, but somehow this novel is not. Yet we have only to consider the fact that while "Mvema" is presented without comment as both a well-known ethnic group and a language, it does not seem to exist as such outside Oyono's novels.[15] We can then wonder to what degree we have a grasp of what is happening in the novel and what the novelist, like his interpreter, might be keeping from us.

Inversely, the interpreter will prefer palatability to his employer over fidelity to the text. In the same scene, he is overly solicitous to Gosier d'Oiseau when Meka, smarting from an eventful night, proudly declares his refusal to "dirty" the white man's hand by shaking it. The interpreter has already advised Meka in the following terms: "*Ne fâche pas le Blanc . . . tu pourras penser tout ce que tu voudras de lui loin d'ici*" (152) ["Don't annoy the white man . . . You can think what you like about him when you are out of here" (137)]. Indeed, keeping the white man happy and withholding information when necessary might well be the summation of his own professional ethos. Unsurprisingly, then, he wisely delivers a version wiped of bitter sarcasm when Gosier d'Oiseau demands, "*Qu'est-ce qu'il raconte?*" (153) ["What is he saying?" (138)]: Meka said only that his hands were muddy. Hampaté Bâ confirms in his preface to *Wangrin* that this sort of prudence is justified; it is far better, as he says, to have Mount Sinai on one's back than the least colonial administrator (10). The interpreter's choices corroborate this—while Gosier d'Oiseau is widely feared for his temper, Meka's anger carries fewer consequences, if any at all. Indeed, when the old man bravely throws himself into an aggressive battle stance upon being ordered from his cell, he only confuses the guards, who find themselves obliged to bundle him up and carry him out in a scene as tense as it is comically anticlimactic. A further declaration that he is not afraid of white men leads the same guards to burst into laughter.

SIZWE BANSI IS DEAD: INFLATING THE TEXT TO SUIT THE CONTEXT

Besides shrinking the message, as happens in Oyono's text, the interpreter may inflate it if the opportunity presents itself. Here, too, overt political power is responsible for the unevenness between the message received and the text transmitted. Fugard's *Sizwe Bansi Is Dead* illustrates this through the power differentials between Africans and European settlers during Apartheid. The play includes an entertaining passage involving Styles the factory worker, General Foreman Mr. "Baas" Bradley, and other African workers. The

---

15. As best as I have been able to verify.

scene is narrated by Styles himself. It all begins with an unfortunate order by Bradley for Styles to "Come translate!" and ends in Styles hijacking the message to amuse his fellow workers:

> "Tell the boys in your language, that this is a very big day in their lives."
> "Gentlemen, this old fool says this is a hell of a big day in our lives."
> The men laughed.
> "They are very happy to hear that, sir."
> "Tell the boys that Mr Henry Ford the Second, the owner of this place, is going to visit us. Tell them Mr Ford is the big Baas. He owns the plant and everything in it."
> "Gentlemen, old Bradley says this Ford is a big bastard. He owns everything in this building, which means you as well."
> A voice came out of the crowd:
> "Is he a bigger fool than Bradley?"
> "They're asking, sir, is he bigger than you?" (6–7).

Bradley's sentences are watered-down commands underscoring his audience's subordination; because he is the *baas* and they are only the boys, he uses the simplest terminology. However, while stylistics are of little importance to him, that is not true for Styles. Bradley's orders include, "Styles, tell the boys that when Mr Henry Ford comes into the plant I want them all to look happy. We will slow down the speed of the line so that they can sing and smile while they are working." Styles obligingly renders this as "Hide your true feelings, brothers. You must sing. The joyous songs of the days of old before we had fools like this one next to me to worry about" (7).

Ironically handpicked by Bradley himself, Styles tacks on extra meaning for the entertainment of his coworkers while cleverly ensuring that the text he gives Bradley matches their reactions. His extra meaning is also political because his reference to the days "of old" signifies the period before settler colonialism. He translates the men's laughter as a sign of joy at the impending visit and replaces the impudent question with a harmless one. On the one hand, Styles comes across as a rogue *cibliste* catering exclusively to the target audience, since he makes Bradley into the butt of the joke by mediating and rerouting the message.

However, in a way, Styles is playing to Bradley's own objectives. Appearances and performance are clearly management's primary aim: Bradley intends to slow down the machinery and have the men carry on as though it were inconceivable to be anything but euphoric while working in Mr. Ford's factory. He wants them to look happy; Styles, by turning the message into a joke and making the men laugh, is already painting the background for that narrative. In fact, despite his own feelings and underneath all the mockery, Styles is careful that Bradley has no cause to be dissatisfied with the situation. The preoccupation with appearances makes further sense if the reader considers that for all his authority, Bradley is beneath Mr. Ford; this will be "a very big day" in his own life. Bradley's anxiety and Styles's embellishments find echoes in preexisting narratives that have set the stage for raising Mr. Ford to the level of royalty. For example, to prepare for a royal visit in 1947, the government of Northern Rhodesia printed instructions for Africans to the effect that "King George is the biggest King in the world . . . He expects to see His subjects on their best behaviour" (Ranger 233). This sort of language simultaneously dumbs down and magnifies the role of the visiting notable for the African audience ("the big Baas"/"the biggest King") and underlines the importance of performance ("they can sing and smile while they are working"/"He expects to see His subjects on their best behaviour"). Where even the familiar representative of settler power, such as Bradley, is eclipsed by another more formidable than him, the interpreter is incited to develop the necessary façades that magnify acceptable behavior and a "sweet" rhetoric above all else.

Overly conscious, therefore, of his superiors' authority, the interpreter must maintain the image of faithfulness to it, if not to the source text itself. This means that the question about fools will never cross his lips in English in Bradley's presence—the same as Oyono's interpreter who refuses to express Meka's indignation to Gosier d'Oiseau in French. Hence, the quasi-bowdlerized text Styles conveys is as appropriate to the occasion as the francophone interpreter's declaration that Meka says his hands are muddy. Indeed, whether it is subversive or not, Styles's humorous imagery may inadvertently serve to cement the message in the workers' minds. Styles is in a position of power relative to his two audiences. He is, however, not withholding information from Fugard's reader or audience. While the workers are aware that the insolent text cannot be verbatim, they will not know exactly what Bradley is saying unless Styles tells them. This time, the humor involves the reader's recognition and involvement in more active ways than in Oyono's passage.

These are situations where verifying information proves inherently difficult or impossible—either for the European or African parties. They can create an atmosphere in which a personality with a bit of inclination toward trickery can truly flourish. *Things Fall Apart* offers another example that speaks to Wangrin's more mercenary traits, when court messengers deliver a modified message to Umuofia after her elders are arrested. The narrator states that 50 of the 250 bags of cowries paid as a fine to "appease" the white man are in fact going into the messengers' pockets. As far as the district commissioner is aware, the amount he judged appropriate has been paid in full, and order has been restored. He is also under the impression that the elders of Umuofia were treated "with respect" while they were detained. Here, too, it is unlikely his messengers will volunteer the truth to him. And should the people of Umuofia care to protest the amount they have been fined, they would still have to go through untruthful intermediaries to do so.

In the above examples, the means of evaluating a "good" interpretation are not the standard scientific, qualitative, and quantitative criteria (Farnoud), but things like ignorance and satisfaction. This means that having gotten onto the path where precision is secondary and having established that inaccuracies can be gotten away with, deliberate textual manipulation along with the dissimulation of facts for personal gain is only par for the course. Hampaté Bâ's Wangrin demonstrates this spectacularly.

114 • TYPOLOGIES OF HUMOR IN AFRICAN LITERATURES

L'ÉTRANGE DESTIN DE WANGRIN: INTERPRETING AS TRADE

Hampaté Bâ's text is subtitled *Les Roueries d'un interprète africain*, translated as "the shrewdness of an African interpreter." Wangrin is a legendary personality who has charged the narrator with writing down his many adventures for posterity. Over the years, Hampaté Bâ would repeat the assertions made by the narrator—that Wangrin truly existed and recounted his life story to him—essentially, that the text is biographical and that Hampaté Bâ is the narrator. Over the course of a very colorful career, Wangrin used his position and knowledge to accumulate wealth—legally but mostly illicitly—from the colonial government and fellow Africans. As an interpreter, he was transferred to different posts and took advantage of all of them. After retiring from the civil service, he became a businessman and continued to live an eventful life until his death. With one of his most notorious affairs consisting of theft, being tried in a colonial court, and then implicating French officers in his place, tales of Wangrin are legendary. The narrator accordingly records the story as told by the eponymous character.[16] Propitiously enough, he happens to be posted to the same places Wangrin worked, which allows him to supplement and verify details.

From time to time, the narrator uses Wangrin's own words, since Wangrin is a talented orator. "*Fort versé dans la tradition, Wangrin savait mettre en pratique les enseignements des adages, proverbes et paraboles*" (119) ["Well-versed in matters traditional, Wangrin knew how to convert adages, proverbs, and parables into practice" (79)]. This is due, in part, to being raised by a formidable Peul father. His deftness with the spoken word increases his renown, much like Tortoise in the folktale, and even inspires a saying: "*La parole de Wangrin est de l'or, et sa promesse de l'airain*" (10) ["Wangrin's words are gold, and his promises are as durable as bronze" (xix)]. That his facility with speech is likened to precious metals is a sign of his ability to transform words into financial resources.

Trained at the *école des otages* in his youth, Wangrin obtains the highest diploma permitted to an African. Not only is his French impeccable, but he has also absorbed the quirks that come with speaking it "authentically":

> *Il avait fait l'école de Kayes et y avait si bien, paraît-il, appris à parler la langue française que, lorsqu'il s'exprimait dans ce dialecte de mange-mil, les blancs-blancs eux-mêmes, nés de femmes blanches de France, s'arrêtaient pour l'écouter.*

---

16. Eponymous to an extent, as Wangrin is a pseudonym.

*Il ne fallait pas, disait-on, moins de dix ans pour apprendre, imparfaite-
ment d'ailleurs, les gestes supports du parler français, dont voici les plus car-
actéristiques: tendre le temps à autre le cou en avant; tantôt écarquiller les yeux,
hausser les épaules, froncer les sourcils; tantôt tenir les bras en équerre, paumes
ouvertes . . . Ignorer comment ces gestes se combinent pour souligner les mots
que la bouche égrène, c'est tomber dans le ridicule dit de « vieux tirailleur».*

Ce ne pouvait pas être le cas de Wangrin (26).

[(He) had done his schooling in Kayes and according to rumors had learned
to speak French so well that when he used that red-tailed-quelia-idiom even
the real Whites, born of real white French women, hearkened to the sound. It
is said that ten years at least are needed to learn the mannerisms that adorn
French utterances, the most typical being as follows; stretching one's neck
forward from time to time, as well as staring, shrugging, and frowning, now
and again folding one's arms at right angles to the torso with the palm of the
hand turned upward . . . Not to know, however, how these gestures should be
timed to emphasize the words that tumble out of the mouth of the speaker is
to be the object of pitiless ridicule.

But this was certainly not the case where Wangrin . . . was concerned (12)].

With these traits, Wangrin as a French speaker, and Frenchmen by extension,
appears to be an odd, twitching mess. Moreover, the extravagant terms the
narrator uses to describe his protagonist would have it that the "real" Frenchman, born of a white Frenchwoman (and in France at that), are impressed
enough to stop in their tracks when he speaks. Fellow Africans from time to
time qualify Wangrin as a *"blanc-noir,"* illustrating the apparent incongruity
of his traits in addition to Michael C. Lambert's observation about educated
francophone Africans: "If the inalienably African characteristic of these men
was their black skin, then, along with *mathematics* and the French language,
these black Frenchmen had internalized French rules and norms" (255).[17]
Indeed, while much is made of the importance of language and his mastery
of it, Wangrin possesses a natural dexterity with numbers and finances that is
equally important to the plot.

---

17. The emphasis is mine.

COMPULSORY TRUST AND TRUST AS A RESOURCE

Cronin is right to point out that the need for an interpreter can be cause for apprehension. Particularly in the colonial period, translating and interpreting require a significant amount of trust on the part of the emitter and receiver, who cannot verify the results themselves. In Achebe's *Arrow of God*, Mr. Wright transitions from mistrusting Moses the "uppity native" to acknowledging that he is useful (77). Similarly, in Nicholas B. Dirks's "Colonial Histories and Native Informants," Colin Mackenzie, a cartographer and surveyor who reconstructed Indian political history in the nineteenth century, "never learned an Indian language" (281). The existence of his records depends in part on native writers and translators who collected and confirmed information for him (289).[18] "Even [though] Mackenzie often doubted the utility and veracity of many of the texts that were faithfully reproduced," he still "felt that every 'traditional account' contained some potentially useful historical information" (289–290). His eventual choice shows that when future gains outweigh present suspicion toward colonial interpreters, suspicion must be overcome.

To aid in this, certain presuppositions can help to make the process seem less risky. Translating and interpreting have long been considered subordinate fields because their purpose is to "repeat" an original message. Historically, as Claudia V. Angelelli and Brian James Baer state, the "secondary status of the translator/interpreter was reinforced in the Romantic Age, which constructed the translator as the defining other of the 'original' writer—a mere imitator" (8). This notion can find itself expressed in rather curious ways—for instance, in a question put to "men interpreters" even in today's conference settings: "The question itself is a sexist one, harking back to times when men were supposed to have responsible, decision-making functions and women were supposed to have subordinate jobs with a secretarial, non-executive function. It is, 'Isn't it frustrating for a man to be in a job where you don't manage something, where you don't have an executive function?'" (Jones 129). French colonial officers in *Wangrin* thus make a dangerous assumption about the interpreter, which is that his aim is an "acceptable" reproduction of their words; that is, one "giving the appearance that it reflects the foreign

---

18. These documents "have since been the single richest archives for the historical, literary, and anthropological study of peninsular India during the centuries immediately preceding British rule" (Dirks, 283).

writer's personality or intention or the essential meaning of the foreign text—the appearance, in other words, that the translation is not in fact a translation, but the 'original'" (Venuti 1).

What is more, this inferior, "womanly" rank finds an echo in the subordinate status of the African during colonialism. The francophone African context was different from indirect rule, as mentioned in chapter 2. Here, policy "considered Africans, collectively and individually, as a tabula rasa onto whom the French could write French values. Colonization was justified as something that would "produce Africans with French cultural values" (Lambert 241). The assimilated African subject "was, like a typical French citizen, governed not by native law and custom but by the French codes. He was . . . expected to have contributed in his own way to the success of the mission civilisatrice in the colony" (Oludare Idowu 205, qtd. in Lambert 242). Ideally, then, he would be a passable reproduction of a Frenchman, bent on aiding France achieve her goals. This means that, "subordinated to the author" of the message (Venuti 9), and by virtue of being a colonized subject, the African interpreter can be said to be secondary twice over. Consequently, in *Wangrin*, the colonizers' trust in their own dominance is buttressed by confidence that they are dealing with a self-effacing repeater of meaning and intentions. It is building on this invisibility that Wangrin, in response to "*Quelle est ta religion?*" asked by a French officer, promptly replies with a statement that recalls the trickster's shape-shifting abilities: "*Je n'en ai pas de bien définie . . . En tant qu'interprète, je dois ménager tout le monde*" (112) ["I don't have any special religion . . . As an interpreter, it's my job to get on with everybody" (74)].

The image that the French present to their colonies is not necessarily the reality either. Saying one thing and doing another enhances the atmosphere of performance that the comic interpreter revels in, so Wangrin regularly camouflages himself in French cultural values while furthering his own agenda. At Diagaramba, the commandant Galandier is easily charmed. During their first meeting, he even takes the highly unusual step of offering Wangrin a seat in his office and confiding his personal impressions of other residents to him. He declares that Wangrin, whom he calls "*mon ami*," is not like the other natives. Wangrin's mission, as stipulated by Galandier, is to be faithful to his promise to serve France wholeheartedly; he owes France a debt and must pay her back by making the local people love her (33).

Wangrin, who is the type of person to see a goldmine in an upcoming international conflict, completely agrees with Galandier and even sets off a fervent chorus of "*Vive la France*" in the building. After this, the commandant

118   •   TYPOLOGIES OF HUMOR IN AFRICAN LITERATURES

opens his doors to Wangrin while he is a teacher and becomes even more accessible when the latter becomes his interpreter. Even better, the infamous Villermoz, Galandier's deputy, hates to be woken before nine and spends most of his office hours horse riding. He decides it makes sense to give Wangrin carte blanche by signing a sheaf of blank requisition and convocation forms; all Wangrin has to do is to fill and stamp the documents with the official seal. Of course, "*Wangrin comprit vite tous les avantages qu'il pouvait tirer de cette confiance inconsidérée . . . Une victime inespérée était venue s'offrir fortuitement*" (64) ["Wangrin was quick to realize the enormous advantage that would accrue to him from such abundant trust . . . Fate had placed at his disposal an un-hoped-for victim" (40)].

Several other shows of naïveté take place in which the reader is aware that Wangrin has his own agenda but the French authorities are not. Garane puts it aptly: the interpreter has "domesticated" the foreign official (4). In another office, Wangrin has learned that the best way to get into the director's good graces is to act like a former soldier. At the first meeting, he snaps to attention and recites his surname, first name, and title. This has a "magical" effect on the director Quinomel, and once again Wangrin is addressed as *mon ami* before getting his wish of being transferred to the post of his dreams (111). There, and after only a month, the commandant Gordane is so pleased with Wangrin's work that he rewards him with a great deal of trust.[19] In an equally naïve fashion, Villermoz, Wangrin's scapegoat, initially considers that Wangrin is not only "*un fonctionnaire expérimenté*" but also "*un modèle de dévouement*" (63) ["both an experienced civil servant and a model of dedication" (39)].

He certainly is these things but not to the profit of a careless count or even "*la France éternelle.*" It is later, when both are on trial for fraud, that Villermoz changes his tune and calls Wangrin "*un fonctionnaire véreux utilisant l'instruction que la France lui a donnée gratuitement pour tromper ses supérieurs et voler ses concitoyens*" (92) ["here is a man who has used the education that France has freely given him to deceive his superiors and to steal from his fellow townsmen" (61)]. What Villermoz had not considered is that Wangrin may have paid even more attention to the lessons taught by the colonial system than indicated on his official record. He might, after all, be motivated by the same French who, as the narrator points out, use their weapons to annihilate armies and subjugate people for their own profit (25). Just like Villermoz, who wants to get the most by doing the least, Wangrin is driven to get

---

19. "Almost total trust!" is how the translation puts it (79).

Interpreter • 119

rich and get ahead. On one hand, that Wangrin can so easily "put on" French identity confirms the idea of the colonized as an empty (black) slate. On the other hand, this ability points to the trickster tendencies that propel many of his actions. It also highlights a pervasive duality.

DUALITY AND DUPLICITY

From the beginning, Wangrin is born under the auspices of what the Peul call "very good and double" news—both mother and child survive the birth, and the child is a boy (16). Years later, he and his accomplices create *"un double réseau de renseignements"* ["a double intelligence network"]. The first network gathers information and the second spreads it, *"tamisées et assaisonnées au goût et dans l'intérêt [de Wangrin] (52)"* ["both sifted and seasoned according to [Wangrin's] wishes and interests" (31)]. Moreover, Wangrin embodies duality in a society divided along the lines of blacks and whites.[20] *Blancs-noirs* refers to those who do not necessarily have European ancestry but who juggle attributes considered peculiar to each race.

Wangrin is under the tutelage of a god whose name he adopts as one of his many pseudonyms. The very ethos of the god, Gongoloma-Sooké, is steeped in an intricate, mythical duality: he can neither be wet by water nor dried by the sun, salted by salt nor cleaned by soap; he is never hot or cold. To the sun he is lunar, while to the moon he is solar. He cries when he hears of a birth or of a wedding but laughs excessively when he learns of a death, a divorce, or any kind of calamity. The reader is told that this "strange god" is all at once good and bad, wise and a libertine. He declares, *"Si je suis Gongoloma-Sooké, le dieu bizarre, je suis par ailleurs le grand confluent des contraires . . . Venez à moi et vous serez servis!"* (21) ["It is true that I am Gongoloma-Sooké, a weird divinity, but I also represent the confluence of all opposites . . . Come to me and your wishes shall be granted" (8)]. Heeding this call, Wangrin performs an elaborate ritual to put himself under the god's protection.

Gongoloma-Sooké's speech is linked to equivocation and uncertainty: *"Sa bouche n'avait pas de langue. Elle était munie de deux mâchoires édentées mais plus tranchantes qu'un rasoir neuf"* (20–21) ["His mouth was tongueless and

---

20. In addition, Hampâté Bâ mentions characters of mixed race, notably in the person of a Martinican judge who holds a grudge against white people but "paradoxically" hates black people just as much (*Wangrin* 85).

furnished with toothless maws—sharper, however, than a brand-new razor" (8)]. This imagery recalls the mouth of the trickster god Esu-Elegbara, which "appears double" and produces a "double-voiced" discourse (Gates, *Signifying Monkey* 7). Wangrin is an incarnation of the god in the way other individual figures, "aspects or topoi of Esu, are fundamental, divine terms of mediation: as tricksters they are mediators, and their mediations are tricks" (5). Throughout, he openly and eagerly depends on the god for spiritual aid.[21]

Wangrin therefore understands better than most that he can be two contrasting things. While exercising his profession, he can declare one thing and do another. Cronin calls this a "monstrous doubleness, the potential duplicity of interpreters" (392), but interpreters are not the only ones to put this into play. Potential duplicity is a feature of multilingual colonial societies and is seen in the Christian prayer that a young Wangrin and other students are obliged to recite upon entering the church. These students, sons of animists and Muslims, reconstruct "*Au nom du Père / du Fils et du Saint-Esprit / Ainsi soit-il*" ["In the name of the Father / and of the Son / and of the Holy Ghost / Amen," into a Bambara declaration of noncompliance: *Quoi que ce soit / Moi, / Ma participation / N'y sera* (30–31) ["Whatever may be/ as for me / there I won't be" (15)]. The foreign schoolmasters suspect no rebellion because, as the black characters in *Le Vieux nègre* and *Sizwe Bansi Is Dead* do, the students perform the requisite actions (the recital and the sign of the cross).

"Interpreters," as Angelelli and Baer state when discussing what they call the positivist view of interpreting, "have frequently been portrayed as neutral conduits of information" (8). Venuti refers to this assumption as the "an illusionistic effect of discourse" (2). Wangrin's illusions have little to do with self-effacement. This most notably after the death of Brildji Madouma Thiala, a respected chief and the richest man in the country. The commandant Gordane, upon hearing the news, asks Wangrin the most appropriate action. Wangrin informs him that since Brildji has already been discreetly buried, the best thing is to send Wangrin to Yagouwahi to offer his condolences and a donation. Gordane follows his advice in good faith. Wangrin visits the deceased's half brother in his court and privately fans his resentment and rivalry. He demands ten kilograms of gold to avenge familial slights. He

---

21. "*Wangrin ne cachait pas qu'il comptait sur Gongoloma-Sooké pour l'inspirer et l'aider quand il déclencherait ce qu'il appelait des « affaires carabinées et où il se trouverait empêtré »*" (22) ["Wangrin did not try to conceal the fact that he counted on Gongoloma-Sooke's inspiration and assistance for the day when he was ready to trigger off what he called the 'stupendous enterprises that would place him in a good many awkward situations'" (9)].

next informs the deceased's son that the commandant has ordered that the body be exhumed for an autopsy. Exhumation is anathema to the community's Muslim and animist beliefs, meaning that the family cannot conceivably comply. Even the French authorities would not entertain such a demand. Later, when Wangrin alludes to exhumation, Gordane reacts violently: "*Tu as osé faire une telle proposition, Wangrin? . . . Espèce d'abruti, imbécile!*" (188) ["You actually dared to suggest that, Wangrin? . . . You fool, you idiot!" (130)].

But the people of Yagouwahi have few ways of knowing what Gordane thinks. Wangrin, after all, is there in his capacity as "*envoyé spécial du grand commandant . . . qui représente le Goforner, qui représente son grand frère Goforner Zeneral, qui représente Franci*" (150–152) ["special envoy of the Senior Commandant . . . who represents the *goforner*, who represents his senior brother the *goforner zenderal*, who represents *Franci*" (102–103)]. After protracted negotiations, where he receives outrageous amounts of gold, silver, slaves, cattle, and sheep, Wangrin proposes a complex solution that restores peace.

The ruse is successful because existing, legitimate considerations are coupled with poor conceptions about the limits of French belief and actions. In a meeting with the deceased's family, Wangrin cites what is by now a familiar trait, "*la bizarre détermination des blancs-blancs à vouloir, coûte que coûte, nous faire vomir nos us et coutumes pour nous gaver des leurs*" (180) ["One must always reckon with the white-Whites, who are curiously determined to make us vomit our ancient customs at all costs and to ram their own down our throats instead" (124)]. He is insinuating that French strangeness is beyond even him to understand, never mind to curb. This makes sense—those gathered can likely point to an incident (historically accurate or misinterpreted) to highlight the colonizers' proclivity for conquest and assimilation. With a setting of uncertainties thus created, nobody contests the excuse that French obsessions could justify disrespecting the body of a revered chief.

Proximity goes both ways, since the French can be equally ignorant of what to expect from the local populace. Wangrin returns to Gordane and manipulates him by painting the local people as unhappy and warlike. The upcoming conflict, if not handled well, will have a terrible effect on the commandant himself, his interpreter, his African "wife," his cook . . . "*Ce sera une guerre entre Peuls*," Wangrin declares seriously. "*Elle peut durer longtemps, causer de nombreuses victimes et entraîner un grand gaspillage d'argent. Le cercle de Yagouwahi connaîtra une perturbation politique importante, motivant l'envoi fréquent d'agent secrets de la Sûreté générale*"(189) ["There will be a Fulbe civil war, which may go on and on, causing numerous deaths and

122 • TYPOLOGIES OF HUMOR IN AFRICAN LITERATURES

considerable waste of money. The Yagouwahi district circle will be shaken by deep political unrest; secret investigating agents as well as administrative inspectors will descend on us in rapid succession" (130)]. Gordane, mindful of his own ignorance, manages the chief's succession as his interpreter suggests.

Each culture has preconceived notions about the other that are, if not completely unfounded, vague enough that Wangrin can exaggerate them to fear-inducing and unrealistic heights. As a rule, the interpreter must know the culture so that he can imbue his text with sense.[22] But in view of Wangrin's take on interpreting, what is culture? Culture and customs appear to be the constellation of the strange things privileged by foreigners. This builds on "Tortoise and the Birds," where the birds readily accept Tortoise's tutorial on the cultural practices of the people of the sky. They even compliment him for his knowledge—like Wangrin, he is widely traveled. Likewise, at the feast, Tortoise encourages the sky people's assumption about the birds' reverence for their "king." Each side assumes that the other has customs that are not necessarily meant to be understood but that must be accepted—and respected. Assumptions have great potential for humor, and another example can be found in Joyce Cary's *Mister Johnson* (1939), a novel set in colonial Nigeria that occasionally comments on the delicacy with which foreign bizarreness must be handled. "Why does he go on like that?" asks Bamu about the odd Mister Johnson, who has recently moved into the area. "They reply, 'He's a stranger, you understand—a foreigner'" (16). Initially, they cannot tell "whether the boy is mad or only a stranger with unusual customs" (7). Foreign customs, even when they suggest insanity, must be approached cautiously, at least until one can be sure whether one is dealing with a madman or just an unfamiliar way of reasoning. That wary expectation of strangeness is useful to the comic interpreter, since his dupes will use their own imagination to reason away his invented scenarios.

Cronin confirms that the control of knowledge is a fundamental issue in interpreting: "The central problem of translation in general and interpretation in particular is the problem of control . . . Proximity is both desired and dreaded. The desire is to manipulate" (392). Since he controls the flow of information, Wangrin seems to be the only one to know that Africans and

---

22. Fella Benabed makes the observation that "mastery of two languages, with their syntactic and semantic features, is not sufficient to make a good translation; awareness of history and ideology is also an essential requirement . . . Translators need to know not only the Source Language (SL) and the Target Language (TL) but also their underlying cultures in order to build a bridge between them" (71).

Europeans are fundamentally the same. Foreign customs and behaviors are not unshakeable traits integral to their practitioners or necessarily incomprehensible to others. This truth, however, is one that he guards jealously; ignorance is at the heart of his practice.

POWER, TRADE, AND INVESTMENT

Even done scrupulously, interpreting is a wellspring of prestige and power. In Achebe's *Arrow of God*, Moses Unachukwu is elevated to an unparalleled station:

> Moses Unachukwu . . . had come forward to organize them and to take words out of the white man's mouth for them . . . Meanwhile Unachukwu's reputation in Umuaro rose to unprecedented heights. It was one thing to claim to speak the white man's tongue and quite another to be seen actually doing it. The story spread throughout the six villages. (77)

As the character Nweke Ukpaka puts it, this situation exists largely because "none of us can say come in the white man's language" (85). Such a rare exploit is admired in Diagaramba as well when war is declared with Germany. Large posters with the declaration and the mobilization decree are published amid clarions and drumming. It happens that after all the pomp, only about ten people can read them (61). For Kourouma, it is impossible for "the youth of today" to comprehend the interpreter's status (Garane 6). Yankah's statement that the "bilingual interpreter was crucial in communication between colonial representatives and the local states" (25) even seems understated in comparison. Wangrin's companions confidently state, "*S'il lui arrivait le moindre mal, nous serions tous rasés au moyen de tessons de bouteilles avant d'être cuits dans une friture chauffée à l'aide de feux puisés dans le septième enfer!*" (155) ["If the least harm were to come to him, we would all have our heads shaved with pieces of broken bottles and our bodies fried on heat fired straight out of the seventh hell!" (106)].[23]

If Angelelli and Baer note that the difference in status between "the

---

23. Racoutié, the previous interpreter, dresses like a king and acts like one, with money "raining" down on him. His wives no longer know where to store their gold and silver jewelry, while his horses eat fine couscous and drink milk. Racoutié eventually disgraces himself and is ousted by Wangrin, who achieves even more than his predecessor.

domain expert" and that of the translator/interpreter is "reflected most blatantly in the salary differential" (8), and Venuti likewise speaks of translators as "seldom recognized, poorly-paid writers" (17), Wangrin's wealth is proportionate only to his renown. At a point, it seems that he engages in his exploits more for stimulation than for more riches. When he must, the interpreter is the commandant's double. In other ways—of which the commandant is ignorant—the interpreter is his superior. Of Romo Sibedi, Wangrin's biggest rival, "*Ne disait-on pas partout que le pays était comparable à un coche traîné par deux étalons, l'un symbolisant le roi, l'autre le commandant de cercle, tandis que Romo était le cocher de cette puissante voiture qu'il conduisait comme il voulait et entendait?*" (113) ["It was said everywhere that the country was like a coach drawn by two stallions—one representing the king and the other, the Commandant—while Romo was the coachman who led that powerful conveyance to any destination and in any manner he chose" (75)]. The French authorities, for all their brute political power, are being led by the nose. The humor is in their complete ignorance of the truth.

Ironically, Gordane, Romo's old commandant, fondly remembers his "*brave vieil interprète docile comme du cuir corroyé . . . qui toute sa vie, n'avait fait que server les Européens et leur obéir comme un robot*" (114) ["amiable old interpreter who had been as pliable as curried leather . . . who had done nothing else all his life but serve Europeans and obey them like a robot" (76)]. He is unaware that there in Goudougaoua, Romo stands above Gordane's own second in command: "*Romo Sibedi, qui était la deuxième personnalité du cercle, venait immédiatement après le grand commandant. Le petit commandant pouvait en effet ignorer certains secrets. Romo Sibedi, aucun. Tout passait par lui*" (102) ["Romo Sibedi was the second most important citizen in the district, second only to the Commandant. It was conceivable that the Junior Commandant might not be told certain secrets, but not so Romo Sibedi. Everything passed through his hands (67–68)].

Cary's *Mister Johnson* offers a lower-stakes humor and serves as a foil. Mister Johnson is convinced of his importance, while to Mister Rudbeck, his employer, Mister Johnson is a clerk "very like any other clerk" (28). With his surface enthusiasm and alacrity, Wangrin appears much like Cary's portrait of an African civil servant. But unlike Wangrin or Romo, who happen to be running an empire next to the colony, Mister Johnson is flimsy. When he presents Mrs. Rudbeck to his hostile wife, Bamu, Mrs. Rudbeck invites Bamu to tea in English. Bamu "glares at Celia and says, 'I don't like tea. Is she going away now?'" Johnson smiles and says, "She says to tank you mam, too much, she proud to be you frien'" (60). Mister Johnson lies to the Englishwoman less as a nod to her power and more because he seems incapable of reporting speech unembellished. Like comic interpreters presented from the point of view of an African writer, Mister Johnson is a liar. But he is not in control even of his lies—"he believes every word as soon as he invents it" (74). Also, he has little awareness of the workings of his community, even if its people are often painted as simpletons as well. That lack, coupled with his halting command over English, means he cannot rise above either culture. As a native interpreter, Cary implies, Mister Johnson is to be approached indulgently.

Conversely, when Wangrin takes an active role, his agency mutates spectacularly. It is, after all, unlikely that the European "can say come" in many African languages either. Much is made in the text of the interpreter's power as the "mouth" of the commandant. Racoutié is described often as the commandant's "mouthpiece" and boasts of his position as the colonial officer's eye, ear, and mouth. *His* mouth, he adds, is closest to the Frenchman's ear (45). The figure is used consistently in the text—for instance, as part of Wangrin's appellations: "*Wangrin, bouche du commandant . . . et oreilles de Moussé Goforner*" (119) ["Wangrin, mouthpiece to our Commandant and earpiece to *Mousse Gofornere*" (80)].

As Wangrin's abuse of Villermoz illustrates, the "mouth" is only one area of vulnerability, and the powerful colonial officer is almost comically dependent on those whose job it is to protect him from danger and not put him in its way themselves. The text draws parallels between the interpreter and stewards and cooks, who, it was feared, might be influenced to feed the white men love or hate potions, or even poison (260). Despite the potential for subversiveness, the comic interpreter is unapologetically self-seeking. Wangrin bluntly says, "*Je suis disposé à servir celui qui saura me payer bien et discrètement*" (148) ["I am prepared to serve well any man who will pay me handsomely, but discreetly" (100)]. In fact, he shows little interest in the end of colonialism—the status quo is his bread and butter. Like a true trickster, he achieves his full potential by cheating both sides and making an imperfect system work for him. He invites the reader to laugh with him at the French but also at fellow Africans.

If the interpreter is the "real" administrator, this explains his audacity, overindulgences, and immoral behavior. Being "*foncièrement bizarre*," in the words of the narrator and in an echo of his god Gongoloma-Sooké, some of Wangrin's most devastating attacks are carried out without provocation. Even the narrator, often enamored of his subject, acknowledges his selfishness and greed. The ease and keenness with which he gives in to his immoral side are a reminder about the problematic nature of morality as lived in the text:

126 • TYPOLOGIES OF HUMOR IN AFRICAN LITERATURES

*A l'époque, le degré de moralité d'un individu se mesurait d'une part à l'impor-
tance des services qu'il avait rendus à la pénétration française et, d'autre part, à
la situation géographique de son pays d'origine. C'est ainsi que les plus moraux
des hommes étaient les Européens blancs. Après eux venaient progressivement
les Martiniquais et Guadeloupéens, puis les Sénégalais autochtones des quatre
communes . . . et enfin, en dernier lieu, le restant de la population.* (49–50)

[At that time, the degree of moral uprightness of an individual was judged,
on the one hand, on the basis of how much he had contributed toward
French penetration and, on the other, by the geographical position of his
country of origin. Accordingly, Europeans were the most moral of men,
followed by the people of Martinique and Guadeloupe, the black Senegalese
from the four communes . . . and finally, at the very end of the line, the rest
of the population. (29)]

Where morality is judged by geographical origins, the African is rarely
right. The colonial administration, as Kortenaar observes, "thus hides from
itself how much it is based on violence and arbitrariness" ("Modern African Tragedy" 91). Colonialism itself is divided at the heart, for France promotes herself as the universal defender of human rights. It is for this reason
that the commandant Galandier reminds Wangrin that the French language
and civilization are the two most beautiful gifts that history has bestowed on
black Africans (34). France's munificence also explains why they announce
war in terms of their status as champions of human rights: "*L'Allemagne vient
d'allumer les poudres en Europe. Son empereur, Guillaume II, veut dominer le
monde. Mais il trouvera devant lui la* France éternelle, *champion de la liberté
et du droit de l'homme. La France demande à tous ses territoires une aide en
hommes, en prières et en matières premières*" (61) ["Germany has set light to
all the gunpowder in Europe. Her emperor, William the Second, wants to
rule the world, but first he will have to face our Eternal France, champion
of freedom and of the rights of man. France demands that all her territories
contribute men, raw materials, and prayers" (38)]. Though their credentials
are laudable on paper, the statement does not acknowledge that the Germans
may wish to do to the French something akin to what the French have done
to Africans. Nor does it see the irony in the French demanding resources and
prayers from countries they have themselves subjugated.

This peculiar interpretation of morality works for the French but also for
Wangrin and his accomplices. One vital rule seems to be that all that counts is

Interpreter • 127

winning. In the story, trade, or giving up something for a thing of more value, is important on many levels. For instance, the French mission is to take away the uncultured parts of Africans and give them something better by making them like Frenchmen. In return, the French themselves have gained incalculable resources and political power. When Wangrin arrives in Diagaramba, he is welcomed and given gifts by people who wish to have good relations with the new schoolteacher; his impeccable French is surely a sign of important things to come. Even Galandier puts a price on Wangrin's loyalty when he seals his demands with two months' salary. In other posts, people offer gifts with the hope of ingratiating themselves with him. This often translates into a constant mass of people in his house. Upon his return from Yagouwahi, his house is full of "*griots, musiciens, quémandeurs des deux sexes, demandeurs et défenseurs de justice, courtisans, représentants de chefs de canton, etc. . . . En effet, pouvoir dire « Je suis bien avec le Grand Interprète du Grand Commandant » équivalait à un titre de noblesse et arrondissait bien des angles dans la vie courante de l'époque coloniale* (191) ["griots, musicians, beggars of both sexes, petitioners and defendants engaged in lawsuits, courtiers, representatives of warrant chiefs, etc. . . . It is a fact that everyone who could claim that 'the great interpreter of the Senior Commandant was his friend' had attained something equivalent to an aristocratic title and was able to smooth many a rough edge in the day-to-day life of colonial times" (132)].

The crowds (so dense and diverse the narrator must resort to an "etc.") underscore the oft-cited picaresque nature of the text. Additionally, no one leaves empty-handed, and the understanding is that they will bring something in return. At each post, Wangrin receives valuable information or specialized services.[24] These exchanges and investments translate into more money. In his own words, "*Je ne suis pas venu . . . pour 'faire la religion' en vue d'un paradis situé dans l'au-delà, mais pour gagner de l'argent*" (148) ["I haven't come . . . to indulge in religious practices with a view to gaining access to paradise. I have come to make money" (100)]. Speaking of religion, spirituality also involves the sale of goodwill. Wangrin offers opulent gifts to powerful marabouts and geomancers to secure spiritual and social protection. "*Wangrin n'était pas un fidèle fervent,*" the narrator explains. "*Il pratiquait une sorte d'opportunisme*

---

24. For example, the young man who steals vital documents from Villermoz is a seasoned thief whose prison sentence Wangrin previously had reduced. At Yagouwahi, Wangrin wins over the commandant's lover by offering her mother a cow, a calf, a trousseau filled with clothes, and a hundred francs. The griot who sings his praises has received rich clothing and money (*Wangrin* 123).

qui lui permettait d'embrasser, sans gêne, la foi de ceux dont il souhaitait l'aide ou le silence" (202) ["Wangrin was no faithful devotee. Rather, he practiced a sort of opportunism that enabled him to embrace without scruples the religion of those whose assistance or silence he needed for his own ends" (140)]. In this way, religion is like other aspects of life, tied to expediency and trade.

INTERPRETING AS ENTREPRENEURSHIP

Given the significance of reciprocity and investment, and the counting of trust and ignorance as resources, it is unsurprising that interpreting, too, is a question of trade. Franz Pöchhacker notes that for some linguists, the etymology of "interpreter" denotes "a 'middleman,' 'intermediary' or 'commercial go-between'" (10). Wangrin as a comic interpreter explodes normal boundaries, including the commercial quality only vaguely hinted at in the meaning of his profession. In *Arrow of God*, Unachukwu "takes" words out of the white man's mouth (Achebe 77). Wangrin likewise masters the commodification and distribution of words and commercializes information. Being "in the middle," as Bruce Anderson says, "has the advantage of power inherent in all positions which control scarce resources" (qtd. in Cronin 392). Wangrin speaks French the color of Bordeaux wine, in Racoutié's words. The older interpreter feels pleased surprise Wangrin's apparent lack of ambition, which implies that his subsequent takeover is unsurprising. In a similar way, a man who approaches Romo to offer a bribe is "perplexed" when, instead of accepting the money at once, the interpreter asks him to bury it in a designated field. Any bashfulness appears aberrant—an interpreter should receive a bribe as his due. Ultimately, taking the pains to learn French is an investment for future gain; it is difficult and time-consuming and makes sense only if fully exploited.

Wangrin does live up to the challenge and in ways Racoutié could not have imagined. The first major event comes to be called the "*affaire des bœufs*," which involves making large illegal requisitions with the count's blank and signed official forms. The scheme, too brazen to be self-sustaining, comes to an end after a surprise audit. Wangrin and Villermoz must be arraigned before a judge, with the understanding that Wangrin, a subject and not a citizen of France, will take the fall. Yet, remarkably, Wangrin is successful, despite the network of Europeans siding with Villermoz because of his race and his powerful family (93). Wangrin, on the other hand, must work around his lack of credibility and overt access to power. He chooses to use that very status quo. In court, his accomplice asserts that Villermoz's involvement—indeed, the mere fact of his existence—legitimated and purified the entire affair: "*Si le petit commandant n'avait pas été dans le coup, j'aurais hésité. Je croyais fermement qu'un Blanc ne saurait ni voler ni mentir, parce qu'il représente la force et la justice et est venu pour éduquer et civiliser*" (92) ["If the Junior Commandant had not been involved, I might have hesitated; but I firmly believed that a white man could neither steal nor lie, since he represents strength and justice, and comes here to educate and civilize" (61)]. The accomplice is speaking like an obedient colonized subject, and the presiding judge can hardly contradict him. He even references the infamous monocle to show that Villermoz is surely unimpeachable.

Wangrin theatrically pulls out the official forms at a tense moment and displays the count's signature, "*une preuve que M. de Villermoz ne pourra récuser*" (94) ["This evidence cannot be refuted by Count de Villermoz" (62)]. He is right. The European justice system must overtly stand by a fair trial for both sides, a place for witnesses, and allowance for material evidence. Given the very public nature of the trial, the court has no choice but to acquit Wangrin and even compensate him for his trouble. The system's inflexibility works to its own disadvantage, and Wangrin can regularly use legitimate paths to accuse French officers of unjustly targeting his all-important human rights. That means that even powered by personal grudges, they find it hard to use their public office to punish him. Unfortunately, Wangrin's proximity to the French, his wide reading, and his experiences mean he knows the law intimately. Indeed, after one of Villermoz's friends arrests him in a fit of anger, Wangrin ensures that the event is made public and even refuses to leave prison without compensation. On such occasions, his enemy colonial officers end up being reprimanded by their superiors for their public displays of "unfairness." By the time he retires from the civil service, Wangrin has acquired a collection of medals for faithful service rendered to the government.

Wangrin's sense of freedom sustains the text's comic atmosphere; there is a lack of serious consequences for his actions. Even his unfortunate end is attributed to a destiny pronounced in his youth. Overall, the text gives the impression that ramifications, even for the most outrageous acts, are far off. Given the lack of consequences and his ability to rebound after crises, the adventures are often reminiscent of folktales. Because Wangrin is regularly transferred to new posts, each becomes a territory to conquer before moving on to the next. He overcomes his antagonists in a seemingly magical manner. These together create the episodic effect of traditional tales, and the text quickly takes on a fantastic quality. It is not for nothing that Wangrin chose his narrator because of his talent for recounting folktales (7).

Because the text places such an emphasis on performance, it hints that being "French" can be reducible to roleplaying. Villermoz is one example of someone who performs "Frenchness" with his ostentatious clothing and mannerisms. What his houseboy imagines about the monocle fits into a narrative involving other mysterious tokens associated with Europeans—whether the phonograph, carbon paper, or the book. Just as the interpreter lets others imagine the justification for strange behavior, it suits the colonial culture to let the colonized imagine that those objects are an "insignia of colonial authority" (Bhabha, "Signs" 144). This feeds into the assertion that by virtue of some intrinsic moral superiority, the colonizer deserves to rule over Africans. "The white man is very clever," states Okonkwo, who has come to perceive that the funniness of foreignness is the ultimate ruse. "We were amused at his foolishness and allowed him to stay. Now . . . He has put a knife on the things that held us together and we have fallen apart" (Achebe, *Things Fall Apart* 115). By encouraging and playing on ignorance, the colonizer is also a trickster.

Wangrin can also perform Europeanness but with a difference. He can easily slip between both worlds, either by playing at being a "*blanc-noir*" or by falling back on the image of a naïve colonial subject. The interpreter can take advantage of the colonizers' reluctance to let go of their very public moral superiority and admit their self-interest. The French are captive to their own rhetoric and weakened by their conviction that their language gives its citizens access to the moral order of the universe. But to the comic interpreter, language is a tool for convincing listeners. That hard assessment of the world is what gives him his own power. That the narrative is presented as nonfiction, "faithfully reported" except for proper nouns, shines a light on a world parallel to the official colonial domain. In this mostly illicit world, there was much cause for laughter.

With the comic interpreter, humor appeals to the reader's understanding of the surface message as well as a hidden one. The various scenarios speak to the reader's knowledge of the different languages or create a form of dramatic irony. Consequently, interpreting becomes a question of performance, juggling lies and half-truths, and keeping a straight face while saying something that may go completely against what the sender has asked to be transmitted. What comes to life is a disconnect between the source text and the target text, fueled by an outward appearance designed to match the "interpreted" text. Language, then, shows how it can say so many things with one statement. There is also an irony in the fact that, though interpreters cast doubt on the message that French or English speakers receive, somehow English and French readers must trust the writers to give us full access to what is said in African languages. Ignorance is a key ingredient and is illustrated in different levels—for instance, in Racoutié, who sees himself as the master but does not know he is a despised comic figure, or in the houseboy, whom the reader can laugh at because of his inaccurate knowledge about French culture. Most remarkably, the French officials are unaware that in practice they are not the real commanding authority at their posts. Comic interpreting thus takes advantage of a propitious sort of vulnerability and gullibility on the part of the colonial officers.

It is often said that folktales are based on a moral and are meant to educate about acceptable conduct. In the case of *Wangrin*, which often plays on its folktale-like aspects, stress is on the chaos implied by Gongoloma-Sooké, the "strange" god that Wangrin is drawn to. The god invites the reader to look beyond questions of morality and of order—indeed, to be suspicious of them—and, rather, to consider the relationship between language, lies, and performance. The resultant freedom, which the interpreter revels in, finds an echo in the subject of the next chapter.

CHAPTER 4

Deviant Norm

In Ola Rotimi's *Our Husband Has Gone Mad Again* (hereafter, *Our Husband*), Rahman Taslim Lejoka-Brown, a former soldier and wealthy cocoa farmer, has set his sights on a major political post in Nigeria. He has little by way of practical plans or experience, but that is beside the point. When Lejoka-Brown throws himself into his campaign, it is so that he can get his slice of the national cake. However, the image evoked by that term—soft, sweet, and dainty pastry—does not quite do justice to his crude personality or humor. Early in the play, he explains his intentions to his best friend, Okonkwo, and shows what politics means to him:

> Politics is the thing now in Nigeria, mate. You want to be famous? Politics. You want to chop life? No, no you want to chop a big slice of the National cake? Na Politics. [*Clears his throat.*] So I said to my party boys when was it? Last week, or so. I said to them . . . I said: [*Striking an oratorical pose.*] Cakes are too soft, Gentlemen. Just you wait! Once we get elected to the top, *wallahi*, we shall stuff ourselves with huge mouthfuls of the National chin-chin [*Munches an imaginary mouthful.*] something you'll eat and eat, brothers, and you know you've eaten something. [*They both laugh, slouching in the settee.*] (4–5)

The loose-limbed, indulgent nature of this and other scenes, combined with the protagonist's loud and unapologetic corporeality, is the thrust of the humor in this comedy. While the trickster, the mimic, and the interpreter are all verbose, the deviant norm exposes an acute cacophony. This typology comes alive in the stories that hold our insistent, embarrassing human bodies and realities against the norms and ideals that appear dignified—on paper, at least—such as national leadership or romantic love. In other words, the deviant norm is found in the back-and-forth between rarefied institutions and awkward, unsophisticated behaviors. This typology shows the humorous

Deviant Norm • 133

interplay between what is qualified as modern, official, or civilized, such as the school, the church, and the courthouse, and the kinds of attitudes occasionally denigrated for being vulgar or "bush."

He also reveals a certain pleasure that comic writers get from contrasting social groups and institutions and mocking one with the features of the other. Perhaps even more than the previous typologies, the deviant norm questions societal standards for politics or education and institutions such as marriage or government; he also interrogates our acceptance of them. This chapter first reads Rotimi's *Our Husband*, which offers much exposition on politics, power, and polygamy in the newly post-colonial state. I then explore similar themes in Soyinka's *The Lion and the Jewel* and Okot p'Bitek's *Song of Lawino*.

A COMIC UNIVERSE: RELIEF, RIDICULE, AND REVELRY

Our Husband Has Gone Mad Again was published in 1977 by Ola Rotimi, a professor and one of Nigeria's best-known playwrights. Lejoka-Brown is the flag bearer for the National Liberation Party (NLP). His proposed strategy for winning the upcoming elections is a dubious army tactic dubbed "Surprise and Attack." He will concentrate the party's campaign in villages while their opponents focus on cities. When their adversaries' guard is lowered, the NLP will swoop into the previously ignored areas and, taking advantage of the resulting surprise to fuel their attack, sweep up the votes. Amid the election hubbub, Liza, a Kenyan whom Lejoka-Brown married in Belgium, makes a surprise trip to Nigeria after completing her medical training in America. There, Liza discovers to her horror that her husband has two other wives: Mama Rashida, a placid woman "inherited" from his late brother and married to him while he was in Belgium, and Sikira, a confrontational younger woman chosen for expediency's sake—her mother is the president of the Market Women's Association, and the marriage is to secure the "women's votes." With her sudden appearance, Liza clashes with her husband, who clashes with his wives, who clash with each other, before forming alliances to more efficiently clash with him.

The play is often referred to as a satire. With its slapstick action and peripeteia, however, any corrective aim is regularly eclipsed by satire's by-product: laughter.[1] If, as a rule, comedy is rooted in immediacy and "doesn't

---

1. Ikenna Kamalu emphasises the play's absurdity; Moji A. Olateju and Yisa Kehinde Yusuf

134 • TYPOLOGIES OF HUMOR IN AFRICAN LITERATURES

provoke reflection" (McGowan 3), this is even truer for its lower forms. The sillier characters in *Our Husband* embody the physical manifestations of "low comedy"—noisy singing, clownishness, buffoonery, and scatological material (Harmon and Holman 279).[2] The largely carefree atmosphere differentiates Rotimi's text from a comedy like *The Blinkards*, even though they share some themes. On many occasions, Rotimi illustrates the description of the satiric scene as "disorderly and crowded," "choked with things," and dominated by "idiocy, foolishness, depravity, and dirt" (qtd. In Ball, 14). Ball notes that though this definition was developed from classical, English, and American examples, it corresponds as well to some postcolonial fictions. Additionally, the play illustrates Robert B. Heilman's take on farce, whose "essential procedure . . . is to deal with people as if they lack, largely or totally, the physical, emotional, intellectual, and moral sensitivity that we think of as 'normal'" (49). The text combines these elements for a buoyant and busy mood. In fact, Noël Carroll might be talking about *Our Husband*'s characters when he describes the residents of the humorous universe:

> The wacky logical inferences so frequently indulged by the denizens of jokes, satires, and burlesques . . . are absurdities, given the laws of logic, again, both deductive and inductive, formal and informal . . . Norms of appropriateness govern almost every aspect of our lives, opening up, thereby, the possibility of humour with respect to sexual behaviour, cleanliness, attire, and much else. We presuppose norms of human intelligence and physical condition. Hence, it is no accident that so many clowns are inhumanly stupid and exceedingly fat or skinny. (22)

Similarly, Critchley reminds us that humor produces a disjunction between reality and representation, with "common sense rationality left in tatters" (1). All these, of course, assume that there is such a thing as common sense, and that we expect it enough to be surprised by its absence or its travesty. It is productive to read the play as the reversal of the norms of human

---

underline its "hilarious and comical effect" (520); Nwaugo Goodseed Ochulor calls it a "hilarious and comical satire" (54).

2. "It is important to recall," Critchley states, "that the succession of tension by relief in humour is an essentially bodily affair. That is, the joke invites a corporeal response, from a chuckle, through a giggle to a guffaw. Laughter is a muscular phenomenon, consisting of spasmodic contraction and relaxation of the facial muscles with corresponding movements in the diaphragm" (7–8).

intelligence. At the same time, "normal" or "appropriate" does not always equate to "rational" in this setting.

Several studies emphasize the link among suffering, ridicule, and the liberation of tension through laughter and unfair power dynamics in the postcolony. Humor and laughter, according to these studies, serve as a coping mechanism for the majority and as an escape from the terrible realities of the African state. In "The Uses of Ridicule: Humour, 'Infrapolitics' and Civil Society in Nigeria," Obadare sums up the argument that humor is "vital to the way in which ordinary people endure social asperities, as well as negotiate, shape, and contest the public domain" (244). He adds, "As post-military 'democracy' across Africa encrusts the same shenanigans that were characteristic of military rule, ridicule has emerged as a means through which people attempt to deconstruct and construct meaning out of a reality that is decidedly surreal" (245). In that way, he echoes an argument of Relief theorists. In "The Freedom of Wit and Humor," Lord Shaftesbury presents an attractive link among relief, repression, and power imbalances: the "natural free spirits of ingenious men, if imprisoned or controlled, will find out other ways of motion to relieve themselves in their constraint; and whether it be in burlesque, mimicry, or buffoonery, they will be glad at any rate to vent themselves, and be revenged upon their constrainers" (qtd. in Morreall 16). Using strikingly similar terms, Reichl and Stein acknowledge that despite the complexity of relationships between center (or centers) and margin, "the specific settings, however diverse, regularly include conditions in which laughter and humour can release some of the tension and relieve some of the potential aggression" (9). For an unstable setting like Lejoka-Brown's Lagos, with its obvious hierarchies of class and gender, and where power is available to those who do not deserve it, the idea of humor as a pressure valve for respite or revenge has merit.

Nonetheless, Relief and similar theories are not without their criticisms, one being their mechanical aspect. For Morreall, to automate emotions, muscular movement, and psychic energy is to reduce laughter "almost to the level of belching and farting" (17). And even more important, humor in texts like *Our Husband* fulfills *and* frequently transcends its function as a tool for revenge or a respite from a cruel world.[3] Humor is not, agrees Critchley, "just

---

3. "The question of whether humor in the postcolony is an expression of 'resistance' or not, whether it is, a priori, opposition, or simply manifestation of hostility toward authority, is thus of secondary importance" (Mbembe 108).

temporary comic relief" (9). Indeed, Reichl and Stein go on to caution against reducing laughter to "laughing back," since humor does more than address power (12). The power differentials certainly end up favorable to humor in *Our Husband*, but while the "center," as it were, appears to be governed by clowns, it is also true that the margins seem occupied by circusgoers.

Mbembe points out that the relationship between the *commandement* and its subjects is best described as convivial (104). Similarly, in *Humor, Silence, and Civil Society in Nigeria*, Obadare mentions that "resistance" and "domination" are not straightforward; they are complicated by questions of complicity and antagonism in the relationship between Nigerian civil society and the state (60). The opening scene of *Our Husband* shows Lejoka-Brown hamming it up in the middle of a campaign procession and surrounded by a swarm of supporters, "cheering underlings," and "banner-flaunting partisans."[4] The party boys are engaged in "aggressively vociferous, coarse chanting" on par with their description by the stage directions as thugs and echoing the signs brandished by other supporters: YOU BEAR THE CHILDREN WE PAY THEIR SCHOOLING or YOU TOO CAN CHOP LIFE. JUST VOTE NLP (x). With the NLP in power, people will not only eat to their fill, they will be free to reproduce unreservedly and without responsibilities. The playwright specifies that there is to be "warm, audience-actor rapport" and that this can be established by the actors going into the audience and distributing some of Lejoka-Brown's tracts. A mutual understanding is thus created between the crowds who consume Lejoka-Brown's rhetoric and the audience, who are invited to do similar. Lejoka-Brown, after all, is promising "freedom for you" and "freedom for me" (viii) to a crowd venting through loud music and vigorous dancing, and to a theatre audience who likely shake their heads and chuckle at what has gone wrong with the post-colonial state not two decades after Nigeria's independence. It is true that laughter is effective against political tyranny, but the play is not so straightforward in naming an enemy. Mbembe again points out that in the postcolony, those laughing are "not necessarily bringing about the collapse of power or even resisting it . . . They are simply bearing witness, often unconsciously, that the grotesque is no more foreign to officialdom than the common man is impervious to the charms of majesty" (110).

---

4. Considering that the play is set smack in the middle of Lagos and that he is already being acclaimed by crowds, the Surprise and Attack tactic, when he unveils it, does not make much sense.

In *Our Husband*, the comic atmosphere defangs the power of the state, its representatives, and potential leaders before they become truly threatening. The play shies from most forms of violence unless it is transformed into slapstick. One scene initially presents as an interlude to the comedy but quickly returns to the default settings: Government soldiers are destroying the house of an old man and assaulting bystanders in the process. Alhaji Mustafa, the "venerable old man," comes to Lejoka-Brown's house to return the gun he borrowed to fight the government "devils." The year 1966, when the play was first produced, was marked with unrest and culminated in two bloody military coups within six months of each other. It seems, therefore, that the play is about to be contaminated by the cold reality of state and military violence. However, not only do the confrontations happen offstage, but the scene also takes the additional step of stripping Alhaji Mustafa of pathos or dignity by reducing his personality to his devout beliefs. The man only dares to enter Lejoka-Brown's house if the wives confirm several times that they are covered literally from head to toe. To be on the safe side, as he cannot bear to see anything scandalous such as an uncovered ear, he enters the scene rump-first while loudly announcing his entry. Only then does he chance turning around to greet them and complain about the government. The emphasis on his buttocks, compounded by his toothless threats to shoot the government officials *and* the fact that he has already accepted compensation for the demolition of his house, means that even the threat of grimness is quickly dispersed by the strong comic mood. Alhaji Mustafa is no dignified foil to government violence.

The emphasis on physicality recalls Bakhtin's observations on the European carnival, particularly what he says about the weeks preceding Lent in early modern Europe. Bakhtin says that for the duration of carnivals and marketplace festivals, the entire society was caught up in the festivities. The carnival's unofficial, humorous atmosphere and practices were considered as valid as the serious, unhumorous manifestations of officialdom, leading to an interesting duality in this society. Since the publication of *Rabelais and His World*, Bakhtin's arguments have sometimes proven controversial, overstated, or ahistorical.[5] Certain features of the carnival, like its universal sway over the "entire" society, have been challenged.

Despite these objections, and even though Bakhtin discusses olden peas-

---

5. See, for example, Richard M. Berrong's *Rabelais and Bakhtin: Popular Culture in Gargantua and Pantagruel*.

138 • TYPOLOGIES OF HUMOR IN AFRICAN LITERATURES

ants and *Our Husband* is set in Lagos, the play shows the interplay between the official and the unofficial in parts of mid-twentieth-century Nigeria.[6] It does not, however, limit humor to one space or time. Lejoka-Brown's home is characterized by strict rules for the women but is quite forgiving of emotional outbursts and bodily urges, provided they are the patriarch's. Conversely, places like the office or the airport demand a certain decorum from everyone; a panel at the airport forbids smoking, while another at the NLP conference room simply reads "Silence" (vi). Officialdom (represented ultimately by the government seat Lejoka-Brown is vying for) is governed by serious laws, regulations, and unforgiving expectations of etiquette. And this is where the problem lies: while these dual spaces exist, the denizens of this comedy rarely respect boundaries, in particular the limits of the formal. When Bakhtin contrasts the carnival with the ecclesiastical or the state-sponsored, it is understood that the aim of the latter is to sanction and reinforce existing patterns. The carnival "is opposed to that one-sided and gloomy official seriousness which is dogmatic and hostile to evolution and change, which seeks to absolutize a given condition of existence or a given social order" (160). Thus, authority figures are deeply serious, unamusing, and generally unamused. In a like manner, seriousness is enshrined in the formal institutions Lejoka-Brown aims to represent. He is in a contract with the voting public. As a nod to his station, members of the press even refer to him as "Mister President."

We may not know what the press or the masses truly believe, but it is made abundantly clear to reader and audience that Lejoka-Brown is ridiculous. While the private and the domestic tend to anticipate and forgive his eruptions into anger and confusion, the formal, at first, appears less so inclined. In practice, though, formal institutions must themselves contend with issues of legitimacy, instability, and some frankly unintelligent choices that chip at the sheen of respectability and official seriousness. When Lejoka-Brown unveils his Surprise and Attack tactic, party executives initially feel compelled by the formal setting to dance around their worries. In one sequence, seven men trip over one another with formulae of politeness, drowning in a series of "Mister President" and "after you." The façade is halted abruptly when the frustrated deputy declares, "Protocol be hanged!" and tears into their flag bearer (52). Where only moments ago he had playfully suggested that they go "one by each," Lejoka-Brown drops

---

6. In her analysis of *Le Vieux nègre*, Christiane Ndiaye argues that Bakhtin can be a solid point of reference for African literature (27).

Deviant Norm • 139

his own veneer of politeness and insults them, calling them "small-small boys" and "book-heads" (52). The scene degenerates into a chaos of raised, passionate voices reminiscent of the same coarse "thugs" who opened the play. The earnest aim of the characters occupying formal spaces is to be the neutral image that comes "first" to mind (as discussed by Genette in the introduction) when one pictures a leader: capable and commanding. They are funny because they deviate from that image; they would like to "control the law" (Mbembe 105) but control very little. Lejoka-Brown's funniness is often in spite of himself and his best intentions. Like Meme Jumai, he illustrates Genette's notion of involuntary comedy.

With such figureheads at its mast, the "official" alternative in the Nigeria of *Our Husband* evokes what Mbembe calls the postcolonial *commandement*, wherein a state is still seeking to institutionalize itself and achieve legitimation and hegemony (103). Mbembe qualifies the *commandement* as a "hollow pretense, a regime of unreality" (108). Using Cameroon as a case study, he argues that the grotesque and the obscene are innate to the postcolony in its official state. Mbembe further mentions "a polity in which the state considered itself simultaneously as indistinguishable from society and as the upholder of the law and keeper of the truth. The state was embodied in a single person, the president. He alone controlled the law" (105). For him, that narrative is a façade; it is an especially flimsy one when "Mister President" is Lejoka-Brown, whose attempts at grandeur are consistently reversed into comedy.

Rather than binaries, Mbembe insists on an atmosphere of conviviality, and the way the comedy leaks across implicit and explicit divides in *Our Husband* supports this. Therefore, the "tacit social contract" that Critchley names as the background to a humorous narrative involves leaders and their wider societies enabling each other (4). Instead of a situation akin to Bakhtin's two-world situation, which would alternate between a reputable (and monolithic and unrealistic) standard and its travesty, Lejoka-Brown must juggle official signs with their travesty. For him, this means having to manage the intrusions of his own body and impulses at moments when the body would best serve him by not calling attention to itself. He therefore offers a different take on Bakhtin's "material bodily principle": instead of the "high" being brought "low" in a sanctioned space and time, the humor comes from his abysmal sense of *timing*. There are moments when it would behoove him to show the "high," protocolary face—dignified bearing, oratorical language, the insight and competence of a democratically elected leader. As he tries to tell his party members during a walkout, "things must be done constitution-like" (52). Yet,

MATTER OVER MIND

The play to a large extent opposes the baseness of the human body to the intelligence of the mind, especially in the portrayal of Lejoka-Brown as larger than life. Party supporters chant that the "reality of Lejoka-Brown's presence itself commands instant awe!" (ix). While they are referring to his political might, such as it may be, the stage directions take care to underline his eye-catching physical presence. When he first appears surrounded by crowds, he is "lavishly adorned in gaudy traditional attire" (ix). Okonkwo is a "spruced up" figure whose Western-style suit, according to the stage directions, lend him dignity (4). Lejoka-Brown, on the other hand, is not very dignified: "husky, broad-shouldered, barrel-chested and hirsute [with] only a loincloth on, buttressing, as it were, the complacent sag of his jumbo-sized potbelly" (4). The potbelly must in some way be related to the gourd of palm wine with which he is "carousing"; Okonkwo is sipping from a bottle (4). The scene is set for an intriguing kind of contrast that runs throughout the play. Lejoka-Brown, presented in a loincloth (of all things) and drinking from a gourd, loudly signals an ease with informal areas that he will not be able to reproduce elsewhere. He also embodies excess and makes others like Okonkwo, and more formal sectors by extension, almost effortlessly symbolize restraint.

Lejoka-Brown sees himself as a fit and virile machine but has gone to seed. This is most obvious when he decides to relive his long-gone soldier days by performing an exercise. Sikira sniggers at her husband's loss of breath, causing Okonkwo to exclaim, "Enough, Major, look—your wife is laughing at you!" (5). His response, between bouts of panting and straining, is that Sikira need not be taken seriously, because she is an ordinary woman. Okonkwo, he adds, has also become soft like a woman. Mbembe shows how the body of the despot (to be fair to Lejoka-Brown, he is yet an aspirant) or, specifically, his "anus is not of something out of this world—although, to everyone's amusement, the official line may treat it as such; instead, people see it as it really is, capable of defecating like any commoner's" (108). One notable scene illustrates just how Lejoka-Brown may be seen by the majority. He is at the airport to intercept and redirect Liza, when Polycarp the steward rushes to inform him that Liza has already found her way to the house and discovered the existence of his other wives. Lejoka-Brown is momentarily overcome. He drops to a crouch as though overtaken by a pressing need, when what he wants is to engage his head to find a solution. At the sight of his friend squatting, Okonkwo amuses himself by sending Polycarp to buy toilet paper:

[POLYCARP *takes off.*]

LEJOKA-BROWN *peremptorily*].
    Hey! What's the matter? Hunh?

[POLYCARP *halts.*]

    Madman, where are you going?
POLYCARP.
    I dey go buy toilet paper sah.
LEJOKA-BROWN.
    I see . . . for who?
POLYCARP [*respectfully*].
    For you sah.
LEJOKA-BROWN.
    Ehen? I see . . . Na so your papa dey take shit? Hunh? Answer. When
    your Papa wan go latrine, he go take shokoto put for nyash; he
    carry damask agbada cover body, take cap knock for head finish,
    then he come butu dey shit for International Airport? (30–31)

For Polycarp to even mention those baser functions makes him a "madman," given Lejoka-Brown's official face: his position, the setting, and his fancy attire. Polycarp should know better than to publicly associate his master with something as appalling as excrement, especially when he is supposed to command "instant awe" in the public space. He is meant to be the opposite of the "*roi pour rire*," Bakhtin's carnival "king" elected in a mimicry of serious ritual. Probably, Lejoka-Brown would like us to associate him with Bakhtin's "classical body"—that is, a finished and perfect frame not at all suggestive of sucking and expelling orifices.

There is straightforward humor in the contrast between the leader and his travesty, decked in damask *agbada* and apparently gearing up to do his business in full view of the world. However, Lejoka-Brown's anger rings false; the text heavily suggests that very few—whether among the audience or the supporters—are holding their breath for him to be respectable. When Okonkwo insists that Polycarp run to buy toilet paper for his master to do the deed, Polycarp seems to reason that doing so is only logical. His overly pragmatic worldview makes sense because he sees beyond his master's Sunday best to the person inside. The steward may be used to worse at home than watching Lejoka-Brown *"sink down, absently, ending up in a vulgar squat"* (30).

Or perhaps Polycarp feels as Bakhtin does, that bodily functions have their place in human life, and one should not feel embarrassed if finding oneself caught by surprise. He manages to address Lejoka-Brown "respectfully" and without guile, and that may be what cuts his master so deep! The expectations that others have of him, even as a potential national leader, are derisorily low. Mbembe addresses the universality of excretion in blunter terms still: "obesity of men in power, their impressive physique or, more crudely, the flow of shit from such a physique—all these appeal to people who can enjoy themselves with mockery and laughter, and, sometimes, even join in the feast" (107). Polycarp, who does not laugh at all at his employer's plight, is possibly skeptical of hierarchies in general. What is more, this scene brings full circle Lejoka-Brown's intention of "eating and eating," although he does not appear to have thought about where the national chin-chin would end up.

Bathroom jokes are often linked to an immature sense of humor, testified to by Okonkwo's "impish delight" when he directs Polycarp (30). In "Scatological Children's Humour: Notes from the Netherlands and Anywhere," Sjaak van der Geest explains that at a young age, children love to joke about "dirty" bodily substances; as they get older, sexual topics become involved (127). Scatology signifies excretion as well as other obscene things, and sexual themes overlap with excretion in scatological humor as they do with the human body (129). Lejoka-Brown and Okonkwo confirm this while engaged in a discussion on seduction techniques before the toilet paper crisis. Okonkwo suggests a method to lower Liza's ire, labeled the Egg Treatment. As dubious as Surprise and Attack, it involves nibbling on and blowing into the woman's ear while talking. Okonkwo unfortunately decides to use a nearby orange seller for a practical demonstration. Far from seduced, she "stares blankly about, baffled" before rushing off as soon as she is paid (29). (They should have taken this as a warning. When Lejoka-Brown tries the Egg Treatment on Liza, she coldly asks if he is hungry.)

TEMPORALITY

Lejoka-Brown's expository speech, an enthusiastic ode to abundance that makes Okonkwo laugh, highlights the importance of eating, or "chopping," not just to satiety but to excess. In pidgin English, "to chop" is a versatile term that appears to take inspiration from some Kwa languages. It refers broadly to consumption in monetary, alimentary, or temporal terms. One can therefore chop food, chop money, or chop (a term as) president. That may be why Lejoka-Brown yokes his ambitions with meat.

Lejoka-Brown tells Okonkwo that politics is the "thing now." That preoccupation with making hay is expressed eloquently in another Nigerian text, Ike Oguine's *A Squatter's Tale*. This is a clever novel, set partly in early 1990s Lagos, which offers more insight into norms, expectations, and their reversal. Obi, a young investment banker, describes how his biggest client, an important businessman, regularly and brazenly defrauds the Nigerian state. His client's apish features, awful breath, and broken English mean he would hardly be welcome in the flashy world of investment banking if not for his money. It also happens that, in the past, the man "suffered" to "supplement his family's diet"; it is understood that hunger excuses larceny. As Obi explains, "Only our country's socialists, radicals and people like that still thought that robbing the government was any sort of crime. Government money was juicy fruit hanging on a tree that belonged to no one; only a fool would, when given the opportunity, not help himself" (84). The "fool" is not so much the person who cannot fulfill his obligations—it is rather the "radical" who allows himself to be held back by abstractions like morality or legality. By showing comically unscrupulous government officials, public figures with no morals, and members of the private sector with equally dodgy business practices, *A Squatter's Tale* explicitly reverses the ethics that a society should ideally build itself on. Like Lejoka-Brown, Obi equates lack to hunger, and ill-gotten money to tempting food that must be plucked and savored, because the chance to overindulge will not always so neatly present itself.

For Bakhtin, the carnival in Europe would happen over a given period in the year. Everyone would participate in it, and there was no life outside of it or escape from its atmosphere. But though Bakhtin considers that it was universal while it happened, the carnival was a special occasion and so had to come to an end for the official way of life to resume. This is equally true of other ancient festivities he cites, such as the Roman Saturnalia, where the servant would become the master, the master would serve the slave, and the "norm" would be turned on its head in a spirit of amusement that was enjoyable but temporary. This surely means that even during the carnival feast, the specter of the legitimate king loomed over the sham king who was crowned for humor's sake. It was understood that the feast presided over by the fool would come to an end, and none must have been as acutely aware of this as the *roi pour rire* himself.

In *Our Husband*, it is unclear if the people Lejoka-Brown aims to govern would know what to do with him if he consistently displayed anything resembling the "classical body" and a comparable mind. Liza and Sikira constantly undermine him and refuse to let his authority take hold. Sikira even parodies his politics: "SIKIRA *yanks a poster off the wall, holds this high above her head like a banner, and starts marching round the living room . . .* LIZA *is half slumped over her sewing machine, convulsed with laughter at this unabashed caricaturing of* LEJOKA-BROWN *and his political antics*" (55). While Sikira indeed caricatures him, he is himself the caricature of an ideal that other characters accept he will never meet. The spectator knows, as well, that there should be better alternatives for leadership. However, the play gives no indication that such a person might be allowed to the fore. After the NLP votes Lejoka-Brown out, the play ends with the revelation of the NLP's new flag bearer, borne high by the same uproarious crowds from the beginning—it is the fiery, equally unsuitable Sikira. Her antics at that moment are hardly distinguishable from the actions she took to parody her husband. Lejoka-Brown dramatically declares that the world has come to an end, though he was hardly any more qualified than her. As W. H. Auden says, in the world of laughter, we are all equal (Critchley 17). That sentiment is echoed by what might be the catchphrase of the entire play, a statement Sikira learns from Liza and that becomes the NLP's new slogan, underscoring what the comedy has hinted at throughout: "Men and women are created equal!" (76).[7] The occupants of the comic universe are, at heart, alike.

TWO WORLDS?

In *Our Husband*, the arrival of the American-educated wife is a catalyst for conflict. Liza occupies space unflinchingly, and her response to Lejoka-

---

7. Typically, their husband violently disagrees with "this schoolgirl arithmetic talk about one Man equals one Woman."

Brown's confrontational "Two bulls can't drink from the same bucket" is an equally combative "We will see!" (44).[8] He is right, though, to point out their sometimes-conflicting values and backgrounds: he is Muslim, she is Catholic; more important, she has received more schooling than he has. Formal education, with its trappings, can create a gulf when taken as a marker of prestige. The conflict between marriage and education is illustrated further decades after Rotimi's play, in another Nigerian text, Lola Shoneyin's *The Secret Lives of Baba Segi's Wives*. This novel revolves around a household structure like Lejoka-Brown's. There, the fact that the fourth wife is university-educated means that the other wives cannot reconcile themselves to her. One of their husband's friends even tells him that since "the woman is educated, she will only listen to people from the world she knows. The place to take her is the hospital" (*Secret Lives* 12).[9] The hospital can be put in the same category as the school, the court of law, or the police station. Those who consider themselves on the fringes of this "world" have trouble relating to it, because the agency of its citizens is admired but also feared, alienating, and ultimately misunderstood (on occasion, even by those who have access to it). The situation can either become pathetic, as it does in Shoneyin's novel, or be used for comedy, as it is in Rotimi's play. When Liza arrives in the Lejoka-Brown household, Sikira, who has been stewing in her resentment, is ready to surprise and attack the overly educated upstart:

[Girds her wrapper tightly, ready for a fight.]

Come on! You say you are a doctor? I will show you who I am!

[Feigns a charge at LIZA.] (24).

Later, when they have become fast friends, Sikira confesses that her antagonism came from fear: "They say when our African women go to England, or to America, or so-so-and-so, they come back wanting to be Headmasters,

---

8. The battles between two "bulls" evoke Bergson's jack-in-the-box analogy or humor from two stubborn sides who refuse to back down: "*Le genre d'amusement qu'il renferme est certainement de tous les temps. C'est le conflit de deux obstinations*" (35) ["The kind of amusement it affords belongs to all time. It is a struggle between two stubborn elements" (23)].

9. Throughout the play, she is labeled variously "an exquisite slice of feminine beauty," with "the erect, self-assured bearing of a young banana plant" (20), "pretty as a young palm tree" (60), and similar.

and kicking everybody round and round" (24). Equally aware of the potential for usurpation is Lejoka-Brown, who confesses that he entered politics to make Liza proud and to measure up to her. He invites Okonkwo to compare the ways an MC might introduce his wife: "'Ladies and Gentlemen, I have pleasure in introducing to you this evening, the Chairlady of this august occasion . . .' People clap pra-pra-pra-pra-pra . . . 'She is the one and only Dr Mrs Elizabeth Lejoka-Brown, MD, MSc, wife of . . . [*Drops his voice.*] . . . an Ijebu-Ijesha cocoa farmer!'" Contrasting this is another scenario, pronounced in a more robust voice: "She is the one and only Dr the Honourable Mrs. Elizabeth Lejoka-Brown, MD (Yale), MSc (Gynaecology), wife of the one and only Federal Government Minister of Agriculture and Housing, Mister the Honourable Major Rahman Taslim Akinjide Lejoka-Brown, ON, MHR, Esquire!" Without waiting for feedback, he declares, "A man must measure up, brother" (28–29). What he does not consider is that each scenario is as ridiculous as the other, since an MC should have little reason to introduce the chairperson's husband—never mind his surplus of titles—if he is not serving any purpose at the function. Lejoka-Brown's self-consciousness is seen again when he improvises a song about university-educated women as "BA women," who are not for the fainthearted and cannot be fully trusted (but are still a coveted source of prestige).

For the most part, Liza suggests physical restraint, at least relative to the exuberant Lejoka-Brown. She tries to exude reserve—for instance, remaining "coolly caustic" in the face of Sikira's insults and "female caterwauling" (24). Liza's demeanor is also contrasted to the wrapper-clad Sikira's provocatively slovenly behavior. The comparison between the women mirrors that between Lejoka-Brown and Okonkwo. Both scenes appear to equate the more "Westernized" person with comparatively more reason, while the less-Westernized person has exaggeratedly embraced unkempt attire and behavior as though to prove a point.

Liza offers another interesting contrast, this time to characters in *The Blinkards*. In Sekyi's play, care must be taken for "modernization" not to turn into "civilization" as Sekyi defines them. Those untouched by formal education are dignified and represent an avenue into a lost past that must be recuperated as much as possible. Those who have received some education, on the other hand, provide the comic material. In *Our Husband*, Liza, who is a medical doctor, is hardly ever ridiculous for her education. Her husband is often the awkward one. The standard that is used to mock either the educated or the uneducated is linked to a particular social vision. In *The Blinkards*, it is subversive because it calls attention to the potential ridiculousness of colonial culture. In Rotimi's text it is equally so but mocks the overly patriarchal household.

Perhaps because she is not familiar with West African pidgin and likely speaks a Kenyan language the others do not understand, Liza communicates in a standard form of English that Lejoka-Brown has not mastered to the same degree. When trying to create camaraderie with reporters, for instance, his casual attempts at correction fall short:

[looks over the shoulder of a reporter, flippantly dictating what he thinks the spelling of polls is.]

Polls—p-o-l-e-s.
REPORTER.
Beg your pardon.
LEJOKA-BROWN.
I said p-o-l-e-s: polls.
BBC CORRESPONDENT.
It's P-o-l-l-s, Mr President.
LEJOKA-BROWN.
I see . . . anyhow, polls is poles. Next question. BBC man, your turn.
(62)

Liza is aware of her advantage and, on one occasion, weaponizes her training. She piles terminology Lejoka-Brown does not understand onto his head in order to frighten him, and his perplexity underscores his role as a bumpkin with a shakier grasp of "correct" English. To him, her overblown medical jargon even sounds like witchcraft (40). Though they may not be spiritual, words spoken in Standard English do have power.[10] Hence, Sikira tries to counteract that power by ridiculing it, feigning an "English accent which comes out in the desperate stammer of a he-goat just before coitus" (19). The humor of these interactions comes from people occupying the same society—and even the same house—but drawing lines between their differ-

---

10. Similarly, Baba Segi's friend tells him that he must handle Bolanle's barrenness with great care lest the authorities get involved: "When she opens her mouth and English begins to pour from it like heated palm oil, the constable will be so captivated, he will throw our friend behind bars!" (11). As the speaker implies, it is not so much what the woman says as how she says it that will decide the case in her favor.

148 • TYPOLOGIES OF HUMOR IN AFRICAN LITERATURES

ent "worlds." The confusion in the household is caused by polygamy, which brings its own conflicts with it.

POLYGAMY AND PROGRESS: *SONG OF LAWINO*

Lejoka-Brown is given the kind of body and manners meant to suggest that he is jolly, more belly than brain, and cares little for propriety. He is like Sareil's ideal comic character: a mix of fantasy and reality, nonchalant and a hearty eater, with no links to the past or worries for the future (66). The playwright's generosity with his protagonist's bulk is also suggestive because it seems to be the purview of polygamous "big" men in literature.[11] Keeping with his personality, Lejoka-Brown has rigid views on gender roles. In his interactions with his Nigerian wives, the women first appear self-effacing and overly respectful—bowing, scraping, and calling him their lord. Their husband takes these acts as his due and even attempts to run his household like the military general he used to be (Sikira responds "Sah!" when she is called; so does Polycarp).

Opoku-Agyemang notes that in literature centered on the family, polygamous marriage is "a fertile arena for discord" (125). Discord is ripe for humor, and a polygamous man may be forced to reveal himself as a natural clown when his futile attempts to cordon off the women's quarrelsomeness ends with him subsumed into the conflict. Furthermore, by introducing Liza into his home after Mama Rashida and Sikira, Lejoka-Brown fits into a type of narrative that uses the natural conflicts in the polygamous home to mirror the conflict between the occupants of the official and unofficial spaces. When a husband pursues a formally educated woman to signal his own prestige or modernity but does not fully reckon with whomever is waiting for him at home, the result can lead to an especially biting humor.

Song of Lawino is a classic illustration of such conflictual polygamous relations. This long narrative poem was published in 1966 by the renowned Ugandan poet Okot p'Bitek; its plot hints at what could have developed

---

11. Any claims Baba Segi might make to cutting an arresting figure are tainted by the slightly gaseous terms used to describe him; upon waking up, for example, he determines that the stomachache that has been bothering him is not due to "hunger or trapped gas." Soon after, he "reinflates his large frame" when he steps out of his car (9). He is ballooned and larger than life, and this impression is compounded by his flatulence, burping, and diarrhea.

Deviant Norm • 149

between Liza and Sikira had they not become friends. It draws and maintains the clear battle lines between the first wife and her rival and, consequently, between "traditional" and "modern" ways of life. The first wife and narrator, Lawino, complains about her husband's obsession with his new wife and, by extension, his rejection of the traditional Acoli values embodied by Lawino herself. Ocol, the husband, does not come across well in Lawino's song. Neither does Clementine, the new wife, whose fruitless aspiration (as Lawino tells it) is to look and act like a white woman. She rather resembles a bloody, ulcerated "wild cat," while her face powder also makes her look like a wizard on his way to "the midnight dance" (lines 127–139).

Lawino maintains her judgmental, aggressive, and comically ironic tone, even while claiming that she is speaking out of concern about Clementine's advanced age and shriveled breasts, that Clementine is beautiful, and that Lawino is not jealous or complaining anyway! Before long, she speculates that the new wife must have thrown aborted fetuses into the latrine, declares that Clementine smells like stale beer and burned rats, testifies that she kisses their husband with a slimy tongue, and attributes many other colorful traits and behaviors to her hapless rival. While Lawino is motivated by dislike, her fight is not so much with the practice of polygamy; it is with the world Clementine represents. The cultural traits Clementine copies do not suit her. More than that, in a text published only four years after Uganda gained independence from England, they are presented as dangerous to the existing African cultures that have already taken a beating over the past several decades.

Lawino believes in cultural authenticity. While the ways of foreigners are opaque to her, she does not despise them, reasoning that a leopard cannot change into a hyena any more than a giraffe can become a monkey. With her critique of the blind mimicry of European culture, Lawino is sometimes reminiscent of a Mr. Onyimdze and his complaints about appropriate clothing:

> At the height of the hot season
> The progressive and civilised ones
> Put on blanket suits
> And woollen socks from Europe,
> Long under-pants
> And woollen vests,
> White shirts;
> They wear dark glasses

150 • TYPOLOGIES OF HUMOR IN AFRICAN LITERATURES

And neck-ties from Europe.
Their waterlogged suits
Drip.
    (lines 515–525)

Lawino, however, is far more hotheaded in her criticism than Mr. Ony-imdze. Her tone, language, and themes are often as crude as she can make them. She associates the so-called civilized with piss, sweat, saliva, farts, vomit, and in one memorable ode, to dung (lines 579–613). These failed mimics are drunks, beggars, or halfwits. As for Clementine, she is a sickness that has turned Ocol from Acoli traditions. Ocol, for his part, is a pale caricature of white culture such that even a Mr. Borɔfosɛm seems staid in comparison (Lawino likens her husband to a hen that must be trapped under a basket, a "mad hyena," or a child-hating wizard). His blind championing of these cultural elements makes him another involuntary comic figure who is almost tragic in his ignorance. In this text, too, the official spaces may be intimidating, but they are misunderstood by members and outsiders alike.

Ocol justifies his wife's criticism by condescending to fellow blacks. His wife's baseness, according to him, stems from her inability to dance "white" dances like the samba, speak English, play the guitar, use imported electrical appliances, or tell time and season with the cuckoo clock. Lawino disdains those practices and items while, age, she reasons, is determined by looking at the person in question. She is also put off by the Protestant practice of eating human flesh and drinking blood from a chalice; the Catholic service, which revolves around meaningless shouting and parroting mad verses, is no better in her eyes. When she asks, "What is all this?" or "Why should I know it?" her frustration is understandable. The world no longer makes sense to her.

The humor in *Song of Lawino* is more malicious than in *Our Husband*. The conflict comes from the characters' clashing social identities. In "*Song of Lawino*: Un cas de contestation en Afrique," G. Daniel comments: "*Par-delà l'opposition mari-femme, par-delà le désaccord sur ce qui est beau, bon à manger, bon à porter, propre, sale (désaccord qui n'est pas innocent non plus, car ces categories font partie intégrante du système conceptuel à partir duquel on organise les objets qui nous entourent), on voit se dessiner une opposition beaucoup plus profonde entre deux systèmes de pensée*" [Beyond the husband-wife conflict, disagreements on what counts as beautiful, good to eat or wear, clean or dirty (disagreements that are not innocent either, since these categories form an integral part of the conceptual system used to organize our surroundings), there is a much deeper opposition between two different ideologies (197)].

Each side believes it has an edge, whether Ocol, who has been saved from savagery; Lawino, who staunchly defends her values; or even the voiceless usurper Clementine, newly wed and trying to live as a civilized person. Were Lawino not controlling this tale and were she not so unimpressed by the trappings of the foreign culture, her song would have a more pathetic bent. Instead, Ocol is a far more pathetic version of Lejoka-Brown: a wretched and misled party who does not deserve power either at home or in public. His authority is built on things that the audience knows not to be particularly true. The lines are blurred between victim and aggressor because Ocol, who has concrete power, is violently abased, while Lawino, the casualty of a forceful sociopolitical change, rarely backs down. On the contrary, her antagonists are browbeaten to the point of pitifulness. This, for example, is how Lawino narrates dances among the civilized crowd:

You meet a big woman
She staggers towards you
And leans on the wall
And before she has untied her dress
She is already pissing;
She forces out the urine
As if she has syphilis.
The stench from the latrine
Knocks you down, from afar!
You enter;
It is as if you have entered
Into a lion's mouth.
The smell of Jeyes
And the smell of dung
Rise to the roof.[12]
 (lines 572–586)

---

12. The association between evening outings, excretion, and sex speaks to a mock-epic scene in Alain Mabanckou and Helen Stevenson's *Verre cassé* (*Broken Glass*), where two potential love interests meet in a bar. The exuberant Robinette challenges Casimir, a newcomer, to a public "pissing competition" with her "fat ass and big tits" on the line. After much peacocking and bawdy language, and over an impressive number of pages, the competitors spray an eye-watering amount of liquid out of their nether regions (62). The taunts increase in time with the excretions and at a point, Casimir draws the map of France in the dust and declares that he can do China as well. Robinette concedes the victory and gives Casimir his promised reward.

The persistent return to bodily functions is Lawino's way of reminding these people that they are no better—are actually much worse—than others, and that their airs are to be pitied. In that way, her husband, who previously crawled, wept, and endured beatings to be allowed to marry her, is like the schoolteacher Lakunle in Soyinka's *The Lion and the Jewel*, which I will discuss in the next section. The little Western education Lakunle has received has made him patronizing and haughty, even toward the girl he desperately wishes to marry, even though his books have taught him that women have smaller brains and thus cannot argue with him. Such prejudices recall the fact that the colonial period prioritized formal education for boys, and many African countries are still trying to correct the problems created by colonial policies and make formal education more accessible to girls. In that light, the idea of women more educated than her husbands can also be viewed as the world reversed. However, by painting the men so badly, the comic reversal is not at the expense of the women. They rather become the touchstone for judgment from the audience, while the patriarchal status quo is painted as dubious.

SEX VS. ROMANCE

At the end of *Our Husband Has Gone Mad Again*, Lejoka-Brown is left with Liza while the "old" wife and the "young" wife are freed to pursue other avenues. Mama Rashida has learned the rudiments of economic theory from Liza and takes her now-bustling poultry business to her village. Sikira marries political pointers picked up from their husband with a slogan learned from Liza and goes into politics. Both women are now free to chop life on a bigger scale.

It should be mentioned that in pidgin, "chopping" can refer to sexual activities as well. Even though sex is important in Rotimi's play, the characters discuss it obliquely for the most part. The audience is made to understand that Mama Rashida was married to Lejoka-Brown by his father out of "pity," as a retirement plan of sorts for her. Lejoka-Brown haltingly sums up their relationship: "I mean, not that I don't like Mama Rashida as a person. I like her and respect her . . . in many ways she is just like Liza herself . . . you know . . . well-mannered, quiet, full of concern: a well-bred, African pigeon. But . . . are you there . . . ? I mean . . . let's face it . . . you know . . . look at it . . . I mean . . . you see . . ." (9). And indeed, the audience does see. Mama Rashida, generally tranquil and staid, is allowed to depart with little objection. As she tells him, "My lord can come to see old Mama Rashida and her chicken farm in Abule Oja whenever he wants" (72). By referring to herself as "old Mama Rashida," she confirms that whatever fondness they might have for each other is mostly platonic, tied to liking the other "as a person."

While Mama Rashida may feel affection, or just a higher level of tolerance for nonsense, Sikira is clearly unhappy with the status quo. She is not only younger and more physically attractive but also more forthcoming about their bedroom life. She eagerly explains to Liza how things can get quite "terrible" in bed, blaming it on the fact that in the middle of the night, Lejoka-Brown will grab his pillow and hoist it like a flag and sing party songs (23). Sikira dresses modestly until Liza disembarks with her sewing machine. For her part, Liza's dress does not match Lejoka-Brown's strict Muslim worldview. It is not clear if she practices Roman Catholicism beyond occasionally blaring the "Hallelujah Chorus" on the radio, but she has no qualms about wearing "provocative" clothes. This, in addition to her more liberal worldview, influences Sikira. In time, Liza makes Sikira "*a tightfitting, micromini snippet of a dress. Other attributes of this: a saucily low neckline exposing much of her back, and a sumptuous sweep of her 'frontal undulations'*" (53). Horrified that she would dress like this in public, and to celebrate his victory at that, Lejoka-Brown reacts violently. Sikira, on the other hand, had thought that he would like it and perhaps thought of the outfit as a seduction tool. Sikira's presence may be necessary for his career, but it is easy to see that their husband does not like her very much "as a person" and is especially discomfited at the thought of her attractiveness being noticed by any other man.

Sexuality spills over into Lejoka-Brown's interactions with Liza as well and hammers the final nail into his political coffin. After the walkout, Lejoka-Brown and his party hastily organize a press conference to quell rumors. The occasion is attended by party executives, local reporters, and a reporter from the BBC. All are men, and Lejoka-Brown seems to have things more or less in hand. While his attempts to appear erudite have fallen short ("polls is poles"), he has not done or said anything scandalous. Then, just as the men are drinking to the NLP's success, and once again displaying the importance of awful timing to the plot, Liza, dressed in a bikini, strolls in from a place called Bar Beach. Lejoka-Brown spots her from afar, panics, and promptly loses his protocolary bearing. He tries to shoo her away, threatens the men with a machete and a gun, and then orders them to dive to the floor and divert their eyes.

"Sex," Carroll states, "particularly in terms of marriage, can provide an indefinitely large number of opportunities for common laughter, since they are so freighted with rules of behaviour just asking to be transgressed" (82).

154 • TYPOLOGIES OF HUMOR IN AFRICAN LITERATURES

For Lejoka-Brown, the rules come from an obsession with modesty: a woman's demeanor should not hint at sex except to her husband and, even then, away from prying eyes. As happens with Alhaji Mustafa, an otherwise serious situation once again turns comic when one of the reporters, in mortal danger and prostrate, still finds it within himself to wolf-whistle at Liza's bikini-clad body. This throws Lejoka-Brown further into a loud but ultimately harmless rage. After a scandalized Liza has retreated, his attitude switches back to jovial, and he invites the disgruntled media men to have another drink as though nothing were amiss. As low as expectations of him may be, even he cannot survive this scandal. Still, a disgraceful end to his career does not faze him as much as others seeing his wife's body.

There is less jealousy between the women. It is not clear what happens between Liza's fight with Sikira, but between the first and second acts, Liza has created a space for herself in the household. She even advises Sikira to stay, telling her that it would be "silly" of her to go running to her mother over marital quarrels. Given Mama Rashida's stoic acceptance and Sikira's resentment, any rivalry or jealousy is superficial. Already accustomed to sharing what is often a difficult, belligerent husband, none of Liza's co-wives especially wants exclusive rights to him. It is thus only normal that when they find alternatives to the marriage, they take them.

That relative indifference is not the case in *Song of Lawino*. Nor is it the case in *The Lion and the Jewel*, where two men from different generations and outlooks vie for the hand of one woman. Soyinka's comedy was first published in 1966. Like *Our Husband* and *Song of Lawino*, it layers marriage with gender-role perceptions, political power, social upheaval, and disparities rooted in the access to formal education and institutions. Lakunle the schoolteacher and Sidi appear on the surface to fit the mold of the conventional young couple of the romantic comedy. She is a "true village belle," even if Lakunle has sworn, as a model young lover should, that "[her] looks do not affect [his] love." He is the ardent young suitor, a cultured teacher with dreams of taking Sidi away to the big city for a new life. He presents himself as the young country's hopes for a future. Sidi is not unwilling: she is ready to marry him "today, next week, or on any day." Some of Lakunle's lines would be appropriate in any romantic comedy: "Oh Sidi, vow to me your own undying love" (8). Their future together, however, is threatened by Baroka, a lecherous older chieftain and "master of self-indulgence" who wants Sidi for himself. Another obstacle to the marriage is money. This setup seems like it

Deviant Norm • 155

should build toward a conflict, resolution, and the marriage that comedies are meant to end in. It is a familiar formula that goes back to European antiquity, prominent in plays by Plautus and Terence:

> _Deux gens qui s'aiment sont menacés d'être séparés, à cause de l'avarice égoïste de deux vieillards (senes), l'un étant le père du jeune homme et l'autre le leno propriétaire de la jeune fille. Concrètement, il faut trouver d'urgence l'argent permettant au jeune homme de racheter la jeune fille._

> [Two young people in love are threatened with separation by the selfish greed of two old men (_senes_); one is the young man's father and the other is the _leno_ who own the young woman. There is an urgent need to find the money that would allow the young man to buy the woman]. (Mortier 26)

The formula persists with some variations over the centuries, inspiring playwrights like Shakespeare, Molière, and Marivaux.[13] However, cracks quickly develop in the framework. Lakunle does not have the shoulders for such a story and deviates comically from the established norm. His conviction that he is too civilized for the village makes him into a clown. He is, himself, the source of their money issues because he dawdles over paying Sidi's bride price. Sidi is adamant that the full price be paid in accordance with custom and to keep her honor intact. Baroka the Bale (the chief) has no qualms about paying it. In the European template, the conflict is resolved with tricks, a clever matchmaker, or _dei ex machina_ if the situation gets too knotty. After a series of twists, the two young people are married and live happily ever after.

While _The Lion and the Jewel_ does end in a marriage celebration, the union is between Sidi and Baroka and with the young woman's enthusiastic consent. It is true that at first, the joke is on the lecherous old man, but not for long. In the Western tradition, the older antagonists are often humiliated. One of Molière's most famous scenes is in _Les Fourberies de Scapin_, where the clever servant tricks his master's intractable father into a sack and thrashes him soundly. For his part, Lakunle is not redeemed by a stock servant character who will obligingly endanger himself for the pleasure of seeing young

---

13. Wodehouse wonderfully parodies this formula in his Bertie Wooster and Jeeves plays. Examples can be found in _The Jeeves Collection_.

love triumph. Lakunle can have no such figure in his life, as he looks down on his "bush" neighbors. The servant, Sadiku, rather, works against him and for the Bale's gratification.

Sidi's beauty inspires poetry and she serves as a photographer's muse. Yet, in her own way, the young woman picks chin-chin over cake. After Baroka tricks her into sleeping with him, Sidi expresses her disbelief that Lakunle would assume she would choose a "book-nourished shrimp" and "beardless version of unripened man" over the Bale's strength and "perpetual youthful zest" (67–68). It turns out that, in all the ways that count, the older man is young enough for her. In other words, the play is still a comedy but one that accords more importance to concerns like sexual fulfillment over sublime fantasies of love and civilization.

Sidi's clear-eyed sensibility means she might be willing enough to marry Lakunle but will not compromise her values for his silly dreams. Unlike the belle in the European template, she is not long suffering for the sake of romance but rather mocks her suitors and delights in their misery. For instance, when she discovers that she is even more famous than Baroka, she threatens Lakunle, who just called her a "mere woman," by saying it would demean her to marry a "mere village school teacher" (14). Sidi tells ribald jokes, is comfortable in her physical appeal, and takes little issue with "lustful" men ogling her. She has a down-to-earth view of life and in several ways, therefore, is like Lawino, who takes pride in her own beauty and local customs.

In reversing European conventions of comedy, the play creates part of its humor out of the disruption of those generic codes. Soyinka is commenting on African difference: in his version of a romantic comedy, elders outwit younger men, impotence is funny, and sexual prowess counts more than love. *The Lion and the Jewel* questions the norms and practices closer to home as well. Soyinka valorizes women's sexual enjoyment, but the way in which Sidi gets hers is problematic, since it is based on a predator's deception. We are meant to sanction trickster-like behavior carried out onstage and even laugh at it. But at the same time, we would condemn those actions if they were done offstage. Additionally, the play was first performed in 1959, a year before Nigeria's independence, and reflects the ambiguities created by the social and political upheaval. On the one hand, it is derisive of the "fizzled" old chief. At the same time, it is critical of difference and may defensively humanize the lecherous chief *and* ridicule the pretentious youth in the same breath. Soyinka shows the humor in the battle between preserving the status quo and contesting it.

Therefore, while the larger-than-life polygamist is an easy target for mockery, the young man's discomfort in the face of blunt sexuality is scorned as readily. Lakunle is stubbornly fixated on civilization but is a shallow caricature of progress. He associates the baser functions of the body with a lack of civilization; his love, he stresses, is "the love of spirit and not of flesh" (64). He is ill at ease in his skin—"dressed in an old-style English suit, threadbare but not ragged, clean but not ironed, obviously a size or two too small" (3). Wearing clothes he has outgrown accentuates the "shrimp's" mental and bodily immaturity, making him seem turned mulishly toward a youth he should have left. The Bale has multiple wives and wants more; Lakunle is awkward and easily flustered. Even seeing Sidi, his supposed fiancée, wrapped in "the familiar broad cloth which is folded just above her breasts," leaves him unhappily excited. He chides her for her uncivilized dressing but even then has trouble finding his words. There is a false start where he tries to name her breasts but ends up referring to "her . . . shoulders," before falling back on the vague-enough term of "that" (5). Later, when he is informed that she is oiling herself up as brides do, his response is not joy, but rather, "I am not impatient / Surely she can wait a day or two at least." He gets increasingly agitated, adding that he must prepare himself, that marriage must come gradually, that his pupils might not be pleased (66).

By choosing the older man, Sidi confirms that intergenerational conflicts are not always meant to be won by the youth. In these comedies, a man who can fulfill his sexual "obligations" is to be celebrated not necessarily because of his age but because he does not suffer from the dreaded curse of impotence. The male who finds himself unable to "satisfy" a woman sexually can become a source of mockery once the secret comes out. In *Our Husband*, this is Lejoka-Brown's heartfelt reply when Okonkwo suggests that he house his wives separately:

I leave these two women here in Idumagbo; next, I hire room and parlour in Surulere for Liza; then I, too, bury my head in a separate room at Abule Ijesha. Abi? I wake up every morning and parade from one house to another visiting these women. That's right! Suddenly, I'm no more a husband; I've become a caretaker! . . . So stop making funny suggestions, brother, I'm in trouble: I mean, look at it . . . I should leave my women open, unprotected, each one camped in a separate tent, while I hide myself away for six whole donkey months . . . What do you think I am? IMPOTENT? (11).

158 • TYPOLOGIES OF HUMOR IN AFRICAN LITERATURES

To him, impotence makes a man a powerless "caretaker" unable to keep his women from predators.[14] Fear can drive laughter and we sometimes even laugh at what we fear. In this case, men will laugh to signal that they belong to the group unaffected by impotence.

The idea that an impotent man is feeble and, thus, a toothless creature to be played with is prominent in *The Lion and the Jewel*. Baroka appears to be the quintessential hypersexual lout begging to be put in his place. When rumors of his impotence begin to circulate, he plays to the image of an aging man paying for a life of hedonism. He uses the ruse of impotence—and its resultant humor—to lower the delighted Sidi's reservations. She feels confident enough to go to his house at night to mock him to his face, as though his lack of sexual "power" means a loss of political power. While she and the audience think he is "harmless," his condition is a source of derision and Sidi is eager to go and "mock the devil." Laughing at his "condition," she says she "longs to see him thwarted, to watch his longing / His twitching hands which this time cannot / Rush to loosen his trouser cords" (36).

"Since sex and sexual behaviour are freighted with so many norms and stereotypes, they too are a natural breeding ground for humour," writes Carroll. Thanks to "our gender stereotypes regarding manliness," when a man turns out differently, some may laugh at him (27). The Bale's ploy works because he knows that "maids would hear of it / And go to mock his plight" (63). Sidi confirms this to be true, saying that the news makes her happy to be a woman. This suggests that impotence is especially funny when the sufferer has based his power on his gender and used that power to oppress others.[15] Robert LeVine addresses those stereotypes in "Sex Roles and Economic Change in Africa," when he observes:

> There are some conspicuous uniformities throughout the agricultural societies of sub-Saharan Africa in the traditional division of labor by sex and the husband-wife relationship. Among most of these peoples, men clear the bush and do other annual heavy tasks, while women have the larger share of

---

14. The specter of the "caretaker" is central to *Baba Segi's Wives* as well. Despite the regular reference to his sexual prowess, the novel's climax is the revelation that Baba Segi is sterile and that none of his children is his: "'Are you saying that . . . all I have been is a temporary caretaker?' . . . 'Indeed, my friend. You have been no more than a doorkeeper'" (183). Baba Segi is forced into a compromise with his three cheating wives to keep the affair quiet.

15. In French for instance, the word "*impuissance*" covers various conceptions of powerlessness, including the sexual.

routine cultivation. Women carry the heavy burdens, usually on their heads, while men occupy their leisure with a variety of prestigeful and important activities . . . Thus women contribute very heavily to the basic economy, but male activities are much more prestigeful and require less routine physical labor. In husband-wife relations, the male is ideally dominant . . . Thus African women have less prestigeful occupations than their husbands and are often subordinated to them in the family in consequence of polygyny, patrilocality, and the ideal of male dominance; nevertheless, women play essential and semi-autonomous roles in the labor force as producers and distributors of goods. (186–187)

While such statements do not always apply, it is true that African women make vital contributions both socially and economically. If, in spite of those, men are considered more "prestigeful" by simple virtue of their gender, then an underlying resentment can fuel schadenfreude in the women when what makes the man "manly" becomes defective. This explains Sidi's otherwise disproportionate glee. It also explains why the young women are more prone to mocking laughter than the men. Regarding gender roles among the Yoruba, LeVine notes a "widespread and intense preoccupation with impotence. Many married men report experiencing impotence, others fear it, and it is an extremely common topic of conversation. Medical practitioners are besieged by impotent men seeking cures" (191). If one reaction from the women is laughter, especially manifested as relentless teasing like Sidi's, one can understand the scramble for a cure.

Relationships between men and women offer a domestic take on center-margin rapports. We can read those who display relative sophistication and cosmopolitanism (like Liza or Lakunle) as creatures of the "center" and put others like Lejoka-Brown or Sidi at the "margins." None of these designations is fixed, and indeed they can be quite flimsy—Lakunle has little of Liza's exposure or education and quite often is the center only in his own head. This means that those with some power, when they consider themselves as the standard, set themselves up for a fall and exposure as being dafter than those on the periphery. Lakunle's scorn, aimed at the villagers for their "bush minds" and "ignorance," is based on his own ridiculous understanding of civilization—high-heeled shoes, stretched hair, and the foxtrot. On the other hand, the perceptions of those who lack that power can be just as inaccurate, such as Lawino's understanding of Western religious symbolism. Each party, ultimately, can be as ludicrous as the other.

Nonetheless, it is worth pointing out another distinction between *The Lion and the Jewel* and *Our Husband*. Throughout Soyinka's text, Lakunle is mocked for how awkwardly his education hangs on him. The non-Western-educated chief, on the other hand, is infinitely more astute. In Rotimi's play, the opposite happens: Lejoka-Brown is constantly mocked, while the most educated character, Liza, is often also the most dignified. This means that the two plays are based on different norms. The educated Lakunle becomes a comic figure because he deviates from the communal norm, while Lejoka-Brown is a comic figure because he deviates from the sophisticated standard set by his wife. In each case, the women show that even if they do not themselves occupy the primary clown positions, their role in creating and highlighting humor is vital to the comedy.

Conclusion

"NOBODY NOSE"

As the Digital Age deepens our familiarity with other cultures and widens interpretative communities across the globe, the objections to the dreary discourses on Africa—the insistence that Africa is not a country, essentially—may eventually become clichéd. In the meantime, to recognize and revel in displays of African humor is also to appreciate the ability of African artists to adequately address humanity's messy complexity. If we do not take care, laughter is one of the first elements to suffer in the literatures and their critical reception. It therefore pays to engage those texts that are not singularly focused on rousing the reader, rubbing his face in gloomy themes, or, inversely, whitewashing those themes in a contrived manner.

That said, it is quite easy to condemn sweeping statements but not so easy to avoid making them! This book has been, first, an invitation to reread a selection of canonical African texts. It is also a signpost to even more instances of humor across a wide variety of genres. It is difficult to overestimate the amount of humorous material in African art and societies, especially with the addition of new material on the internet. Even though I limited the corpus to print texts, I still, by necessity, excluded many examples that deserve a study of their own.[1] The abundance of material across different comic genres means the typologies I have presented cannot claim to be a prescriptive framework that literary texts must contort themselves to fit into; as precise as our aim may be, humor is a wily phenomenon. And if people—especially the charac-

---

1. Christopher Hope's *Darkest England*, Mongo Beti's *Le Pauvre Christ de Bomba*, Ken Saro-Wiwa's *A Forest of Flowers* and *Basi and Company*, and the wonderfully weird *Le Regard du roi*, trapped in a polemic since Camara Laye's death, are only a few.

ter types we have read—have taught us anything, it is to be wary of forcing them to do what they do not want to do. None of that, of course, is to imply that categorization must be so broad as to be meaningless. I argue for character typology in line with Northrop Frye's statement that the "theme of the comic is the integration of society, which usually takes the form of incorporating a central character into it." This character, the comic hero, "will get his triumph whether what he has done is sensible or silly, honest or rascally" (43). That triumph, as I have tried to show, may involve its own impish categorization wherein the butt of the joke and the reader are placed in one bracket. Humor hints that just as the comic hero laughs at others, the comic writer, in the end, could very well be laughing at us.

The enjoyable uncertainties inherent to the typologies manifest in the relationship among multilingualism, implicit and explicit differences, and hierarchies. Hierarchies can be among Ananse-type characters and rules, upper and lower classes, colonizers and the colonized, Wangrin and everybody, leaders and followers, men and women, the youth and their elders, pastors and congregants. For their part, modern African literatures frequently inhabit a space between orality and literacy; between local languages spoken by many characters and the English or French (or Portuguese) used by a narration; between local cultures and state-sponsored modernity. To produce a certain effect in its consumers, the literature often relies on their familiarity with both spaces. Therefore, textual mediation is reflective of a kind of cultural mediation. The trickster showcases tensions between institutions and conceptions of morality. The mimic quite literally opposes black to white. The interpreter pits mutually unintelligible languages against each other. The deviant norm embodies the interplay between serious conventions and deviancy. Given these unending negotiations, the comic character is a possible *figure* of the African text.

If categorization should not be overly expansive, it must not be so narrow as to reduce African humor into another sort of essentialism. African literatures themselves are best placed to orient us toward their humorous facets, which are revealed when we privilege their literariness and aesthetics. In *Come to Laugh*, Bame mentions "the habit of dramatization and a focus for laughter which Ghanaians share with other Africans and indeed with other peoples of the world" (5). Such reminders, about the universality of humorous laughter, speak to an issue in some studies that do focus on African humor. Many betray an anxious tendency, almost at every turn, to recite the reasons Africans should *not* be laughing. It is as though something Africans do every

Conclusion • 163

day were a wonder, and as though the study of that phenomenon were itself a guilty pleasure. I have referred to Bergson's "momentary anesthesia of the heart," which, he explains, is necessary for appreciating the comic. Pushing that concept further in this setting reveals a particularly intentional perspective of the world. I am not suggesting a humorous predisposition innate to all Africans but, rather, the presence of an attitude or cultivated "habit" like the one Bame proposes.

I touched on the importance of existent, indigenous approaches to laughter, and orality can be illuminating in this regard. Barbara Christian notes, eloquently, that "people of color have always theorized . . . often in narrative forms, in the stories we create, in riddles and proverbs, in the play with language, because dynamic rather than fixed ideas seem more to our liking" (68). There must be at least as many proverbs about humor or laughter as there are African languages. I limit myself once more to Akan in the Mfantse saying *Fa bi yɛ serew*—literally, "turn some of it into laughter." *Fa bi yɛ serew* is a prompt to find something "in there" to laugh at, to laugh regardless but not arbitrarily or thoughtlessly. It is not passively defaulting to laughter because the only alternative is crying or raging, but a clear-eyed admonition to seek the amusing—not the stubbornly positive; it is not a call to complacency—for one's own sake and to refuse to take one's ultimately ridiculous neighbors, circumstances, or oneself too seriously. It highlights the deliberate rejection of a humorless vision of one's world and is why some storytellers look *beyond* the better known but less sympathetic versions of these typologies—inhumane fraudsters, tragic mimics, a shamefully treacherous comprador bourgeoisie, and wicked dictators—and turn some of what they see there into laughter.

While looking backward we can simultaneously look forward at new forms of storytelling in the proliferation of humorous genres on social media and digital sharing platforms.[2] Many offer original takes on themes that by now should be familiar, such as the following skit starring the comedian Mark Angel and his partner, the child actress Emmanuella. At a film audition somewhere in Nigeria, children are seated in front of a meal that, according to the plot they are given, has been poisoned by their stepmother.[3] Each child is supposed to "die" while eating. Halfway through some rice and stew, one boy dies dutifully, if unconvincingly. When it is her turn, Emmanuella, who

---

2. There is a growing body of work on African digital literatures and their humor.

3. "The Audition, Episode 105." *YouTube*, uploaded by MarkAngelComedy, 17 March 2017, https://www.youtube.com/watch?v=Qhnn8cLnwVs

was dragged along, hungry, by her pushy uncle Mark, verifies that she can eat the food "real" but that she will not die "real-real." The film crew tell her, indulgently, that it is her story. At that, Emmanuella transforms into a ravenous sinkhole. She gorges herself as capably as any competitive eater, showing no signs of distress or dying. The crew are stunned into silence while her desperate uncle hisses at his money ticket to "die! Emmanuella! Die! Die! Die!" Emmanuella refuses to do any such thing until she has licked the bowls and gulped down water. Only then does she begin to convulse spectacularly. The story ends on this dialogue:

> DIRECTOR: Cut! Cut! He said your stepmother put poison in the food! Eat it and die while eating! But you finished the food and even drank water before dying.
> EMMANUELLA (*licking her chops*): But the poison was not in the food. It was in the water.
> DIRECTOR: No! Your stepmother put the poison in the food, and not the water.
> EMMANUELLA (*gesticulating defensively*): Is it your stepmother? Is it not my stepmother? It's my story, *na*.

This video is a drop in the bucket of online comedies but I selected it for a few reasons. First of all, it highlights a female lead taking charge of a comic narrative and not just adapting to it. Furthermore, this sketch embraces old trickster qualities but with a difference—here, the "new" trickster is even a girl. The trickster in the age of the internet shows the continued centrality of orality and of indigenous attitudes to humor. Today's texts lay the foundation for texts of the future, and humor provides an avenue for understanding the nature of African intertextuality. The Mark Angel video also renews the theme of the hungry, abused, and exploited African child but, in the spirit of *Fa bi ye serew*, finds something funny even "in there." In a similar vein, it shows that African humor involves self-reflection as well as a wry self-deprecation toward the narrative tendencies of African stories, such as overused Nollywood tropes around wicked stepmothers. And, finally, the truth is that it was impossible to resist sharing one last, brilliantly funny story.

This book considers that humor is best addressed by a multipronged approach. Essentially, humor expresses doubleness, ambivalence, or doubt. Ambivalence gives an edge to things: look at it this way and you see one thing; look at it another, and you see something else. In fact, it will have struck the reader that the typologies I employ are quite porous. Over the course of the analyses, it becomes evident that some of the "mimics" could make the criteria for "interpreters," just as many "interpreters" could fit comfortably under the category of "trickster." In fact, at heart, all of the character types display trickster tendencies.

The trickster mind-set highlights different kinds of incongruity. This may be in terms of resource access and distribution (scarcity and plenty, affluence and indigence). Incongruity also has to do with the vulgarity of man, especially the failings of the human body that provoke judgment from the reader or audience, who are assumed to be arbiters of better taste and yet who still laugh. It is in the difference between content and the treatment that a writer might choose. Incongruity likewise manifests in the differences between home and abroad. The trickster-interpreter emphasizes the hypocrisy of the colonial powers. But though he is dishonest, he is celebrated and rarely condemned. Perhaps the narrator also thinks that claims to civilization and transcendent morality are false and hypocritical. In the end, the colonizers themselves show that there is only ever self-interest. The trickster mind-set comes through, as well, in the attitude people take to their heads of parties, households, and other organizations. Furthermore, the wife manipulating the man while making him think he is in charge is the trickster mentality transposed onto the domestic scene.

At heart, it seems that trickster stories are a comment on the nature of society. The trickster believes that claims to know-how, education, or edification based on qualification are a cover. In the end, he seems to say, everyone is on the same level. For that reason, hierarchies are to be viewed with deep suspicion. This is a subversive kind of knowledge; it is potentially liberating but also a profoundly cynical view of human relations. The trickster's laughter is partly based on the superiority that comes from recognizing this but also on his clear-sighted worldview that looks beyond self-righteousness and that recognizes that few have an unshakeable claim to authority, moral or otherwise. There is, therefore, humor in the contrast between rigid rules and crafty improvisation. Noble, unfunny rhetoric and rigid morality are consistently reduced to sources of humor. This humor seems to imply that heroism and stiff uprightness are hollow. That may even explain why a significant portion of African writing is not humorous. A lot of African literature is read through the lens of historicity, mimetics, and didacticism. It insists on morality, courage, uprightness, and all virtuous things as a way of holding the unjust world to account. But comic writing reminds us that inflexible morality is not enough, that power is what makes the world we live in, and power is rarely a question of virtue.

"There is no other subject," as Max Eastman says, "besides God and laughter, toward which the scientific mind has ever advocated so explicit and particular a humility" (134). God and laughter are indeed to be approached with caution not only because they cannot be pinned down but also because they can quite easily humble whoever tries to ride roughshod over them. Thus, if a sense of uncertainty colors our role as readers so that we are unsure where the writer is coming from; if a person laughing can as easily become a source of laughter; if words can be denuded of their meanings; if, indeed, we find things funny but cannot unerringly say why, then the trickster is quite right to encourage us to laugh anyway—*yɛmfa bi nyɛ serew*—because "only God nose" anything with any certainty.

REFERENCES

Abarry, Abu Shardow. "The Significance of Names in Ghanaian Drama." *Journal of Black Studies* 22, no. 2 (1991): 157–167.

Achebe, Chinua. *Arrow of God*, 2nd ed., rev. Heinemann, 1992.

Achebe, Chinua. "The Novelist as Teacher." *Hopes and Impediments: Selected Essays.* Anchor Books, 1990: 40–31. Achebe, Chinua. *Things Fall Apart.* Heinemann, 1996.

Adichie, Chimamanda. *Americanah. 2013. Anchor Books, 2014.*

Adu-Amankwah, David. "Akan Humor." In *Encyclopedia of Humor Studies*, edited by Salvatore Attardo. SAGE Publications, 2014.

Agualusa, José Eduardo. *My Father's Wives.* Arcadia Books, 2008.

Angelelli, Claudia V., and Brian James Baer, eds. *Researching Translation and Interpreting.* Routledge, 2015.

Ansah, Kwaw, dir. *Heritage Africa.* Film Africa Limited, 1988.

Ansah, Kwaw, dir. *Praising the Lord Plus One.* Film Africa Limited, 2013.

Aristotle. *Nicomachean Ethics.* Translated by D. P. Chase. Cosimo Classics, 2007.

Aristotle. *Rhetoric.* Translated by W. Rhys Roberts. Courier Corporation, 2004.

Ashcroft, Bill, Gareth Griffiths, and Helen Tiffin, eds. *The Post-Colonial Studies Reader.* Taylor & Francis, 2006.

Asiedu, Awo Mana. "The Enduring Relevance of Kobina Sekyi's *The Blinkards* in Twenty-First-Century Ghana." In *African Literatures and Beyond: A Florilegium*, edited by Bernth Lindfors, 39–54. Rodopi, 2013.

Astruc, Rémi. "Transformations de l'Afrique, transformations du rire." *Humoresques* 38 (2013): 5–13.

Attardo, Salvatore, ed. *The Routledge Handbook of Language and Humor.* Taylor & Francis, 2017.

Bakhtin, Mikhail Mikhaïlovich. *Rabelais and His World.* Indiana University Press, 1984.

Ball, John Clement. *Satire and the Postcolonial Novel: VS Naipaul, Chinua Achebe, Salman Rushdie.* Routledge, 2003.

Bame, Kwabena N. *Come to Laugh: African Traditional Theatre in Ghana.* Lilian Barber Press, 1985.

168 • *References*

Basamalah, Salah. "L-Aphilosophie de la traduction ladmiralienne." *Spirale* 258 (2016): 31–33.

Bassnett, Susan, and André Lefevere. "General Editors' Preface." In *The Translator's Invisibility: A History of Translation*, edited by Lawrence Venuti, vii–viii. Routledge, 1995.

Baudelaire, Charles. *De L'Essence du rire et généralement du comique dans les arts plastiques.* Collections Litteratura.com, 1855.

Belmessous, Saliha, ed. *Empire by Treaty: Negotiating European Expansion, 1600–1900.* Oxford University Press, 2014.

Benabed, Fella. "Ethnotextual Mental Translation and Self-Translation in African Literature." *Ars Aeterna* 9, no. 2 (2017): 71–80.

Bergson, Henri. *Le Rire: Essai sur la signification du comique.* Chicoutimi: Les Classiques des sciences sociales, 2002.

Bergson, Henri. *Laughter: An Essay on the Meaning of the Comic.* Temple of the Earth Publishing, 2008.

Berman, Antoine, Isabelle Berman, and Valentina Sommella. *Jacques Amyot, Traducteur français: Essai sur les origines de la traduction en France.* 2012.

Berrong, Richard M. *Rabelais and Bakhtin: Popular Culture in Gargantua and Pantagruel.* University of Nebraska Press, 1986.

Beti, Mongo. *Le Pauvre Christ de Bomba.* Présence africaine, 1976.

Bhabha, Homi. *The Location of Culture.* Routledge, 2012.

Bhabha, Homi. "Signs Taken for Wonders: Questions of Ambivalence and Authority under a Tree outside Delhi, May 1817." *Critical Inquiry* 12, no. 1 (1985): 144–165.

Block, Elizabeth. *The Effects of Divine Manifestation on the Reader's Perspective in Vergil's Aeneid.* Ayer Company, 1984.

Bühler, Alex. "Translation as Interpreting." In *Translation Studies: Perspectives on an Emerging Discipline*, edited by Alessandra Riccardi. Cambridge University Press, 2002: 56–74.

Burton, Tim, dir. *Sweeney Todd: The Demon Barber of Fleet Street.* DreamWorks Pictures, 2007.

Carroll, Noël. *Humour: A Very Short Introduction.* Oxford University Press, 2014.

Cary, Joyce. *Mister Johnson.* 1939. Michael Joseph, 1961.

Casely Hayford, Joseph Ephraim. *Ethiopia Unbound: Studies in Race Emancipation.* C. M. Philips, 1911.

Casely Hayford, Joseph Ephraim. *The Truth about the West African Land Question.* C. M. Philips, 1913.

Chambers, Robert. *Cyclopaedia of English literature.* Vol. 1. Chambers, 1858.

Chaplin, Charlie, dir. *The Gold Rush.* Charlie Chaplin Productions, 1925.

Chapman, Antony, and Hugh Foot, eds. *Humour and Laughter: Theory, Research and Applications.* 1911. John Wiley, 1976.

Chevrier, Jacques. "La ruse dans L'Étrange destin de Wangrin." In *Lectures de l'œuvre d'Hampaté Bâ*, edited by Robert Jouanny, 41–52. L'Harmattan, 1992.

Christian, Barbara. "The Race for Theory." *Feminist Studies* 14, no. 1 (Spring 1988): 67–79.

Cole, Catherine M. *Ghana's Concert Party Theatre*. Indiana University Press, 2001.

Critchley, Simon. *On Humour*. Routledge, 2002.

Cronin, Michael. "The Empire Talks Back: Orality, Heteronomy, and the Cultural Turn in Interpreting Studies." In *The Interpreting Studies Reader*, edited by Franz Pöchhacker and Miriam Shlesinger, 387–397. Routledge, 2002.

Daniel, G. "Song of Lawino: Un cas de contestation en Afrique." *Canadian Journal of African Studies/La Revue canadienne des études africaines* 5, no. 2 (1971): 193–212.

Davis, Jessica Milner. "Farce." In *Encyclopedia of Humor Studies*, edited by Salvatore Attardo. SAGE Publications, 2014.

Deloria, Vine, Jr. *Spirit & Reason: The Vine Deloria, Jr. Reader*. Fulcrum Publishing, 1999.

Delisle, Jean, and Judith Woodsworth. *Les Traducteurs dans l'histoire*. Vol. 3. Les Presses de l'Université Laval, 2014.

de Moraes, Farias Paulo F., and Karin Barber, eds. *Self-assertion and Brokerage: Early Cultural Nationalism in West Africa*. University of Birmingham Press, 1990.

de Sousa, Ronald. *The Rationality of Emotion*. MIT Press, 1987.

de Souza, Pascale. "Trickster Strategies in Alain Mabanckou's *Black Bazar*." *Research in African Literatures* 42, no. 1 (2011): 102–119.

Dirks, Nicholas B. "Colonial Histories and Native Informants: Biography of an Archive." In *Orientalism and the Postcolonial Predicament: Perspectives on South Asia*, edited by Carol A. Breckenridge and Peter Van Der Veer, 279–313. University of Pennsylvania Press, 1993.

Eastman, Max. *The Sense of Humor*. C. Scribner's Sons, 1921.

Evwierhoma, Mabel. "Pastoral Verbal Performance and Visual Aesthetics: Brother Jero's Cape as Sign." *Matatu* 39 (2011): 493–502.

Farnoud, Esmaeel. "Methodologie de la critique des traductions." *Linguistic and Philosophical Investigations* 13 (2014): 272–280.

Finnegan, Ruth. *Oral Literature in Africa*. Open Book Publishers, 2012.

Forster, Edward Morgan. *Aspects of the Novel*. Arnold, 1927.

Freud, Sigmund. *Wit and Its Relation to the Unconscious: An Authorized English Edition*. Kegan Paul, Trench, Trubner and Co., 1917.

Frye, Northrop. *Anatomy of Criticism*. Princeton University Press, 1957.

Fugard, Athol. *Sizwe Bansi Is Dead and The Island*. Viking Press, 1987.

Garane, Jeanne. "The Invisibility of the African Interpreter." *Translation: A Transdisciplinary Journal* (Fall 2015): 1–33, https://sc.edu/study/colleges_schools/artsandscien ces/dllc/our_people/garane_jeanne.php

Gates, Henry Louis. *The Signifying Monkey: A Theory of African American Literary Criticism*. Oxford University Press, 2014.

Gates, Henry Louis. "Writing 'Race' and the Difference It Makes." *Critical Inquiry* 12, no. 1 (1985): 1–20.

Genette, Gérard. "Morts de rire." *Des Genres et des œuvres*. Seuil, 2012, 411–522.

170 • *References*

Gérard, Albert S. "1500 Years of Creative Writing in Black Africa." *Research in African Literatures* 12, no. 2 (1981): 147–161.

Gibbs, James. "Seeking the Founding Father: The Story of Kobina Sekyi's *The Blinkards* (1916)." In *African Theatre: Histories 1850–1950*, edited by Yvette Hutchison and Jane Plastow, 23–37. James Currey, 2010.

Gikandi, Simon. *Encyclopedia of African Literature*. Routledge, 2003.

Haliburton, Gordon M. "Mark Christian Hayford: A Non-Success Story." *Journal of Religion in Africa* 12, no. 1 (1981): 20–37.

Hampâté Bâ, Amadou. *The Fortunes of Wangrin*. Translated by Aina Pavolini Taylor. Indiana University Press, 1999.

Hampâté Bâ, Amadou. *L'Etrange destin de Wangrin ou Les Roueries d'un interprète africain*. Édition 10/18, 1973.

Harmon, William, and C. Hugh Holman. *A Handbook to Literature*. Longman, 2012.

Harrison, Helen L. "Myths and Metaphors of Food in Oyono's *Une Vie de boy*." *French Review* 74, no. 5 (2001): 924–933.

Heilman, Robert B. "The *Taming* Untamed, or, The Return of the Shrew." In *The Taming of the Shrew: Critical Essays*, edited by Dana E. Aspinall, 45–57. Routledge, 2002.

Hobbes, Thomas. *Leviathan, or, the Matter, Forme and Power of a Commonwealth Ecclesiasticall and Civil*. Touchstone, 2008.

Hokenson, Jan. *The Idea of Comedy: History, Theory, Critique*. Fairleigh Dickinson University Press, 2006.

Hope, Christopher. *Darkest England*. Atlantic Books Ltd, 2015.

Hyde, Lewis. *Trickster Makes This World: Mischief, Myth, and Art*. Macmillan, 1997.

Irele, Abiola. *The African Imagination*. Oxford University Press, 2001.

Jakobson, Roman. "On Linguistic Aspects of Translation." In *On Translation*, edited by Reuben Arthur, 233–239. Harvard University Press, 1959.

Johnston, Andrew James. "The Exegetics of Laughter: Religious Parody in Chaucer's *Miller's Tale*." In *A History of English Laughter: Laughter from Beowulf to Beckett and Beyond*, edited by Manfred Pfister, 17–33. Rodopi, 2002.

Jones, Roderick. *Conference Interpreting Explained*. Routledge, 2014.

Jung, Carl. *The Archetypes and the Collective Unconscious*. 1959. Taylor & Francis, 2014.

Jungwha, Choi. "The Interpretive Theory of Translation and Its Current Applications." Hankuk University of Foreign Studies, 2003.

Kamalu, Ikenna. "Metaphor and the Absurd: Reimagining the Discourse on Nationhood in Ola Rotimi's Plays. *Journal of English and Literature* 2, no.8 (2011): 182–189.

Konadu, Kwasi, and Clifford C. Campbell, eds. *The Ghana Reader: History, Culture, Politics*. Duke University Press, 2016.

Kortenaar, Neil ten. "Law and Literature in the Postcolony." *Cambridge Journal of Postcolonial Literary Inquiry* 2, no. 1 (2015): 1–4.

Kortenaar, Neil ten. "Chinua Achebe and the Question of Modern African Tragedy." *Philosophia Africana* 9, no.2 (2006): 83–101.

Kourouma, Ahmadou. *Les Soleils des indépendances*. Seuil, 2013.

Ladmiral, Jean-René. "Préface." In *Traduire, transmettre ou trahir?: Réflexions sur la traduction en sciences humaines*, edited by Stephanie Schwerter, xi–xvi. Maison des Sciences de l'homme, 2013.

Ladmiral, Jean-René. *Sourcier ou cibliste*. Les Belles Lettres, 2014.

Lambert, Michael C. "From Citizenship to Négritude: 'Making a Difference' in Elite Ideologies of Colonized Francophone West Africa." *Comparative Studies in Society and History* 35, no. 2 (1993): 239–262.

Langley, Ayo, Introduction to Sekyi, Kobina. *The Blinkards: A Comedy*. Readwide Publishers/Heinemann Educational, 1997: xiii–xxix.

Larson, Charles. "Heroic Ethnocentrism: The Idea of Universality in Literature." *The Post-Colonial Studies Reader*, edited by Bill Ashcroft, Gareth Griffiths, and Helen Tiffin, 62–65. Taylor & Francis, 2006.

Laye, Camara. *Le Regard du roi: roman*. Pocket, 1975.

Lederer, Marianne, and Danica Seleskovitch. *Interpréter pour traduire*. Les Belles Lettres, 2014.

LeVine, Robert A. "Sex Roles and Economic Change in Africa." *Ethnology* 5, no. 2 (1966): 186–193.

Lindfors, Bernth. "Politics, Culture and Literary Form in Black Africa." *Colby Quarterly* 15, no. 4 (1979): 240–251.

Lippitt, John. "Philosophical Perspectives on Humour and Laughter." PhD Diss. Duke University, 1991.

Lunel, Ernest. *Le Théâtre et la Révolution*. Slatkine, 1970.

Luske, Hamilton, dir. *Mickey and the Beanstalk*. Disney, 1947.

Lynn, Thomas Jay. "Postcolonial Encounters Re-Envisioned: Kojo Laing's Woman of the Aeroplanes as Trickster Narrative." *Tradition and Change in East and West African Fiction*, edited by Ogaga Okuyade, 153–166. Rodopi, 2014.

Mabanckou, Alain. "'The Song of The Migrating Bird': For a World Literature in French." Translated by Dominic Thomas. *Forum for Modern Language Studies* 45, no. 2 (2008): 144–150.

Mabanckou, Alain, and Helen Stevenson. *Broken Glass*. Serpent's Tail, 2010.

Macaulay, Thomas Babington, and H. Woodrow. *Macaulay's Minutes on Education in India: Written in the Years 1835, 1836, and 1837 and Now First Collected from Records in the Department of Public Instruction*. CB Lewis, at the Baptist Mission Press, 1862.

Mbembe, Achille. *On the Postcolony*. University of California Press, 2001.

McGowan, Todd. *Only a Joke Can Save Us: A Theory Of Comedy*. Northwestern University Press, 2017.

Mda, Zakes. *Ways of Dying*. Picador, 2007.

Migeot, François, and François Baverey, eds. *Texte, lecture et interprétation: Hommage à Thomas Aron*. Diffusion les belles lettres, 1991.

Milbury-Steen, Sarah L. *European and African Stereotypes in Twentieth-Century Fiction*. Springer, 1980.

172 • *References*

Molière. *Œuvres complètes*. Ed. Georges Forestier. Vol. I & II. Gallimard–Bibliothèque de la Pléiade, 2010.

Molière. "Le Bourgeois gentilhomme." *Œuvres complètes*. Ed. Georges Forestier. Vol. I. Gallimard–Bibliothèque de la Pléiade, 2010.

Molière. "Les Femmes savantes." *Œuvres complètes*. Ed. Georges Forestier. Vol. II. Gallimard–Bibliothèque de la Pléiade, 2010.

Molière. "Les Fourberies de Scapin." *Œuvres complètes*. Ed. Georges Forestier. Vol. II. Gallimard–Bibliothèque de la Pléiade, 2010.

Morreall, John. *Comic Relief: A Comprehensive Philosophy of Humor*. John Wiley & Sons, 2011.

Mortier, Daniel. *Le Triomphe du valet de comédie: Plaute, Goldoni, Beaumarchais, Hofmannsthal*. Champion, 2000.

Mounin, Georges. *Les Belles infidèles*. 1955. Presses Universitaires du Septentrion, 2016.

Naipaul, V. S. *A House for Mr. Biswas*. 1961. Picador, 2003.

Ndebele, Njabulo Simakahle. *South African Literature and Culture: Rediscovery of the Ordinary*. Manchester University Press, 1994.

Ndiaye, Christiane. "Ceci n'est pas un vieux nègre. Le corps ambivalent chez Oyono." *Etudes* françaises 3, no. 1 (1995): 23–38.

Newell, Stephanie. *Literary Culture in Colonial Ghana: How to Play the Game of Life*. Indiana University Press, 2002.

Newell, Stephanie. "Local Cosmopolitans in Colonial West Africa." *Journal of Commonwealth Literature* 46, no. 1 (2011): 103–117.

Ngũgĩ wa Thiong'o. *Decolonising the Mind: The Politics of Language in African Literature*. 1986. East African Publishers, 1992.

Nicholson, Nancy Schweda. "Translation and Interpretation." *Annual Review of Applied Linguistics* 15 (1995): 42–62.

Nola, Bienvenu. *Le Vieux nègre et la médaille: Essai d'analyse argumentative*. Harmattan, 2008.

Noonan, Will. "Reflecting Back, or, What Can the French Tell the English about Humour?" *Sydney Studies in English* 37 (2011): 92–115.

Nwokolo, Chuma. *Diaries of a Dead African*. Gwandustan, Kindle Edition, 2003.

Obadare, Ebenezer. *Humor, Silence, and Civil Society in Nigeria*. Boydell & Brewer, 2016.

Obadare, Ebenezer. "The Uses of Ridicule: Humour, 'Infrapolitics' and Civil Society in Nigeria." *African Affairs* 108, no. 431 (2009): 241–261.

Ochulor, Nwaugo Goodseed. "A Pragmatic Approach to the Ideological and Power Perspectives in *Our Husband Has Gone Mad Again* by Ola Rotimi." *Journal of Humanities and Social Sciences* 20, no. 8 (2015): 52–62.

Oguine, Ike. *A Squatter's Tale*. Heinemann, 2000.

Ogungbesan, Kolawole. "Politics and the African Writer." *African Studies Review* 17, no. 1 (1974): 43–53.

Olateju, Moji A., and Yisa Kehinde Yusuf. "Backchannel Communication in Ola

Rotimi's *Our Husband Has Gone Mad Again.*" *Nordic Journal of African Studies* 15, no. 4 (2006): 520–535.

Opoku-Agyemang, Naana Jane. "Gender-Role Perceptions in the Akan Folktale." *Research in African Literatures* 30, no. 1 (1999): 116–139.

Oriola, Taiwo A. "Advance Fee Fraud on the Internet: Nigeria's Regulatory Response." *Computer Law & Security Review* 21, no. 3 (2005): 237–248.

Oyono, Ferdinand. *Le Vieux nègre et la médaille.* Julliard, 1956.

Oyono, Ferdinand. *The Old Man and the Medal.* Translated by John Reed. Heinemann, 1967.

Palmer, Jerry. *Taking Humour Seriously.* Routledge, 2003.

p'Bitek, Okot. *Song of Lawino and Song of Ocol.* Heinemann, 1985.

Pelton, Robert D. *The Trickster in West Africa: A Study of Mythic Irony and Sacred Delight.* University of California Press, 1989.

Perego, Elizabeth M. "Emasculating Humor from Algeria's Dark Decade, 1991–2002." *International Journal of Middle East Studies* 52, no. 1 (2020): 67–86.

Perks, Lisa Glebatis. "The Ancient Roots of Humor Theory." *Humor* 25, no. 2 (2012): 119–132.

Plaatje, Sol T. "The Essential Interpreter." In *Selected Writings*, edited by Sol T. Plaatje and Brian Willan, 50–61. Witwatersrand University Press, 1996.

Plato, and Alan Bloom. *Philebus.* Global Grey e-books, 2018.

Plato, and Alan Bloom. *The Republic of Plato. Translated with Notes and an Interpretive Essay.* HarperCollins, 1968.

Pöchhacker, Franz. *Introducing Interpreting Studies.* Routledge, 2016.

Prest, Julia. *Controversy in French Drama: Molière's* Tartuffe *and the Struggle for Influence.* Palgrave Macmillan, 2014.

Price-Mars, Jean. *Ainsi parla l'Oncle suivi de Revisiter l'Oncle.* Mémoire d'encrier, 2009.

Provine, Robert R. "Laughter." *American Scientist* 84, no.1 (1996): 38–45.

Pype, Katrien. "Of Fools and False Pastors: Tricksters in Kinshasa's Television Fiction." *Visual Anthropology* 23, no. 2 (2010): 115–135.

Quayson, Ato. *Oxford Street.* Duke University Press, 2014.

Quayson, Ato. *Strategic Transformations in Nigerian Writing.* James Currey, 1997.

Ranger, Terence. "The Invention of Tradition in Colonial Africa." In *The Invention of Tradition*, edited by Eric Hopsbawm and Terence Ranger, 211–262. Cambridge University Press, 2012.

Rao, Sathya. "L'Etrange destin de Wangrin or the Political Accommodation of Interpretation." In *Translating and Interpreting Conflict*, edited by Myriam Salama-Carr, 221–232. Brill, 2007.

Ray, Carina E. *Crossing the Color Line: Race, Sex, and the Contested Politics of Colonialism in Ghana.* Ohio University Press, 2015.

Reichl, Susanne, and Mark Stein, eds. *Cheeky Fictions: Laughter and the Postcolonial.* Rodopi, 2005.

174 • *References*

Rivera, Maria M. "Invisibility vs. Transparency." *Un Idioma: Professional Language Group*, 02 (Jan. 2013).

Ross, Alison. *The Language of Humour*. Routledge, 2005.

Rotimi, Ola. *Our Husband Has Gone Mad Again*. Twentieth-Century Drama Full Text Database, 2006, http://collections.chadwyck.com.myaccess.library.utoronto.ca

Sareil, Jean. *L'Écriture comique*. Presses Universitaires de France, 1984.

Sareil, Jean. "La Démolition comique de l'idéologie." *Romanic Review* 75, no. 1 (1984): 1–9.

Saro-Wiwa, Ken. *A Forest of Flowers. Longman, 1995*.

Saro-Wiwa, Ken. *Basi and Company: A Modern African Folktale*. Saros International, 1987.

Schaeffer, Neil. *The Art of Laughter*. Columbia University Press, 1981

Schilling, Bernard Nicholas. *The Comic Spirit, Boccaccio to Thomas Mann: Giovanni Boccaccio, Charles Dickens, Henry Fielding, Israel Zangwill, Thomas Mann*. Wayne State University Press, 1965.

Sekyi, H. V. H. Foreword to Sekyi, Kobina. In *The Blinkards: A Comedy*. Readwide Publishers/Heinemann Educational, 1997: vii–xi.

Sekyi, Kobina. *The Blinkards: A Comedy*. Readwide Publishers/Heinemann Educational, 1997.

Shipley, Jesse Weaver. "Comedians, Pastors, and the Miraculous Agency of Charisma in Ghana." *Cultural Anthropology* 24, no. 3 (2009): 523–552.

Shoba, Jo Arthur, and Kari Dako. "'Locally Acquired Foreign Accent' (LAFA) in Contemporary Ghana." *World Englishes* 32, no. 2 (2013): 230–242.

Shoneyin, Lola. *The Secret Lives of Baba Segi's Wives*. HarperCollins e-books, 2010.

Shumway, Rebecca. "Palavers and Treaty Making in the British Acquisition of the Gold Coast Colony (West Africa)." In *Empire by Treaty: Negotiating European Expansion, 1600–1900*, edited by Saliha Belmessous, Oxford University Press, 2014: 161–185.

Souriau, Étienne. *Les Deux cent mille situations dramatiques*. Flammarion, 1951.

Soyinka, Wole. *The Interpreters*. 1965. Africana Publishing Corp., 1972.

Soyinka, Wole. *The Jero Plays*. Eyre Methuen, 1973.

Soyinka, Wole. *Jero's Metamorphosis*. 1971. In Soyinka, *The Jero Plays*. Eyre Methuen, 1973.

Soyinka, Wole. *The Lion and the Jewel*. 1966. Alexander Street Press LLC, 2016.

Soyinka, Wole. *The Trials of Brother Jero*. 1963. In Soyinka, *The Jero Plays*. Eyre Methuen, 1973.

Spencer, Herbert. "The Physiology of Laughter." *Macmillan's Magazine, 1859–1907* 1, no. 5 (1860): 395–402.

Tenkorang, S. "The Founding of Mfantsipim 1905–1908." *Transactions of the Historical Society of Ghana* 15, no. 2 (1974): 165–175.

Utudjian, Eliane Saint-André. "Uses and Misuses of English in *The Blinkards* by Kobina Sekyi." *Commonwealth (Dijon)* 20, no. 1 (1997): 23–31.

van der Geest, Sjaak. "Scatological Children's Humour: Notes from the Netherlands and Anywhere." *Humor* 28, no. 1 (2016): 127–140.

Venuti, Lawrence, *The Translator's Invisibility: A History of Translation*. Routledge, 2008.

Voltaire. *Dictionnaire philosophique*. Le Chasseur abstrait, 2005.

Weems, Scott. *Ha!: The Science of When We Laugh and Why*. Basic Books, 2014.

Wittenberg, Hermann. "The Boer and the Jackal: Satire and Resistance in Khoi Orature." *Critical Arts* 28, no. 4 (2014): 593–609.

Wodehouse, Pelham Grenville. *The Jeeves Collection*. Douglas Editions, 2010

Yankah, Kwesi. *Speaking for the Chief: Okyeame and the Politics of Akan Royal Oratory*. Indiana University Press, 1995.

INDEX

Aborigines' Rights Protection Society, 63,
    71, 73
aborɔfosɛm, 65, 67
    See also foreign cultures and insanities
accents, 147
    locally acquired but foreign, 61, 75, 76
Achebe, Chinua
    Arrow of God, 31, 116, 123, 128
    "The Novelist as Teacher," 63
    Things Fall Apart 3, 10, 22, 32, 79, 87,
        100, 102–107, 113, 130
advance-fee fraud, 24, 25, 29
    See also con men
African borders, 9
    See also Partition of Africa
African diversity, 6, 135
African traditions, 72, 150
aggression, 5, 11, 56, 135
Akan 1, 3, 20, 21, 61, 66, 72, 77, 103, 163
    See also Fanti; Mfantse; Twi
ambivalence, 8, 20, 30
    toward mimics 64, 77
    toward tricksters 26, 58
amorality, 20, 42, 45, 100
    See also immorality; morality
Ananse, Kweku, 20, 21, 26, 41, 162
animism, 120, 121
Ansah, Kwaw, 51
Anthropocene, 4
anticlimax, 25, 109, 110
Apartheid, 102, 110
appetite, 20, 33, 34, 46
    See also starvation

approximations, 6
Aristotle, 11, 16, 17, 18
attack, 16, 32, 48, 49, 97
    See also satire; Surprise and Attack
audience, 1, 2, 3, 5–10, 13, 18, 26, 33, 45,
        47—50, 55–59, 68, 69, 72, 75, 76, 79,
        103, 100, 138, 142, 151, 152, 158, 165
    jeering, 53, 60, 110
    intended, 84, 86, 88, 109
    rapport, 47, 48, 50, 99, 136
authority of foreign texts, 80, 81
autobiography, 29
    See also self-narrated humor
awkwardness, 4, 21, 56, 60, 90, 108, 132,
    146, 157, 160

Bakhtin, Mikhail
    Rabelais and His World, 19, 34, 51–55,
        58, 59, 95, 137–143
Ball, John, 4, 5
Bame, Kwabena
    Come to Laugh, 3, 84, 162, 163
Barber, Karin, 67, 78
barefaced lies, 110-113, 117
bathos, 49
Benigni, Roberto, 5
Bergson, Henri
    *Le Rire: Essai sur la signification du
        comique*, 27, 30, 35, 43, 44, 46, 55,
        68, 82, 91
Beti, Mongo
    Le Pauvre Christ de Bomba, 5, 19, 161
Bible, 2, 51, 53, 81

178 • *Index*

Big Men, 10
   See also polygamy
black and white. *See* Manicheanism
black Frenchmen, 115
   See also policy of assimilation
bodily functions, 34, 55, 94, 138, 142, 152
   See also scatology
boredom, 6, 14, 109
bovarysme collectif, 81
buffoonery, 134, 135
butt of the joke, 111, 162

Cape Coast, 66–72, 80, 82, 84, 87, 90
   See also Ghana; Gold Coast
caricature, 49, 82, 144, 150, 157
carnival, 51, 53, 54, 55, 59
Carroll, Noël, 14, 16, 30, 134, 53, 158
Cary, Joyce
   Mister Johnson, 122, 125, 125
center, 19, 60, 63, 64, 135, 136, 159
   See also periphery
Chabon, Michael, 39
Chapman, Anthony, 13
children, 36, 46, 56, 79, 119, 136, 142, 163
Christianity, 42, 54, 60
   inspiration from, 21, 48, 51, 52, 120
   power of, 51, 53, 77
   takes on laughter, 15, 52
   See also monotheism; polytheism
cibliste, 105, 106, 107, 111
   See also sourcier
class, 8, 67, 70, 71, 72, 79, 90, 135, 162
classics, 5, 6, 61, 92
clownishness, 7, 8, 134, 136, 148, 155, 160
clumsiness, 61, 64, 67, 70, 80, 98
codes, 42, 52, 156
   foreign, 94, 117
   formal, 20
   societal, 26, 85, 101, 160
code switching, 9
Cole, Catherine
   Ghana's Concert Party Theatre, 72, 77, 84
colonial functionaries, 6, 92, 99, 104, 106, 114–117, 125, 129, 131

   See also commandants
colonialism, 6, 9, 52, 62– 64, 95, 97, 111, 117, 126
   impact of, 5, 65, 67, 101, 102
   resistance to 19, 88, 125
commandants, 97, 117, 118, 121, 124–129
commandement, 95, 136, 139
common sense, 70, 101, 134
communication, 6, 21, 51, 99, 101, 105, 107, 108, 109, 123
community, 1, 3, 26, 38, 42, 54, 56, 58, 125
concert party theatre, 2, 3, 8, 9
condescension, 10, 48, 150
con men, 21, 24, 25, 27
context for humor, 38
conviviality, 136, 139
copycatting, 70, 86
corruption, 132, 143
Cosmopolitan Club, 72, 73, 74, 76, 80, 82, 85
costumes, 69, 82, 83, 140, 146
courtrooms 102, 109, 114, 129, 133, 135
Critchley, Simon 101, 134, 135, 139, 144
Cronin, Michael 104, 120, 122, 128
crowds, 20, 24, 93, 104, 111, 134, 136, 144
crudeness, 65, 67, 85, 150
cultural confusion, 98
culture hero, 28, 40, 53, 77

d'Ablancourt, Nicolas Perrot, 106
decolonization, 4
Deloria Jr., Vine, 26
democracy, 135
desacralization, 52, 55
despots, 140
deviancy, 137, 138, 141, 143, 144
dictionaries, 1, 14, 65, 79
didacticism, 5, 22, 165
dishonesty, 8, 100, 165
domesticity, 118, 138, 159, 165
drama, 43, 59, 90, 99, 108, 144
   as opposed to the comic, 10, 12, 36, 40
dramatic irony, 99, 130
duality, 138

Index · 179

dullness, 29, 85
duplicity, 27, 119, 120

educated natives, 63, 69
Egg Treatment, the, 142
elitism, 65, 67, 79
Englishes 36, 37
   See also Pidgin
ennui, 6, 108, 156
entrepreneurship, 114, 123, 127, 128
Europeanness, 131
exaggeration, 22, 27, 65, 70, 95, 122, 146
excesses, 15, 16, 34, 45, 50, 70, 71, 119, 140, 143
extraecclesiastical, 58

factions, 8, 83
Fanti, 67, 71, 75, 79, 82–89
farce, 33, 96, 134
feminine "stubbornness," 46, 47, 48, 54,
   140, 163, 164
feminine "wiles," 46, 52, 137, 152
   See also sex
fidelity in translation, 100, 106, 107, 110
Finnegan, Ruth, 53
flat characters, 61, 97
Foot, Hugh, 13
foreign cultures and insanities, 62, 86, 99,
   116, 117, 122, 123, 130, 149
formal education, 40, 42, 145, 146, 148,
   152, 154
formal settings, 8, 20, 21, 37, 70, 73, 138,
   139, 154
Forster, E. M., 65
foulness, 45, 46
French Sudan and French West Africa, 98
Freud, Sigmund, 15, 17, 20, 23
Frye, Northrop, 162
Fugard, Athol
   Sizwe Bansi is Dead, 110–113

gaudiness, 140
generational conflict, 87, 154, 156
gender equality, 22, 144, 162
gender-role perceptions and stereotypes,
   135, 148, 154, 159

Genette, Gérard, 12, 19, 27, 36, 38, 139
Ghana, 2, 37, 52, 67
   See also Gold Coast
Ghanaians 1, 3, 61, 69, 162
gibberish, 7, 50
   See also communication
gods, 31, 51, 104, 119, 125, 131
Gold Coast, 52, 62, 66, 69, 71, 78, 90, 94
Gone Fantee, 69
greed 20, 30, 43, 44, 155
   See also hunger and deprivation;
     money
griots, 103, 127
   See ɔkyeame
grotesque, 95, 136, 139
grotesque realism, 94
Guggisberg, Gordon, 69, 78

Hampaté Bâ, Amadou
   L'Etrange destin de Wangrin
     context of, 98–102, 114, 115
     heroism in, 127, 128, 129
     resources in, 123–131
     treachery in, 116–123, 130
Hayford, J. E. Casely, 61
   *Ethiopia Unbound: Studies in Race
     Emancipation,* 64, 69
   *The Truth About the West African Land
     Question,* 61
Heinemann Publishers, 89
Hobbes, Thomas, 15
homophones, 2
honor amongst thieves, 42, 43
humor studies 3, 14
hunger and deprivation, 30
Hutcheson, Francis, 16
Hyde, Lewis, 26, 27, 28, 34, 39, 42, 46
hypocrisy, 57, 58

idealism, 68, 87, 87, 88, 90
Igbo, 10, 103
immorality, 42, 125
impotence, 156–159
   See also sex
incompetence, 105

Index

incomprehension, 123
Incongruity theory of laughter, 17, 64
Indirect Rule, 78, 117
indoctrination, 79
informal education, 21
informal settings, 21, 37, 140
inside jokes, 10, 108, 111
internet humor, 4, 51, 69, 161, 163, 164
involuntary comedy, 38, 39, 139
Irele, Abiola, 101, 104
irony, 25, 43, 126, 131
Islam 120, 121, 137, 145, 153

Jones, Roderick, 100, 101, 116
judgment, 46, 50

Kant, Immanuel, 17, 18
Kinaata, Kofi, 2, 3, 18, 20
Konadu, Kwesi, 79
Kortenaar, Neil ten, 21, 64, 102, 126
Kourouma, Ahmadou, 59, 123

Ladmiral, Jean-René, 105, 106, 108
Lagos, 70, 135, 136, 138, 143
Lambert, Michael C., 115, 117
lampoon, 3
    See also satire
laughing back, 136
Leuk-le-lièvre, 26
    See also Ananse, Kweku
liminality, 28, 42, 60
Lindfors, Bernth, 5
linguistics, 2, 9, 21, 35, 36, 75, 99, 101, 103
Lippitt, John, 15
literacy, 37, 38
    dangers of, 73, 79–82
    transformative power of, 76–79, 162
logic, 33, 84, 142
    peculiar forms of, 27, 43, 59, 106, 134
Lunel, Ernest, 46
Lynn, Thomas, 27, 53, 59

Mabanckou, Alain, 5, 28, 151
Mackenzie, Colin, 116
Manicheanism, 61, 63, 97

manliness, 140, 158, 159
    See also Big Men
Mark Angel, 163, 164
marriage, 62, 67, 72, 133, 145, 148, 153–
    157
    See also polygamy
Maslow, Abraham, 30
material bodily principle, 95, 139
Mbembe, Achille, 19, 52, 59, 63, 82, 95,
    136, 139, 140, 142
mediation, 21, 67, 91, 104,120, 162
Ménage, Gilles, 106
Mfantse, 1, 2, 3, 8, 66, 67, 69, 163
Mfantisipim School, 71
    See also Cape Coast
military coups, 137
miscegenation, 62
miscommunication 99, 110, 111
missionaries, 10, 53, 67
modernity, 9, 64, 70, 100, 148, 162
modern women, 149, 150, 151, 153
Molière, 20, 55, 90, 99, 155
    L'Avare 68, 91
    Le Bourgeois Gentilhomme 70
    Les Femmes savants 55, 70
    Les Fourberies de Scapin 47, 155
money, 24, 34, 39, 41, 59, 98, 122, 127, 143,
    154, 164
    See also greed; entrepreneurship
monotheism, 42
Moraes, Farias de, 67, 78
moral authority, 126
morality, 24, 26, 33, 42–44
Morreall, John, 16, 17, 27, 36, 43, 47, 56,
    64, 135
Mounin, Georges, 105
mugu 40, 41, 43
multilingualism, 2, 9, 99, 102, 120, 162

Naipaul, V. S., 68, 76
naming and nomenclature, 33, 50, 72, 77,
    79, 91, 91, 103
nation/narration, 4
national cake, 132
    See also greed

National Congress of British West Africa, 71

nationalism, 21, 63, 78

Ndebele, Njabulo, 12, 97

neocolonialism, 19

neo-traditions, 83, 86

Newell, Stephanie

    Literary Culture in Colonial Ghana, 52, 69, 73, 78, 86, 87, 88, 90, 91, 97

    "Local Cosmopolitans in Colonial West Africa," 85, 86

Ngũgĩ wa Thiong'o, 53, 56, 77, 107

Nigeria, 24, 38, 45, 54, 67, 70, 132–148, 156, 163

    Civil War, 45

    Criminal Code, 24

    English, 9, 37

Nigerians, 75, 87

Noah, Trevor, 18

Nollywood, 164

Noonan, Will, 11, 13

Nwokolo, Chuma

    Diaries of a Dead African

        ethics in, 42–44

        scamming in, 24–27, 41

        style of, 36, 37, 38

        writing in, 28–34, 38–41

Obadare, Ebenezer, 4, 31, 135, 136

Obama, Barack, 7

    See also protocol

ɔboronyi, 87

    See also Western conventions

obscenity, 17, 95, 141

    See also scatological humor

officialdom, 8, 51, 131, 136, 138

Oguine, Ike, 143

ɔkyeame, 103, 104

    See also communication

overt justice, 128

Oyono, Ferdinand

    atmosphere of, 91–97

    dichotomies in, 66, 93

    interpreters of, 6, 108–110

    Le Vieux nègre et la médaille, 120

parodia sacra, 49

parody, 8, 52, 80, 81, 144

partition of Africa, 62

pastors, 1, 2, 3, 20, 21, 22, 40, 162

    authoritative, 81

    sham 49, 50, 54, 59

pathetic, 30, 47, 90, 145, 151

pathos, 87, 137

p'Biket, Okot

    Song of Lawino, 22, 133

    relationships in 148–152

Pelton, Robert, 24, 26, 27, 28, 51, 53, 56, 57

periphery, 19, 63, 64

physical laughter, 13, 16

physicality, 17, 29, 45, 46, 95, 134, 137, 140, 156

picaresque, 129

Pidgin English, 9, 37, 49, 58, 143, 147, 152

Plaatje, Sol, 102, 109

Plato, 15, 31

Pöchhacker, Franz, 100, 128

Policy of Assimilation, 94, 121

political humor, 52, 53, 54, 95

politics, 5, 67, 132–152,

polygamy, 67, 133, 148, 149, 157

polytheism 55

    See also god

postcolonialism, 4, 5, 10, 19, 20, 139

postcolonial literature, 5, 35, 70, 88, 134

post-colonial states, 63, 133, 136

post-independence, 4

practical jokes, 27

Price-Mars, Jean, 81

problematic kissing, 71, 80, 84, 85, 149

props, 79, 82, 84

protocol, 7, 8, 138, 139, 153

proto-nationalism, 73

proverbs 29, 37, 87, 103, 114, 163

Quayson, Ato, 37, 56

racism 6, 62, 97, 102

Radin, Paul, 26

Ranger, Terence, 83, 86, 112

Rao, Sathya, 100

Index

Raskin, Victor, 11
rationality, 101, 134, 135
readers, 5, 13, 23, 33, 36, 56, 72, 96, 97, 99
  diegetic, 38, 40, 73–77
  enjoyment by, 12, 29, 30, 100
  trust, 39, 41, 46, 112, 118, 125
  uncertainty of, 10, 22, 108, 109, 131, 162, 166
reading, 119, 130, 138, 161, 165
realism, 96
referentiality, 5
Reichl, Susanne, 4, 13, 35, 135, 136
Relief theory of laughter, 16, 17
religion, 31, 42, 54, 55, 60, 61, 81, 117, 127, 128
religious language and rituals, 48, 49, 51
religious persons, 8, 31, 52, 81
  See also pastors
repetition, 49, 70, 75, 103, 114, 116, 117
restraint, 140, 146
revenge, 16, 34, 121, 135
reversal 56–60, 94, 95, 134, 143, 152
rhetorical devices, 4, 25, 109, 112
Rhodesia, 112
romance 5, 80, 81, 152–160
Rotimi, Ola
  Our Husband Has Gone Mad Again
    contrast in, 140–148
    conviviality in, 133–140
    marriage in, 152, 153, 154
    politics in, 132, 133, 136

Sagan, Françoise, 39, 46
Saint Jerome, 105
Sareil, Jean, 19
  "La Démolition comique de l'idéolo-
    gie," 13, 14
  L'Écriture comique, 14, 16, 25, 35, 40, 45, 46, 55, 56
Saro-Wiwa, Ken, 50, 161
satire, 5, 64, 71, 88, 133
Saturnalia, 143
scandals, 85, 137, 153, 154
scapegoat, 118
Scapinade, 47, 155

scatological humor, 94, 95, 97, 134, 141, 142
schadenfreude, 159
Schopenhauer, Arthur, 17
segregation, 62, 92
  See also racism
Sekyi, Kobina Esuman-Gwira
  The Blinkards, 21
    background to, 61–63, 66–71
    culture in, 79–88
    duality in, 63–66
    lessons of, 85–91
Sekyi, H. V. H., 89, 91
self-narrated humor. See Nwokolo, Chuma
senses of humor, 2, 11, 15, 52, 142
seriousness, 12, 46, 51, 102, 138
sex, 32, 142, 151, 152–160
sexism, 116, 156
Shakespeare, 71, 85, 155
signs for wonders, 98, 106, 129, 130
skits, 61, 163, 163
slavery, 42, 43, 121, 143
sloganeering, 37, 144, 152
social order, 138
sourcier, 105, 106, 107
Souriau, Étienne, 12
Souza, Pascale de, 27, 42
Sousa, Ronald de, 59
Soyinka, Wole, 8, 21, 27
  The Lion and the Jewel, 133, 152
    conventions in, 154, 155, 156
    love in, 154, 157
  The Trials of Brother Jero and Jero's
    Metamorphosis
    conviviality in, 45–51
    scamming in, 48, 49, 51–60
Spencer, Herbert, 16
state violence, 137
Stein, Mark, 4, 13, 35, 135, 136
stereotypes, 40, 62, 70, 158
stock characters, 97
subjectivity, 11, 14, 22
subordination, 22, 34, 51, 62, 107, 111, 116, 117
subtleness 22, 72, 89, 92

Index • 183

subversiveness 8, 10, 54, 64, 100, 112, 125, 147, 165
Superiority theory of laughter, 15, 47
supernaturalness, 81, 98
Surprise and Attack, 133. 136, 138, 142, 145
surprise, 37, 134, 142
survival, 10, 43, 53

tension, 2, 9, 10, 20, 45, 135
theatricality, 69, 129
theories of humor, 13–18
theories of translation, 100–104
thinkers, 90. *See* boredom
tongue-in-cheek humor, 6, 94
  See also irony
trade and investment, 25, 127, 128, 147
traditional folktales, 41, 55, 102, 103
tragedy, 10, 12, 31, 33
translation and interpretation studies ,106
tropes and clichés, 2, 30, 68, 84, 161, 164

Twi, 10
tyranny, 136

Uganda, 148
unease 67, 68, 91, 105, 109
unseriousness, 11

Venuti, Lawrence, 107, 117, 120, 124
victimhood, 8, 15, 19, 42, 43, 58, 59, 151
  See also butt of the joke; *mugu*
violence, 6, 53, 95, 126, 137

weirdness, 20, 99
Western conventions, 86, 90
witchcraft, 30, 31, 147
Wodehouse, P. G., 11, 155
writers, 8, 9, 11, 22, 92, 125, 163
  ambivalent, 22, 41, 90, 91
  impish, 39, 46, 131, 133, 163, 166
  teaching, 5, 63, 65